INSURRECTIONS

INSURRECTIONS

Approaches to Resistance in Composition Studies

edited by

ANDREA GREENBAUM

foreword by

GARY A. OLSON

afterword by

DALE BAUER

State University
of New York
Press

Published by
State University of New York Press, Albany

© 2001 State University of New York

Printed in the United States of America

For information, address State University of New York Press,
90 State Street, Suite 700, Albany, NY 12207

Production by Susan Geraghty
Marketing by Fran Keneston

Library of Congress Cataloging-in-Publication Data

Insurrections : approaches to resistance in composition studies / edited by Andrea
Greenbaum ; foreword by Gary A. Olson.
    p. cm.
  Includes bibliographical references and index.
  ISBN 0-7914-4923-8 (alk. paper) — ISBN 0-7914-4924-6 (pbk. : alk. paper)
    1. English language—Rhetoric—Study and teaching. 2. English
language—Rhetoric—Study and teaching—Technological innovations. 3. English
language—Rhetoric—Study and teaching—Political aspects. 4. English
language—Rhetoric—Study and teaching—Social aspects. I. Greenbaum, Andrea.

PE1404 .I48 2001
808′.042′071—dc21
                                                              00-040018

10 9 8 7 6 5 4 3 2 1

For Neil, Ari, and Yarden

CONTENTS

ACKNOWLEDGMENTS

An edited collection is a collaborative endeavor, and there are many individuals who assisted me in coordinating this book. I want to thank Gary Olson, who encouraged me to pursue this project and who provided astute editorial advice along the way. I would also like to thank Ira Shor, Joseph Harris, and Henry Giroux, who reviewed this project early in its inception. I am also indebted to the book's contributors, who put their trust and energy into this work.

FOREWORD

Resistance and the Work of Theory

Gary A. Olson

In his chapter in this book, John Trimbur points out that although the term "resistance" is ubiquitous in composition scholarship, it has become a floating signifier: a term that everyone recognizes in its contexts of use but that is hard, nonetheless, to pin down. Yet, for those of us who define composition studies as a field committed to critical (not just functional) literacy, who take seriously the connections between the acquisition of critical literacy and the ability to resist systems of oppression and domination, resistance remains a central if polyvalent concept. Thus, if compositionists fail to come to terms with this important and resonant term, it will float into oblivion, becoming yet another disciplinary cliché devoid of meaning—like "process" or "discourse community." *Insurrections: Approaches to Resistance in Composition Studies* makes a serious and sustained effort to theorize resistance, to examine its intricacies, and to develop a language with which to "think" this key notion.

The essays in this collection trace and attempt to clarify several principal understandings of resistance. From examining political history to discussing the politics of race, from exploring pedagogies of resistance to analyzing opposition to the technologized classroom, the essays in *Insurrections* together offer a compelling, insightful, and provocative analysis of one of the most important concepts in contemporary composition scholarship.

This book is particularly timely, emerging as it does at a time of increasing hegemonic struggle over how the field of composition studies should be defined. Just as we are experiencing a renewed backlash against feminism—as Beth Flynn so poignantly describes in her chapter—composition is also witnessing a revitalized backlash against theoretical scholarship, especially that associated with critical literacy and with efforts to draw connections between the work we do in composition and the critical work done in other disciplines. For example, one might read the special issue of *College Composition and Communication* on "teaching writing creatively" (51.1, 1999) as an opening salvo in what undoubtedly will come to be known as "the new theory wars." The attempt to drag composition back to its expressivist roots constitutes a direct assault not only on a two-decade-long tradition of substantive theoretical scholarship but also on a particular *kind* of work: that which attempts to lead the field *away* from a debilitating preoccupation with individual psychology, "genius," "talent," and "creativity" and *toward* a recognition of how and why dominant discourse enacts a kind of violence on many of us, particularly women, minorities, and members of other groups who do not share fully, if at all, in the privileges that society reserves for the few.

Given the vigor with which a powerful handful in composition (Jim Sledd calls them "boss compositionists") are struggling desperately to set back our disciplinary clock, we simply must continue and intensify the valuable and empowering work we have been doing for twenty years. *Insurrections: Approaches to Resistance in Composition Studies* serves as a major statement that theoretical scholarship and work in critical literacy will continue to enrich our pedagogies and our understandings of the workings of discourse. Not merely a thorough examination of resistance, this book is itself an enactment of resistance—resistance against unthinking expressivism, against the growing anti-intellectualism in the field, and against those boss compositionists who have a vested interest in the status quo and who dread theoretical challenges to it. I'm certain that *Insurrections* will inspire many of us to carry on this important work.

INTRODUCTION

Andrea Greenbaum

At the 1999 Popular Education and Social Change conference in New York City, conference administrator and long-time union organizer, Stanley Aronowitz, spoke lovingly about the "radical democratic humanism of Paulo Freire," whose work—especially *Pedagogy of the Oppressed* and *Pedagogy of Freedom*—has been instrumental in guiding academics and social activists toward creating a more equitable, socially conscious, humane society. Moreover, Aronowitz argued that Freire, drawing on the work of Marx, Hegel, and Fromm, understood that the "problem of freedom always entails the collective of individuals to throw off oppressors and see themselves as the subject of their own identity." In paraphrasing Freire, Aronowitz makes evident that the quest for subjectivity is invariably a move toward emancipation, and such transformation must always occur within the inevitable context of antagonism and resistance.

This rhetoric of emancipation and resistance has pollinated the discipline of composition and has, within the field itself, flowered into various areas of interest to writing teachers—including, but not limited to, broad investigations in postcolonial studies, gender studies, cultural studies, working-class studies, neosophistic rhetoric, eco-composition, and techno-composition. While these intellectual projects are varied, they are harmonized by the familiar Freirean melody of emancipation. One could argue (and many have—James Berlin, Ira Shor, Patricia Bizzell, Linda Brodkey, and bell hooks, for example) that it was Freire's influence that forever altered the field of rhetoric and composition, broadening disciplinary objectives to include a pedagogical foundation based on emancipation and resistance, with composition evolving into a field dedicated to teaching students how to create critical texts and to engage in self-conscious writing practices that always consider context— history, locale, politics, culture, gender, race, and class.

For the last twenty years, scholars have drawn on Freire's work in advocating critical teaching as an integral component of education. Freire's concept of *conscientização*—critical consciousness, which invariably leads people to analyze their reality in order to alter social inequity—is the *sine qua non* of critical pedagogy. Freire defines it as "learning to perceive social, political, and economic contradictions, and to take action against the oppressive elements of reality" (19). For Freire, education without social consciousness is merely indoctrination, the primary vehicle for the reproduction of dominant ideologies—ideologies that are almost always sexist, racist, and classist. Further, in the Freirean model, it is not enough to gain class consciousness: one is socially and ethically compelled to act upon this knowledge, to resist oppression and work toward creating a more equitable system.

This notion of resistance to the hegemony of dominant ideologies is manifested in a variety of ways within the academy, and the creation of oppositional discourse within the infrastructure of the academy has emerged as a central concern in composition studies. For instance, in 1991, Mark Hurlbert and Michael Blitz's *Composition and Resistance* examined the disparate practices of resistance inside and outside the academy. They proposed,

> Educators teach composition and literature in order to encourage class actions, resistances in our classrooms, profession, and private lives that any of us will make against those who use money, access to information, administrative rank, traditional privilege (male, white, heterosexual), to control other people, to deny them freedom and safety and equality and their voice, or to distract them/us from noticing the dangers of these conditions. This action demands that composition teachers resist teaching writing as something for a classroom. (172–73)

Writing, then, becomes writing in context, in relationships connected to discourses within and outside the classroom, shattering the quiet belief that composition may be taught as a discrete skill, separated from class, race, or gender.

Henry Giroux, Joseph Harris, James Berlin, and Ira Shor have articulated both the theoretical and pedagogical value of incorporating cultural critique as a form of resistance into the writing class and have argued that teaching students concepts of semiotics and representation may be useful for instructing them in how to read and write a multiplicity of texts, broadening and expanding students' concepts of literacy. Another perspective is that this expanded view of literacy has significant implications for all students, but particularly so for African Americans (Gilyard; Smitherman) and basic writers (Lu; Fox), who often not only struggle with the very material effects of having to support themselves through school, and therefore have less time to devote to the luxury of academic pursuits, but who must also grapple with the psychological consequences of feeling "illiterate" and therefore inadequate to produce substantial academic work (Greenbaum).

Insurrections: Approaches to Resistance in Composition Studies explores how conceptions of resistance have been reconfigured for the twenty-first century. The book is divided into four parts, with each section detailing a thematic understanding of resistance. The essays in the first part, "Theorizing Resistance," provide foundational definitions of resistance, while simultaneously recognizing that the term itself is amorphous and tends to encompass wide areas of discourse. John Trimbur considers resistance as an appealing metaphor for writing teachers, since student resistance "gives expressions to our own hedges, evasions, challenges," and that we are able to locate ourselves in these various pedagogical projects. But he also cautions that despite the honorific, romantic mystique that resistance offers, the historical tracing of resistance (the Bolshevik Revolution, the Spanish Civil War, the Shanghai Uprising, for example) has been fraught with danger, death, and ultimately, tragedy. If writing teachers are to continue to engage in the rhetoric of resistance, it is Trimbur's contention that we remain cognizant of the trope's historical roots.

Elizabeth Flynn suggests that we examine resistance in three ways: as strategic, counter-strategic, and reactive. "Strategic" resistance is planned and acts in direct opposition to oppression. While the term does not necessarily refer to collective opposition, strategic oppositional strategies include "writing, speaking, protesting, fighting, marching, willful and public violation of laws, refusal to comply with policies or accepted modes of behavior, or more subtle or less visual activities such as sabotage and withdrawal." "Counter-strategic" resistance is one that disrupts liberatory practices, and Flynn argues that the recent backlash against feminism takes this form. The third component in this triumvirate of resistance, "reactive resistance," is a spontaneous and emotional reaction, as often occurs in the classroom, especially in the feminist classroom, where students are faced with navigating through the choppy waters of counter-hegemonic discourse.

In Part 2, "Race and the Politics of Literacy," the authors address how the intersections of race and literacy are codified in the composition classroom. Keith Gilyard and Elaine Richardson assess the use of African American Vernacular English (AAVE) in basic writing classes taught between 1996 through 1998. Their classes, which were structured from an African-centric perspective, are a study in the practical application of the 1974 College Composition and Communication's Students' Rights to Their Own Language Resolution. Gilyard and Richardson offer a critique of the nuances of AAVE discourse strategies in composition and provide an expansionist view of academic literacy.

Stephen Brown faced similar challenges of broadening conventions of literacy when he taught Athabascan Indians on a reservation in Alaska. These students had not yet learned to rely on their native discourse, and as a result, Brown notes, "resistance in the borderland classroom assumes many guises." His essay explores the wide vocabulary of passive resistance displayed by these culturally exiled students—strangers to their own heritage and disenfranchised from the mainstream.

Tom Fox, like Gilyard and Richardson, examines African American discourse within an academy that is "generally hostile to people of color." His essay suggests expanding our categories of assessment and literacy, and recognizes that opposition takes shape in various forms, often appearing as conformity rather than resistance.

Part 3, "Technology and Rhetoric," is concerned with how computers and composition have created a new writing frontier of technorhetoricians who are often faced with resistance by other faculty members, administrators, and students themselves. Ellen Strenski recognizes the "contentious battle over educational uses of computer technology to our collective peril." Strenski sees the technological debate in terms of electronic circuitry—power as energy rather than domination. Her chapter examines the symbiotic relationship between resistant faculty, those who refuse to explore technology, and administrators who are seeking to use technology within a corporate paradigm, and have, at least to those resistant faculty members, blurred the line between education and business.

Likewise, Janice Walker examines the myriad ways in which authority is revealed and veiled in computer-aided instruction. She argues that within the computer-assisted classroom, teachers need to be willing to relinquish or at least distribute some of their authority, since once students enter the world of cyberspace they are able to effectively circumvent and resist the teacher's authority. Walker proposes that despite this usurpation, the computer classroom offers the option for teachers to create "alternatives to existing pedagogical structures" that foster critical thinking and a connection to a larger, literate community.

In Part 4, "Toward a Pedagogy of Resistance," the essays suggest examining strategies of resistance, and studies the means by which students can learn to use resistance as a discursive form of communication. Susan Wells examines the classroom in the Habermasian context of a public sphere, as a location where desire and agency can be articulated. Of particular concern to Wells are representations of social class, and how students, through exposure to a variety of readings, learn to critically examine the often obfuscated dynamic of class in the classroom.

My essay investigates how argumentation theory, as articulated in speech communication, may be applicable in composition studies in teaching students, particularly women, how to engage effectively in agonistic discourse, and to resist the social prohibition against argumentation. Such resistance, I believe, will enable students to become more persuasive rhetors.

Finally, Bruce Horner explores the ambivalence over the use of "academic" writing in composition classes. In recent years, Horner notes, compositionists have attempted to make their writing classes more relevant, concerned with real, political and economic significance, but he argues that such efforts mistake the purpose of academic knowledge and "may end up reinforcing, rather than challenging" dominant approaches to such categories.

My hope is that *Insurrections: Approaches to Resistance in Composition Studies* contributes to the discussion generated so thoroughly by Ira Shor, Henry Giroux, Pierre Bourdieu, Mark Hurlbert, and Michael Blitz. The rhetoric of resistance is the rhetoric of possibility— that which is *not*, but may which someday come to be. And it is with this sense of optimism, what Giroux calls a "pedagogy of hope," that this book is written.

WORKS CITED

Aronowitz, Stanley. "Paulo Freire: An Introduction to His Thought." A Roundtable Dialogue. Popular Education and Social Change Conference. Borough of Manhattan Community College, New York. 4 June. 1999.

Berlin, James. "Composition and Cultural Studies." *Composition and Resistance*. Ed. C. Mark Hurlbert and Michael Blitz. Portsmouth, NH: Boynton, 1991.

———. *Rhetorics, Poetics, and Cultures*. Urbana: NCTE, 1996.

Bizzell, Patricia. *Academic Discourse and Critical Consciousness*. Pittsburgh: U of Pittsburgh P, 1992.

Bourdieu, Pierre. *Acts of Resistance: Against the Tyranny of the Market*. Trans. Richard Nice. New York: New P, 1998.

Brodkey, Linda. "On the Subjects of Class and Gender in 'The Literacy Letters.'" *College English* 51 (1989): 125–41.

Fox, Tom. "Basic Writing as Cultural Conflict." *Journal of Education* 172 (1990): 65–83.

———. *The Social Uses of Writing: Politics and Pedagogy*. Norwood, NJ: Ablex, 1990.

Giroux, Henry. "Resisting Difference: Cultural Studies and the Discourse of Critical Pedagogy." *Cultural Studies*. Ed. Lawrence Grossberg, Cary Nelson, and Paula Treichler. London: Routledge, 1992. 199–212.

————. *Pedagogy and the Politics of Hope.* New York: Westview P, 1997.

Gilyard, Keith. *Voices of the Self: A Study of Language Competence.* Detroit: Wayne State UP, 1991.

Greenbaum, Andrea. "'Wat'cha Think? I Can't Spell?': Constructing Literacy in the Postcolonial Classroom." *Composition Forum* 9 (1998): 1–9.

Harris, Joseph. "Teaching Writing as Cultural Criticism." *Composition and Resistance.* Ed. C. Mark Hurlbert and Michael Blitz. Portsmouth, NH: Boynton, 1991.

Hooks, Bell. "Confronting Class in the Classroom." *Teaching to Transgress.* New York: Routledge, 1994. 177–89.

————. "Engaged Pedagogy." *Women/Writing/Teaching.* Albany: State U of New York P, 1998. 231–38.

Hurlbert, C. Mark, and Michael Blitz, eds. *Composition and Resistance.* Portsmouth, NH: Boynton, 1991.

Lu, Min-Zhan. "Conflict and Struggle: The Enemies or Preconditions of Basic Writing?" *College English* 54 (1992): 887–913.

Shor, Ira. *Critical Teaching in Everyday Life.* Boston: South End P, 1980.

Smitherman, Geneva. "CCCC's Role in the Struggle for Language Rights." *College Composition and Communication* 50 (1999): 349–76.

PART 1

Theorizing Resistance

CHAPTER 1

Resistance as a Tragic Trope

John Trimbur

The term "resistance" has become a commonplace in the study and teaching of writing, turning up in the titles of articles ("Accommodation, Resistance, and the Politics of Student Writing," "Resistance and the Writing Teacher"), collections (*Composition and Resistance*), conference papers, and informal teacher talk. Though the term is used widely and frequently, there has been surprisingly little debate about what it means. Unlike other keywords in the composition vernacular, such as "process," "academic discourse," or "expressive," the term "resistance" is not exactly a contested one. (In fact, it is not even an entry in *The Encyclopedia of Rhetoric and Composition* or listed in the index.) Instead, its various meanings and uses just seem to slide across the field of composition, a kind of floating signifier that everyone recognizes in its contexts of use but that is hard, nonetheless, to pin down.

To make it into a question, is the "resistance," say, of male students to a feminist teacher the same notion that is used to make sense of the "resistance" of fundamentalist students to critical thinking about the authority of the printed word or of gay and lesbian students to a normatively heterosexual student culture of dating, fraternity parties, boyfriends and girlfriends? What about the calculated compliance whereby students give the teacher "what he wants" while withholding consent or investment in the activity? Or the students who avoid, to the extent they are able, taking classes with writing assignments, but who spend lots of time doing such self-sponsored writing as e-mail, poetry, journal-keeping, or even writing for the student newspaper? In each of these cases, somebody seems to be "resisting" something, but the instances are so dissimilar that "resistance" is in danger of turning up anywhere and everywhere—a description that can serve as the starting point for analysis but hardly seems capable of investing any explanatory value in the term "resistance" itself.

One solution to this problem, of course, is to stipulate a definition that qualifies certain forms of behavior as "really" resistant, while disqualifying others as something else. Perhaps the best-known example of this strategy is Henry Giroux's distinction between "truly" resistant behaviors that challenge in meaningful ways the dominant logic of schooling and "merely" oppositional ones that appear to be transgressive but ultimately are contained within (and often serve to reinforce) the prevailing social relations. For Giroux, theorizing resistance in this way accomplishes a number of things. For one, it rejects traditional explanations of school failure as a matter of deviance or individual pathology and identifies student outcomes instead as complexly mediated cultural and political events that take place where schooling and society intersect. For another, Giroux's distinction thereby lifts the term "resistance" above a simple description of what students do in school by turning it into an "analytical construct and mode of inquiry" carried out in order to identify the radical potentialities in specific situations and behaviors for emancipation, critical consciousness, and transformative collective action.

There is no question in my mind that the "fleeting images of freedom" that Giroux imagines in "creative acts of resistance" do indeed, as he says, express deep hopes for transcendence and radical transformation. At the same time, however, I want to hold off for a moment, not to "resist" these hopes, which I certainly share, but to see them as warranted not so much by a theory or stipulative definition as by a sensibility and structure of feeling that makes "resistance" attractive and invests it with transformative powers. My interest at this point is not to pin down the term "resistance" or to argue about how it should be used. Instead, I want to think about why and how it has become so popular and what its various manifestations have been. My suspicion is that the circulation of ill-defined terms such as "resistance" goes beyond problems of terminological clarification in research projects and teaching practices (to straighten out terms, apply them correctly, and get to work). There is something more to be said about the very appeal of the term "resistance"—not only in terms of what it signifies but also in terms of what its significations call up in us.

One of the problems with the term "resistance," and surely part of its attraction, is its ubiquity. It turns up both as observable behavior and, more important, as a satisfying account of what is taking place. Part of the allure of the term "resistance" is that it puts events, attitudes, and identities in a system that makes them more knowable. It gives writing teachers, researchers, and theorists a handle on things, a way of understanding occurrences that might otherwise be registered as a quirk, an affront, an anomaly, or simply escape notice altogether. Resistance is one of those things that once you start to see it, you can't stop finding more and more instances.

Here are some of its usual places:

- Resistance to school. The classic case is Paul Willis' *Learning to Labour*, his study of how British working-class "lads" resist the official and hidden curriculum of secondary school (and especially the primacy of mental over manual labor) through a peer culture based on masculinist shop-floor traditions of "us" and "them." This is the resistance of what Willis calls "counter-school culture"—counter-identities to fend off the demands, meanings, labels, values, and preferred ways of doing and being in school. There are, of course, other students who resist in less overt ways, working out "underlife" behaviors and identities (see Brooke) that enable them to evade the subjectivities ascribed by schooling while still acquiring at least some of the cultural capital it offers.

- Resistance to courses. Anyone who has administered a first-year writing requirement knows about this resistance. There is probably a law of physics operating that could be represented in an equation relating placement results to mandated course assignment to individual resistance to writing instruction. As Mike Rose points out, there are other sources of resistance to courses beside the mandate that plagues freshman English. Students' "conceptualization of disciplines," Rose says, may be "out of sync with academic reality" (191)—as in the case of students who think that an Introduction to Psychology course is going to treat human behavior and personality development only to discover that it spends more time on animal studies, neurophysiology, and computer models.

- Resistance to teachers and classroom practices. Here, again, there is a classic defining instance—namely Dale Bauer's account of student resistance to her feminist perspective in "The Other 'F' Word: The Feminist in the Classroom." This is the dark, unsettling underside of resistance because students in these cases are not resisting institutions and their oppressive demands but us, the teachers who believe we have their best interests at heart. In fact, as C. H. Knoblauch suggests, this kind of resistance can be heartbreaking, in part because it reminds teachers that students may well believe, from the perspective of class advantage, that they have little to gain from "critical reflectiveness" or "troubling self-awareness" (19).

- Resistance to texts. This resistance ranges from encounters with unfamiliar (and perhaps intimidating) texts and genres that students mark as "boring" to rejection of academic controversy as "pointless hairsplitting" to a reluctance to question the printed word as an authoritative source ("if it's written down, it must be true"). This kind of resistance has been seized on as a key site for pedagogical intervention, as exemplified by Richard Miller in "Fault Lines in the Contact Zone," but it can also take more public form, such as the "agnosis" (or avoidance of knowing) that James Moffett finds among the West Virginian textbook protesters seeking to ban a new language arts series from local schools.

- Resistance to Peers. This kind of resistance typically occurs in collaborative learning, group projects, and jointly authored writing assignments. It's not just a matter of students encountering personality conflicts or having someone in the group who doesn't pull his or her weight. As Kenneth A. Bruffee has argued, there is something systemic at work. The competitive ethos and reward system of schooling have taught students to be wary of each other as academic performers vying for the limited resources of high grades, institutional recognition, and personal success. Thus, the demand to collaborate may well, Bruffee says, precipitate a crisis in the teacher's authority, on the one hand, and a crisis of intimacy, on the other, as students are, in effect, called on to invest authority in each other as colearners and coworkers (33–34).

- Resistance to parents. To my knowledge, this is a neglected aspect of resistance, at least within composition studies. Nonetheless, I believe it points to very real moments of resistance, when students defy their parents' wishes, say, by switching from a "practical" major such as premed or management or engineering to literature or anthropology. On the other hand, being in college at all, say for women from traditional ethnic-class cultures, may itself be a departure from parental wishes and expectations.

I do not mean this list of examples to be a taxonomy of all imaginable types of resistance or to pretend that it registers the varying degrees and nuances of behaviors, attitudes, and identities that might be called resistant. Instead, I hope to suggest something about the sheer variety and heterogeneity of events that can be marked with the sign of resistance. In certain respects, my point begins with the range and dissimilarity of these examples—and how the term "resistance" appears capable of accounting for so many different moments of noncompliance, evasion, or outright rebellion. From this perspective, one of the main attractions of the notion of resistance is that its various manifestations reveal the divergent ways individuals and groups seize a degree of relative autonomy within the institutions of schooling, articulating identities and purposes that in one way or another withhold consent from the dominant enterprise and its hegemonic aims. To put it in other words, the term "resistance" brings with it the reassuring news that school doesn't totally "work"—that students are persistently inventing safety valves and escape hatches to evade their subjectification as "pupils."

Now, of course, there is something ironic that this perception of how students create and inhabit gaps and fissures in schooling should give us such pleasure, for, as teachers and faculty members, we are, after all, representatives of the institutions of schooling. But that seems to me a source of the pleasure: our interest in the dynamics of resistance gives expression to our own hedges, evasions, challenges, and attempted subversions of the dominant educational mission. The term "resistance," that is, enables us to locate ourselves and our pedagogical projects within and against the curriculum—to clarify the ways, as Greg Myers puts it, that "our interests are not the same as the institutions that employ us" (169).

Of all college and university faculty, writing teachers as a group may be unique in how they like to take on the ambiguous status of being simultaneously insiders and outsiders, using the institutional spaces of higher learning not so much to initiate students into a field of study as to negotiate the border between school and society. Whether they would put it this way or not, writing teachers, I believe, like to think of themselves in a liminal position, at a cusp in social experience where they and their students can momentarily step out of the normal order of things, suspending the rules of school in order to examine them, to determine the complex relations among education, home, popular culture, class society, and the workplace. In this sense, beliefs and views that are largely proscribed in the traditional classroom—by middle-class canons of politeness and good taste, on one hand, and by the specialized methods of the disciplines, on the other—may be actively invited by writing teachers as part of composition's carnivalesque suspension of the official curriculum. Even displays of class entitlement, racism, sexism, homophobia, or First Worldism that we find personally upsetting and politically reactionary can be thematized as resistance and thereby made available for deliberation and struggle (instead of remaining underground where they go unchallenged, exerting a silent, taken-for-granted influence).

The pull of resistance, in its simplest and most direct sense, then, is that it promises to put us in touch with our students' lived experience in all of its messiness, contradiction, and mixed motives. To get this close to how students actually experience and manage the demands of a writing classroom, it should be easy to see, has an obvious appeal to a field of teachers who cherish a collective self-image as student-centered faculty, perpetually balancing their role as gatekeepers against a profound desire to be allies and advocates of student aspirations. But I don't want to make it sound as if the term "resistance" just appeared one day to fit seamlessly into the theoretical and pedagogical repertoire of writing instruction. Instead, I think there is something notable about its moment of appearance in the composition archive, marked symbolically by the publication in 1988 of Geoffrey Chase's *College Composition and Communication* article, "Accommodation, Resistance, and the Politics of Student Writing."

To put it as bluntly as I can, the appearance of the term "resistance" (and its imputed ability to explain both students' and teachers' experience of puzzling and difficult events in the writing classroom) signifies a moment of crisis in the process movement. What no one quite realized in 1988 is that the term "resistance" was immediately usable in part because it helped compositionists deal with their own frustrations when the unimaginable happened—when process teaching reached its limits or outright broke down. Resistance, in other words, gave writing teachers a way to recover their equilibrium when all we had to offer failed to repair the damage we imagined the English teacher's red pen and the authoritarian prescriptiveness of the five-paragraph theme had done to students.

There was a certain shocking recognition that, despite our best intentions, removing the oppressive formalism of current-traditional rhetoric was not automatically turning students into willing and fluent composers. Some of the canniest students complied, producing versions of what they correctly understood to be the kind of sincere and authentic voice their teachers valued but without really consenting to the pedagogical assumption that through writing they could discover a true self. Others balked at the sense of social entitlement and cultural self-confidence in the personal essay favored by the process movement, failing to recognize themselves in the class-inflected prose that process teachers had mistakenly identified with writing itself. Still others, as Lisa Delpit says of African American students, were estranged from the facilitative indirection characteristic of process pedagogy. The tragedy of the process movement, as Delpit points out, is that its attempts to reduce the "power differential" in the composition classroom only served to mask the workings of the culture of power, thereby making it difficult for those raised in non-middle-class homes to acquire the forms of "cultural capital" that were never explicitly named.

[handwritten: connection b/w resistance & CP]

When resistance theory arrived around 1988 (just in time, I've been suggesting, to name some of the oversights, omissions, and blasted hopes of the process movement), it could not be taken up simply as an analytical term in the technical vocabulary of a discipline, as is the case, say, in physics, where the term specifies the quality of nonconductivity in materials. Instead, for writing teachers, to utter the term "resistance" was to call up a whole history of its denominations—in psychoanalysis, immunology, education, Foucauldian critical theory, cultural studies, feminism, and traditions of left-wing politics. I will leave it to someone else to untangle the multiple, overlapping, and sometimes contradictory senses of the term as it enters the composition lexicon. (There are interesting and difficult questions involved, for the meaning of the term can range from the "resistance" to infection that wards off disease to the analysand's "resistance" to therapy that may be part of the illness itself.) My goal is more limited here: if the term "resistance" seems to have pressed itself on writing teachers seeking to understand a moment of crisis in the process movement, then why the term was invested with such a romantic aura still needs to be explained. *[handwritten: romanticizing resistance]*

A simple and readily available explanation is that the term "resistance" brought with it, for left-wing writing teachers taking the "social turn" in the late 1980s, a powerfully persuasive history in radical political movements. Perhaps the most obvious examples are the anti-Nazi movements of World War II, most notably the French Resistance of Jean-Paul Sartre's generation, the partisans who refused to collaborate with the Vichy regime and fought the Nazi occupation through an underground press, sabotage, sheltering Jews and helping them escape, behind-the-lines intelligence work for the Allies, and armed struggle. Composed of workers, peasants, intellectuals, artists, and others, the men and women of the French Resistance loom in the annals of the left as courageous and self-sacrificing figures, exemplary fighters against tyranny. In France, as well as the other occupied European countries, to have been a member of the Resistance became a badge of honor in the postwar period, a reminder that even in the most difficult conditions the forces of liberation will gather and act. A political mystique continues to surround the Resistance, celebrated in novels such as Marge Piercy's *Gone to Soldiers* and films such as Marcel Ophul's *The Sorrow and the Pity* and Alain Resnais' *La Guerre Est Finie*. *[handwritten: Les Mis.?]*

Now I am quite aware that this brief presentation of the anti-Nazi resistance movements verges on the rhapsodic (and fails to take into account such things as the internal struggles in France between Communists and Gaullists, for example). But in a sense, this is my point: we receive the term "resistance" as an already thoroughly mythologized one that conjures up images of unreconciled freedom fighters and legendary stalwarts of the left. There are traditions of principled struggle the term "resistance" taps into—the Paris Commune of 1871, Rosa Luxembourg and Karl Liebknecht's opposition to the Social Democratic parties' support of their national governments during World War I, the Catalonian anarchists during the Spanish Civil War, the Hungarian uprising against the stalinized state in 1956, and the French worker-student alliance of 1968. Readers will no doubt compile their own histories of resistance, but what I mean to suggest is that the term is necessarily a heroic and honorific one, in my version part of the Old World romance of a workers' commonwealth and an internationalist, anticapitalist, and anti-Stalinist left.

It is no wonder, then, and in an important respect revealing that the young men who burned their draft cards and refused to cooperate with the Selective Service during the Vietnam War, along with their supporters, called their movement the Resistance. They wanted to invest their antidraft organizing with the moral authority the term "resistance" made available and to distinguish their movement from the traditional pacifist "conscientious objection" to war, with its implied acceptance of "alternative service" and the legitimacy of the state's claim to conscript its citizens. Instead, they advocated a politics of noncooperation that withheld recognition of the state's power, refused any degree of compliance with the war machine, disobeyed its demands, and attempted, at least symbolically, to shut it down.

The point I am working toward here is that actual moments of resistance invariably involve very real dangers—of death, torture, jail. What makes such acts heroic is the recognition that, no matter the consequences, there are times when resistance is unavoidable. It comes with the history one is living within, and to act otherwise would be, in a profound moral and political sense, to fail to live up to one's ideals and to betray the principle of solidarity that links lives together in the collective struggle for justice and human emancipation. Acts of resistance occur, that is, from the perspective of the resisting subject, as given by the force of necessity, and yet, from the perspective of others—family, loved ones, teachers—as risky and potentially self-destructive. These acts are charged because they seem to court disaster: by being true to yourself, you put yourself in a position of jeopardy. In this sense, resistance figures in the heroic tales of working-class uprisings and the European resistance movements (think of how Rossellini represents the captured partisan as a Christ-figure in *Open City*) as a tragic trope.

The term "resistance," I am urging writing teachers to see, is tied in tightly to the narrativity of its telling. Much of the allure of resistance—and the source of its moral seriousness—is the way it makes sense of the defeat of left-wing movements by valorizing the ethical commitments of the fallen heroes, the men and women who quite literally put their bodies on the line. This is why the history of the left is filled with martyrs who, like the early Christians or the Protestants recorded in John Foxe's *Book of Martyrs*, have given their lives to a revolutionary cause. And similarly, like the martyrs of religious conscience, the martyrs of the left are redeemed in memory. To tell the story of their resistance as a tragic one is, as Raymond Williams puts it, to "read back life from the fact of death" and to make their martyrdom "not only the focus but the source of our values" (56).

Isaac Deutscher's epic trilogy of Leon Trotsky's life—*The Prophet Armed, The Prophet Unarmed,* and *The Prophet Outcast*—is perhaps the fullest modern expression of this tragic view of revolutionary struggle, as it recounts the possibilities of emancipation released by the Bolshevik Revolution, the moment of crisis when the Left Opposition formed against Stalin's betrayals, and the subsequent failure of Trotsky and his comrades to redirect the disastrous policies of the Third International in the decisive events of the interwar period, such as the Shanghai uprising of 1927, Hitler's rise to power, and the Spanish Civil War. Deutscher casts Trotsky, as the titles of the trilogy indicate, as a prophet whose theory of permanent revolution enabled him to foresee in 1917 proletarian revolution emerging from the overthrow of czarism, whose jeremiads in the name of revolutionary internationalism called Stalin's "socialism in one country" into account for abandoning the classical Marxist commitment to the oppressed and working masses worldwide, and whose exile and assassination mark his tragic isolation and ultimate defeat by the forces of Stalinism. What makes the trilogy so moving is that the plot of Deutscher's narrative unfolds as a revelation of how Trotsky, despite his fumblings and miscalculations, could have altered the course of history had his warnings about Hitler and his criticisms of Stalin been heeded. In this sense, as the title of Deutscher's postscript and final vindicating judgment has it, Trotsky achieves "Victory in Defeat." As the closing lines of the trilogy put it, although the masses may allow "those who urge [humanity] forward to be abused, vilified, and trampled to death" in their lifetime, there will come nonetheless the moment of recognition, the "rueful tribute" to the revolutionists' memory and the gratitude "for every drop of blood they gave—for . . . with their blood they nourished the seed of the future" (*Prophet Outcast* 523).

It would be irresponsible at this point, despite the grandeur (and the seductiveness) of Deutscher's sweeping tragic narrative, not to point out some of the difficulties it poses. For one thing, it falls into the old habit, in Willliams' words, of "attaching significant suffering to (social) nobility," thereby risking the separation of elevated tragic sacrifice by revolutionists from the "mere suffering" of ordinary people in everyday life (48). Second, it risks separating individual redemption from social change, producing a story that pays honor to the heroes of the left while simultaneously compensating for the larger collective defeat by apotheo-sizing the fallen as tragic figures. Third, it makes death the ultimate term of resistance: in the ancient pattern of the dying fertility gods, the spilling of blood guarantees the future. Taken together, these difficulties point to the problem of maintaining a certain critical and ethical tension that locates the sources of tragedy not only in the heroic resistance of individuals but also in what Williams calls "the existence of a disorder that cannot but move and involve"—the actual sufferings of real people and their consequences (77).

I believe that this tragic sense of resistance hovers over its uses in composition, education, and cultural studies in ways that have not been fully appreciated. One can sense it, for example, in the subtitle to Willis' *Learning to Labour*—"how working class kids get working class jobs." By their all-too-understandable alienation from and resistance to school-ing, Willis's "lads" (and their all-too-understandable allegiances to a masculinist shop-floor culture) virtually guarantee the reproduction of class relations and their own formation as labor power subjugated to capital.

The standard critique of resistance theory is that the studies of working class and youth culture resistance, which have appeared under the auspices of British cultural studies—such as Willis's *Learning to Labour*, Stuart Hall and Tony Jefferson's collection *Resistance Through Rituals*, and Dick Hebdige's *Subculture: The Meaning of Style*—idealize apolitical cultural styles whose remarkably inventive affronts to bour-geois sensibilities sometimes draw on racist, sexist, and national chau-vinist themes. This is a fair enough comment: it is true that a celebratory tone often inflects resistance studies. But for me the problem is not to deny the obvious attractions of subcultures that range from the Teddy Boys, mods, and hippies of the 1960s to the Rastas, grunge kids, Goths, and rappers of the 1990s. What needs to be registered is how resistance, in its attempts to extend the boundaries of cultural expression, uses the powerlessness of subordinate groups as a catalyst for new identities that rely on the common bond of social marginalization.

To my mind, such a tragic sense of resistance provides a needed per-spective that recognizes the inventive agency in what Michel de Certeau calls the "practices of everyday life," while simultaneously keeping in view the disorder and contradictions of class society that press in on ordinary people. The metaphors of conflict that run through de Certeau's analyses—the mobile tactics of guerrilla warfare, poaching, ruses, and trickeries—delineate, as he says, "an art of the weak" (37) that subverts the established order by redirecting its resources toward popular uses. It is indeed important to acknowledge, as John Fiske does, that "resistant popular practices refuse to lie down and die even in such tightly controlled contexts as the workshop or the classroom" (211). In fact, as de Certeau and Fiske argue, ordinary people are wonderfully canny at playing the system, making do, and getting over in ways that carve out a measure of autonomy under the boss's or teacher's nose by using tools, texts, commodities, and places for their own ends. But what de Certeau and Fiske do not always foreground adequately is the unjust and oppressive social order that makes such popular redistribution necessary in the first place, precisely because as an organized system of living class society is failing to meet human needs.

Moreover, when, as in the case of de Certeau and Fiske, such a tragic sense of contemporary existence is lacking, there is the unacknowledged danger that the tricksters and semiotic guerrillas of popular resistance will simply turn into operators, wise guys, or dealers—with their identities tied to their ability to tweak the system or maneuver in its interstices. One of the main pleasures of resistance, of course, is getting away with it, but this pleasure is only available as long as the system itself is in place and the resisting trickster is in a position of subordination, acting at the margins or as an underground figure, to reverse temporarily the power differential of the dominant institutions.

To use the term "resistance" responsibly, we must recognize, I believe, that it is tragic in a double sense, for it names both the experience of disorder and suffering that makes resistance necessary in the first place and the consequences that follow acts of resistance. I do not mean that resistance will always backfire on the resister, reproducing conditions of exploitation and marginalization, on one hand, or the addictive and disempowering pleasures of getting away with it, on the other. All I wish to suggest is there are dangers and risks involved that need to be taken into account. And one of these, it's important to note, may well be the writing teacher's own fondness for noncomformists, rebels, bad boys and girls, beautiful losers. The danger, as we can see in Deutscher's trilogy, is not so much that of finding victory in defeat—that is simply part of drawing out the lessons of revolutionary struggles—but of finding victory *only* in defeat.

At a historical moment in the United States when revolutionary energies are largely blocked, mass social movements virtually nonexistent, and the fall of the degenerated workers states in Russia and Eastern Europe the main legacy of the twentieth-century left, it can be all too easy to adjust to these setbacks and retreats by valorizing oppositional behavior that is at best apolitical or prepolitical and at worst antisocial.

The task for radical teachers is to help students understand the sources of resistance and opposition in the tragic disorder and suffering of class society, as well as the consequences of refusal, withdrawal, and counter-identities. Most of all, it is not a matter of calling on alienated students to believe in the system—even the radical teacher's version of it—but of helping them manage a tragic sense of the social order that refuses to accept either its claims or their own alienation.

WORKS CITED

Bauer, Dale. "The Other 'F' Word: The Feminist in the Classroom." *College English* 52 (1990): 385–96.

Brooke, Robert. "Underlife and Writing Instruction." *College Composition and Communication* 38 (1987): 141–53.

Bruffee, Kenneth A. *Collaborative Learning: Higher Education, Interdependence, and the Authority of Knowledge.* Baltimore: Johns Hopkins UP, 1993.

Chase, Geoffrey. "Accommodation, Resistance, and the Politics of Student Writing." *College Composition and Communication* 39 (1988): 13–22.

de Certeau, Michel. *The Practice of Everyday Life.* Berkeley: U of California P, 1984.

Delpit, Lisa. *Other People's Children: Cultural Conflict in the Classroom.* New York: New P, 1995.

Deutscher, Isaac. *The Prophet Armed. Trotsky: 1879–1921.* New York: Vintage, 1954.

———. *The Prophet Unarmed. Trotsky: 1921–1929.* New York: Vintage, 1959.

———. *The Prophet Outcast. Trotsky: 1929–1940.* New York: Vintage, 1963.

Enos, Theresa, ed. *Encyclopedia of Rhetoric and Composition.* New York: Garland, 1996.

Fiske, John. *Understanding Popular Culture.* London: Unwin Hyman, 1989.

Giroux, Henry A. *Theory and Resistance in Education: A Pedagogy for the Opposition.* South Hadley, MA: Bergin and Garvey, 1983.

Hall, Stuart and Tony Jefferson, eds. *Resistance through Rituals: Youth Subcultures in Post-War Britain.* London: Unwin Hyman, 1976.

Hebdige, Dick. *Subculture: The Meaning of Style.* London: Metheun, 1979.

Hurlbert, C. Mark, and Michael Blitz, eds. *Composition and Resistance.* Portsmouth, NH: Heinemann, 1991.

Knoblauch, C. H. "Critical Teaching and Dominant Culture." Hurlbert and Blitz, 12–21.

Miller, Richard. "Fault Lines in the Contact Zone." *College English* 56 (1994): 389–408.

Miraglia, Eric. "Resistance and the Writing Teacher." *JAC: A Journal of Composition Theory* 17 (1997): 415–36.

Moffett, James. *Storm in the Mountains: A Case Study of Censorship, Conflict, and Consciousness.* Carbondale, IL: Southern Illinois UP, 1988.

Myers, Greg. "Reality, Consensus, and Reform in the Rhetoric of Composition Teaching." *College English* 48 (1986): 154–74.

Ophuls, Marcel, dir. *The Sorrow and the Pity.* Facets Multimedia, 1996.

Piercy, Marge. *Gone to Soldiers.* New York: Summit Books, 1987.

Resnais, Alain, dir. *La Guerre Est Finie.* Brandon Films, 1996.

Rose, Mike. *Lives on the Boundary.* New York: Penguin, 1989.

Williams, Raymond. *Modern Tragedy.* Stanford: Stanford UP, 1966.

Willis, Paul. *Learning to Labour: How Working Class Kids Get Working Class Jobs.* New York: Columbia UP, 1977.

CHAPTER 2

Strategic, Counter-Strategic, and Reactive Resistance in the Feminist Classroom

Elizabeth Flynn

When I did a search for books on "resistance and learning" in the electronic catalog of Michigan Tech's library in preparation for the essay, I came up with nothing, so I tried searching for books on "resistance" and was amused by the results: books on topics such as resistance heating, resistance of plants to disease, resistance to insecticides, and resistance welding. Of course, I did not pursue these books since they were far afield of what I was looking for. The exercise did demonstrate, though, that resistance has been used in a wide variety of ways in a wide variety of fields and that often the term has very positive connotations. Resistance to disease is obviously a good thing as is resistance to insecticides and even electric resistance or welding resistance.

In the humanities, resistance is also often used in a positive way, as a necessary response to intolerable circumstances. Numerous books and articles have been written in which "resistance" has been used to describe opposition to alienating or oppressive conditions. Judith Fetterley in *The Resisting Reader*, for instance, urges women readers to resist the canonical white, male, middle-class tradition of nineteenth- and twentieth-century American literature (ix). In this context, resistance becomes an important and necessary response to texts that are alienating for women readers. Fetterley suggests in her foreword to Mark Hulbert and Michael Blitz's *Composition and Resistance*, however, that although she used the term resistance in a positive way in *The*

Julia Jasken provided very useful comments on a draft of this essay.

Resisting Reader, she has discovered that resistance in a pedagogical context can obstruct liberatory goals. She points out that the resistance of some of her male students to her feminist pedagogy can be counter-productive and disruptive. She wonders what happens to the concept of resistance when a male student invokes the model of feminism as resistance in order to resist feminism itself and the feminist teacher (xi). The situation Fetterley describes is no doubt quite common. Students, after all, often bring mainstream values to the classroom and hence become the equivalent of the white, male, middle-class canonical authors that Fetterley thinks women readers need to resist.

We might conclude, then, that resistance to that which is dangerous or oppressive is important and necessary, while resistance to that which is liberatory is debilitating. The male students who resist Fetterley's feminist pedagogy are challenging her authority and jeopardizing the learning of others in the class. I will argue here that it is useful to make distinctions among three different types of resistance: the first involves planned and positive action in opposition to oppression, which I will call "strategic resistance"; the second involves resistance that deliberately disrupts liberatory practices, which I will call "counter-strategic resistance"; and the third involves resistance that is a spontaneous and emotional reaction that may have multiple and conflicting motivations and effects, which I will call "reactive resistance." I will then describe how strategic and reactive resistance can play themselves out in the feminist classroom. It might initially seem as if strategic resistance is desirable and reactive resistance undesirable. I will make clear, however, that reactive resistance can sometimes be productive rather than destructive.[1] I do not mean to suggest that the three types of resistance I identify here can always be clearly delineated. Often, their boundaries blur; their identities also shift from context to context. It is nevertheless useful to name them, if only provisionally, because doing so can help clarify how resistance can be destructive or useful in classroom contexts. Strategic resistance is conscious and deliberate opposition to an oppressive situation. The opposition need not necessarily be collective, though it is usually the result of careful deliberation. Oppositional actions might take the form of writing, speaking, protesting, fighting, marching, willful and public violation of laws, refusal to comply with policies or accepted modes of behavior, or more subtle or less visual activities such as sabotage and withdrawal. Strategic resisters have demonstrated, petitioned, engaged in Ghandi-like passive resistance, and created human barriers in opposition to policies that are seen as harmful to the environment. Counter-strategic resistance involves deliberate attempts by the group in power to oppose or undermine strategic resistance. There are numerous examples of attempts to oppose progressive movements such as the Civil

Rights movement, the Feminist movement, and the Gay Rights movement through strategic action. Opposition sometimes takes the form of protests, written documents, hate speech, threats, and violence. Leaders of liberatory movements such as those mentioned above are often denounced and maligned. Sometimes they are murdered. Attempts are made to sabotage the efforts of activist groups in order to ensure that their goals are not reached. Reactive resistance is a spontaneous and often momentary reaction that can be individual or collective but is not necessarily conscious and may be a result of multiple and conflicting motives. In this scenario, an individual or group disrupts or interrupts in an unexpected way thereby calling attention to themselves. Often, reactive resistance involves action that results from dissatisfaction or discomfort but that has not been carefully thought through.

STRATEGIC RESISTANCE

Pierre Bourdieu provides numerous examples of strategic resistance in his recent book, *Acts of Resistance*. The book itself is a way of resisting what Bourdieu calls neo-liberalism—individualistic and universalistic approaches to the solution of social and economic problems. Bourdieu tells us in his note to the reader that the book is a collection of essays originally written or spoken as contributions to movements and moments of resistance (vii). He explains that he hopes the essays will provide "useful weapons to all those who are striving to resist the scourge of neo-liberalism" (vii). He also explains that he was motivated to take public positions by a "kind of legitimate rage" and something like "a sense of duty" (vi). For Bourdieu, essays can be effective means of resistance because they are action in the symbolic realm as they are policy decisions to an extent (3). The neo-liberal policies and practices he thinks need to be resisted are the return to individualism (7); narrow-minded, regressive, security-minded, xenophobic attitudes toward foreigners in modern democracies such as France (18); the abuse of power by advocates of reason (19); universalist messages of liberation (31); the "casualization" or downsizing of work forces that result in unemployment and job security (82); and the domination of a small number of nations over a whole set of financial markets in the name of globalization (38).

In addition to the act of writing, Bourdieu mentions a number of other acts of resistance that clearly involve careful planning and strategizing. One of the pieces in the collection is a talk given at the time of the occupation of the Ecole Normale Superieure by the unemployed. Bourdieu speaks of the protest movement by the unemployed as a result of "the tireless work of individuals and associations which has encouraged, supported and organized the movement" (88). He sees that the movement itself pulls the unemployed "out of invisibility, isolation, silence, in short, out of non-existence" (89). For Bourdieu, mobilization means a rejection of political fatalism (90).

Bourdieu also sees that intellectual life itself is a form of resistance and finds that "There is no genuine democracy without genuine opposing critical powers" (8). He thinks writers, artists, philosophers and scientists should enter into public decision-making and that the logic or intellectual life should be extended to public life (9). As it is, too often the logic of political life in the form of denunciation and slander and the falsification of the adversary's thought finds its way into intellectual life instead (9). Intellectuals, in turn, can help nonprofessionals equip themselves with weapons of resistance in order to combat the effects of authority and the grip of television (57).

Bourdieu also thinks researchers can resist neo-liberal discourse, which individualizes everything, by analyzing the production and circulation of it (29). He argues that an "economics of happiness" should replace neo-liberal approaches to economics (40), which he defines narrowly as financial profitability of shareholders and investors (40). An economics of happiness, in contrast, would also take into consideration the material and symbolic costs of inactivity or precarious employment (40).

Ultimately, Bourdieu calls for a new internationalism among trade unions, intellectuals, and the people of Europe (65). This will necessitate mobilization of the people (65) through a critique of representations of dominant groups in the media such as false statistics and myths about full employment in Britain and the United States (66). He also thinks it is necessary to act on and through the national states toward the goal of social harmonization (67). More specific objectives include defining a minimum wage, opposing minimum wages and tax fraud, giving priority to strategies aimed at safeguarding nonrenewable resources and the environment, developing public housing and urban regeneration, investment in research and development in health, and the financing of new activities such as small businesses and self-employment (68).

Julia Kristeva also emphasizes the importance of the intellectual in political resistance in her essay "A New Type of Intellectual: The Dissident." She sees that it is crucial to break out of the opposition that has arisen between the intellectual and the masses and to recast the relationship (293). Kristeva discusses types of dissidents such as the rebel, the psychoanalyst, the writer, and women (295). Kristeva finds that the approach of the rebel is ineffective in that a rebel is oppositional and hence remains within the limits of the "master-slave couple" (295). She thinks, though, that psychoanalysis remains an active site of resistance to an all-embracing rationality" (295). The playful language of the writer is also effective in that it gives rise to a law that is "overturned, violated and pluralized" (295). Kristeva recognizes that women can either support or subvert established structures, or support and subvert those structures at the same time, given that a woman is at once the guarantee of a society's stability and a threat to that stability (297). While she sees that certain forms of feminism are characterized by "sulking isolation" rather than political protest or dissidence, she finds that real female innovation can come about "when maternity, female creation and the link between them are better understood" (298). Finally, though, she focuses on the exile as dissident. The exile, according to Kristeva, is already a dissident, and writing is impossible without some kind of exile (298). She concludes that the work of a dissident is a process of "ruthless and irreverent dismantling of the workings of discourse, thought, and existence" (299). The dissident can "attempt to bring about multiple sublations of the unnamable, the unrepresentable, the void" (300).

Intellectuals or individuals engaged in collective political action obviously employ carefully thought out strategies to carry out their resistant practices. As previously mentioned, individual workers can also engage in resistant practices. James C. Scott in *Weapons of the Weak: Everyday Forms of Peasant Resistance*, for instance, describes the acts of resistance of peasant workers in a Malaysian village in which he lived for two years in 1978–1980. Scott discusses their resistance in the context of class struggle and ideological domination, describing the situation in the village as one in which the rich have gotten richer and the poor have remained poor or grown poorer (xvii). The symbolic resistance Scott speaks of involves rewarding those whose conduct corresponds with their values and undercutting the moral authority of their enemies by undermining their reputations and social prestige (236). He finds that the symbolic barrier that is created is a real obstacle to the designs of the rich (236). The peasants resist by refusing to accept the definition of the situation provided by those in power and by refusing to condone their own social and ritual marginalization (240).

Scott also describes nonsymbolic acts of resistance, though he explains that open, collective resistance is too dangerous an undertaking. If the act of resistance is open, it is not collective, and if it is collective, it is not open (242). One covert form of resistance he mentions involves the work of rice threshers. The threshers realize that they can work faster, and hence earn more money, if they do not beat each sheaf thoroughly (256). Also, the threshers' wives can return and collect that which has been left behind if all of the rice is not harvested (257). The workers also resist by being alert to news of farmers paying fractionally more than the rate for the previous season and by using this information to argue for higher wages (258). Or they can threaten to walk off the job or actually do so (259). Scott emphasizes, however, that the activities he describes require little coordination or political organization (273). He says, "They are the stubborn bedrock upon which other forms of resistance may grow" (273).

Strategic resistance, then, can be individual as well as collective; it can involve a minimum of planning or years of coordination, it can involve active opposition or silent protest; it can involve powerful leaders or powerless workers.

Always, though, it involves opposition to injustice or unfairness in the form of action that is deliberate and conscious. The strategic resister identifies a problem and takes action to mitigate or eliminate the problem. In a pedagogical context, courses are often designed as acts of strategic resistance. Teachers attempt to make students aware of social injustice and sometimes encourage them to take action to oppose it.

COUNTER-STRATEGIC RESISTANCE

Opposition to feminism provides a good example of counter-strategic resistance. The movement poses a threat to individuals benefiting from the status quo and so they take action to impede the movement's progress. The backlash against feminism is recounted in VèVè Clark, Shirley Nelson Garner, Margaret Higgonet, and Ketu H. Katrak's *Antifeminism in the Academy* and in Susan Faludi's *Backlash*. In their introduction and in the eight essays in the volume, the contributors to *Antifeminism in the Academy* identify a number of ways in which feminist goals are subverted in the academy including what the authors call intellectual harassment, antilesbianism, ageism, student resistance, and antifeminism in scholarship and publishing.

Intellectual harassment, according to the editors, is methodical assault on feminism that is broad and collective (ix). It includes "use of vilification and distortion or even violence to repress certain areas of research and forms of inquiry" (x). In the introduction, the editors quote a definition of intellectual harassment that was produced at the 1991 MLA convention in San Francisco:

> Antifeminist intellectual harassment, a serious threat to academic freedom, occurs when (1) any policy, action, statement, and/or behavior has the effect of discouraging or preventing women's freedom or lawful action, freedom of thought, and freedom of expression; (2) or when any policy, action, statement, and/or behavior creates an environment

in which the appropriate application of feminist theories or methodologies to research, scholarship, and teaching is devalued, discouraged,
or altogether thwarted; (3) *or* when any policy, action, statement,
and/or behavior creates an environment in which research, scholarship,
and teaching pertaining to women, gender, or gender inequities are
devalued, discouraged, or altogether thwarted. (xii)

The editors also mention the formidable backlash that has assumed center stage in the 1990s media and has been promoted by right-wing ide-
ologues such as Allan Bloom, Dinesh D'Souza, and Camille Paglia (xiv).

Moira Ferguson, Ketu Katrak, and Valerie Miner in "Feminism and
Antifeminism: From Civil Rights to Culture Wars" identify the culture
wars of the 1980s and 1990s as including feminism and feminists among
their targets (48). They identify a number of ways in which feminism is
attacked—intellectual devaluing and ridicule of feminist ideas, political
baiting of feminists, and physical threats (48)—and illustrate the point
by invoking the man who gunned down fourteen women in a University
of Montreal classroom because they were feminists (49). Ferguson,
Katrak, and Miner find that contemporary antifeminism began in the
late seventies among the religious Right and then moved to the White
House with the presidency of Ronald Reagan in the eighties (50). Other
benchmarks include the defeat of the Equal Rights Amendment in 1982
and increased use of the media in antifeminist campaigns. Conservative
talk shows identify feminist goals of autonomy and independence as
causes of women's problems such as depression, unemployment, or
teenage pregnancy (51). Ferguson, Katrak, and Miner also mention violent attacks on abortion clinics and physicians who perform abortions
(51) and the activities of the conservative National Association of Scholars. All of the activities they mention are strategic in that they are deliberate attempts to impede the progress women have made, and involve
planning and considerable deliberative effort, often of a collective
nature.

Susan Faludi in *Backlash* describes what she calls the New Right's
war on women (229). Faludi says that every backlash movement has its
preferred scapegoat—Catholics, Jews, Blacks. For the New Right,
according to Faludi, it is women (232). Rooted in conservative politics
and fundamentalist religion, the New Right finds women's liberation
threatening to its fundamental tenets and therefore promotes traditional
family values and opposes women's entry into the workplace. Faludi
makes clear the considerable bureaucracy that lies behind the New
Right's attack on feminism in her discussions on the work of Connie
Marshner of the New Right's Heritage Foundation and of Beverley La
Haye, founder of the New Right's Concerned Women for America.
Faludi also points out the irony that both Marshner and La Haye were

aggressive career women who did not remain at home to raise their children. Rather, they coordinated large organizations, traveled extensively to make public speaking engagements, and wrote books. Both women worked actively to oppose public support of day care, abortion, and women's rights.

Faludi discusses numerous other manifestations of the backlash against feminism in the late 1980s including media representations, the fashion industry, national politics, and antifeminist books. She argues, for instance, that although Allan Bloom's *The Closing of the American Mind* is ostensibly about the decline of American education, it is actually an assault on the women's movement (290). She sees his book as identifying the same problem again and again: "the feminist transformation of society that has filled women with demands and desires and depleted men of vim and vigor" (290). Faludi sees Bloom as focusing his book on "the rising female terror" (291). Women pose a serious threat because they have triumphed over the family, led to the suppression of modesty, and freed women from the dictates of the male will (291). Faludi finds that for Bloom feminists rule American campuses with "iron-fisted authority" (292). She reports that according to Bloom most faculty jobs and publication rights are now reserved for feminist women (293). Faludi counters this claim with statistics that indicate that women account for a mere 10 percent of the tenured faculty at all four-year institutions and that five times more women with Ph.D.s are unemployed than men (293). Bloom's main complaint, according to Faludi, is that feminism has decimated the basic identity of men (295). But she sees it as little more than a complaint, given that it is not backed up by research, evidence, or quotations that would support his assertions about the contemporary situation between the sexes (296).

Although counter-strategic resistance is possible in a pedagogical context, I would argue that it is not widespread. Fetterley's students, invoking feminism itself, actively oppose her efforts to create a feminist classroom. Their resistance is probably a mild form of counter-strategic resistance, however, if it is counter-strategic resistance at all. It is unlikely that the students are conspiratorial in their opposition, and their efforts to disrupt her class probably do not involve much planning if they involve any at all.

REACTIVE RESISTANCE

The resistance we sometimes encounter in the feminist classroom is often reactive rather than counter-strategic. Students react in a spontaneous way to our pedagogies because they conflict with their own ideological perspectives, but their reactions are not usually carefully planned or even intentional. Dale Bauer and Katherine Rhoades provide good examples of reactive resistance in their contribution to *Antifeminism in the Academy*, "The Meanings and Metaphors of Student Resistance." While mentioning violent expressions of student resistance in the form of heckling, defacing of posters and office doors, and public displays of belittling or defamatory material (96), Bauer and Rhoades focus primarily on their frustrations as exemplified by their teaching evaluations. According to Bauer and Rhoades, because students value neutrality and objectivity, they are often critical of feminist approaches to the material being studied. They exhibit a range of emotions in describing their feelings about their feminist teacher; they can become "upset, . . . exhilarated, exhausted, scared, frustrated, annoyed, troubled, angry, tranquil, and cared for" (97). Bauer and Rhoades suggest that feminist teachers should respond to such resistance by teaching dialogically, i.e., constructing a classroom climate and curriculum which allows students to generate questions fueling the course (109). Dialogical teaching also involves establishing common ground with students (109) and attempting to negotiate the private-public split (110).

Reactive resistance in a pedagogical context is similar in many ways to what Kathleen Dixon in *Outbursts in Academe* calls an "outburst." She defines an outburst as,

> A moment when the often latent conflicts among faculty and among students, between students and faculty, or within individuals bubble to the surface, erupting in class discussions, small-group work, office-hour conversations, conference presentations, evaluations of teachers, written assignments, academic publications, or email conferencing. An outburst is a response to a conflict that expresses a person's orientation to that conflict and to the social and political conditions that underlie it. (xi)

She explains that outbursts are often unexpected and therefore often take an unexpected form (xi). She says:

> They may be loud and short, like a shout, or long and monotonous, like hectoring. They may be gestural or even pre-gestural (e.g. a blush, a stammer). We may believe that we see the traces of an outburst in an absence (e.g. a student who drops a course; the silence that greets one person's outburst). (xi)

Dixon speaks of an outburst as an isolatable, researchable moment in the lives of teachers and students (ix). She makes clear, however, that outbursts, while not always productive, can, at times, lead to useful expression of opinions and learning. For Dixon, the present moment within the academy is one in which there may be less political cohesion but in which more voices are being heard (x). She speaks of the university as an animated and confusing "site of struggle" among students and faculty. Although Dixon makes clear that outbursts are sometimes regressive or both progressive and regressive, she finds that they have the potential, at least, of creating dialogue across groups separated by various and complicated power differences and hence can expand democracy (xiii).

The essays in Dixon's collection provide an extended definition of the term "outburst." Carol Winkelman in "Cyborg Bodies: Race, Class, Gender, and Communications Technology," for instance, describes a number of different kinds of outbursts. The essay is a description of electronic interaction between students in her electronic literacy course and women in a shelter home for abused women; it focuses especially on the situation of one of the women, whom she calls Sheila. Winkelman finds that her white, middle- and upper-middle-class students resist her race, class, and gender analyses of the problems of computer culture, but almost always politely, despite occasional outbursts (5). Her examples of student outbursts, responses to a narrative cowritten by Winkelman and Sheila, are barely detectable as such. One student wrote to Sheila, "I feel really awkward writing to you because I've never even met you" (12). Another writes that Sheilia's daughter, who became pregnant and dropped out of college, "is smart enough to know what she did and the consequences. She is even strong enough to deal with them" (12).

Winkelman describes the shelter, however, as a place of frequent outbursts (5), some quite dramatic. Sheila, for instance, "closed the door of her room, laid down on her bed, and overdosed on drugs. She was hustled out of the shelter by a white-jacketed medical team" (14). Her outburst led to other outbursts, especially by the staff who were livid that she brought illicit drugs into the shelter and that the ambulance and sirens had frightened the children in the shelter. Winkelman wonders if Sheila's suicide attempt was triggered by the interaction with her students but resists this interpretation, concluding that she and her students had to believe that the act of storytelling was not self-destructive (14–15). But Winkelman's telling of the story in conference papers that she delivered resulted in other outbursts: an Asian woman "harangued me about the ethics of making available the private life of African American Shelia for the public scrutiny of white students" (16). Winkelman responded to the attack by explaining that Sheila was a co-author rather than a silent object. She freely chose to initiate the electronic conversation (16). Winkelman concludes that many people, including students and academics, have outbursts when poor and marginalized women speak up (18). She also concludes that her goal was to enable her students and the women in the shelter to see the potential of writing as "weaving, networking, affinity, and social action" (20). Winkelman calls this kind of writing "writing as outburst," an activity she supports (20). Dixon, in her essay, "Revisiting White Feminist Authority, or Gang Life in the University Classroom," admits that her use of the term "gang life" to describe conflict in her classes between and among middle-class women and men is tongue-in-cheek. According to Dixon, the university classroom is usually considered to be gang free (48). She does so because the stories she tells involve groups of students ganging up on other students. Sometimes groups of men gang up on women. Sometimes gangs of white women go after other white women. Sometimes white women group together to act against women of color (48). Dixon describes a class in which "anxious young men devoid of a male master enact rules of mock battle upon a public territory they feel they have a right to claim as their own" (57). She also describes a graduate seminar in which women students objected to some of the course readings on the grounds that they were theoretical, and theory is inherently male and patriarchal (50). Finally, Dixon describes the marginalization of a Native American student in a collaborative group comprised primarily of white, middle-class women (64–65).

Other essays in the volume describe outbursts that also involve reactive resistance. Jacqueline Anderson in "Essays That Never Were: Deaf Identity and Resistance in the Mainstream Classroom" finds that deaf students resist traditional assignments by writing against expectations that they will conform to majority patterns (85). Scott Lyons in "A Captivity Narrative: Indians, Mixedbloods, and 'White' Academe" tells several stories of what he calls "mixedbloods"—who are divergent thinkers who resist convergence (91). They are "racially designated beings who both resist and perform 'racializing'" (91) and are "fluid, porous, mobile—and also schizophrenic, cloistered, captive" (91). Doreen Starke-Meyerring in "Lost and Melted in the Pot: Multicultural Literacy in Predominantly White Classrooms" describes the results of a survey she conducted of 171 composition students on the topic of multiculturalism. According to Starke-Meyerring, the survey provided a forum for comments and outbursts (135–36).

STRATEGIC AND REACTIVE RESISTANCE IN "LITERATURE AND COMPOSITION"

The feminist classroom is quite obviously itself a form of strategic resistance. Teachers attempt to counter oppressive circumstances in society by making students aware of them and even enlisting their assistance in countering them. As Bauer and Rhoades and others point out, however, students often resist feminist teachers and feminist agendas in the classroom. Here I will describe a course I taught recently, "Literature and Composition," as a way of illustrating strategic resistance and discuss the reactive resistance of some students to the course. As the examples make clear, students' reactive resistance can sometimes have beneficial effects.

Although a hybrid, the upper-level course is listed as a literature course and can be taken to fulfill general education requirements or requirements for our major in scientific and technical communication or liberal arts with an English concentration. Described in the Michigan Tech undergraduate catalog as an "Investigation of the composing process in writing through a study of selected rhetoric and literature," its purpose, as stated on my syllabus, is to,

> Explore relationships between reading and writing by focusing on the contexts in which they frequently take place. Jacqueline Bobo's *Black Women as Cultural Readers* will provide an introduction to theories of reading while Peter Elbow's *What Is English?* Will provide an introduction to English studies, the academic area that focuses on developing approaches to reading and writing. We also read two novels, Terry McMillan's *Waiting to Exhale* and Alice Walker's *The Color Purple*, and watch the film versions of these books.

I have taught the course a number of times in a number of different ways, though the past few times I have used Bobo's study of Black women's responses to works such as *Waiting to Exhale* and both the novel and film versions of *The Color Purple* along with Elbow's *What is English?* In addition to daily in-class and weekly out-of-class journal entries, there are two writing assignments in the course. The first asked students to provide background material that would help the class understand *Waiting to Exhale* or *The Color Purple*. They were free to focus on topics such as the cultural background of the novel, its setting, or the author's biography. They were encouraged to work collaboratively on this assignment. The second was a description of the reading or writing processes of an individual or group, broadly defined to include members of e-mail lists, participants in student critique groups, audiences, etc. In their descriptions, they were to draw on material on reading and writing in the Bobo or Elbow books. Students presented summaries of both papers in five-minute presentations. Though comprised predominantly of white students, the class included one Black student and one Native American student.

The course design is an example of strategic resistance in that it aimed to introduce students to reading, writing, and interpreting as cultural, political, and linguistic processes and focused, especially, on relationships between language use and gender. The first book that we read, McMillan's best-selling novel *Waiting to Exhale*, describes the stress-filled lives of four middle-class Black women who are successful in their careers but not in their relationships with men. For instance, Bernadine, a mother of two, is informed by her husband early in the novel that he is leaving her for his white bookkeeper. Much of her energy is devoted to attempting to obtain a fair divorce settlement in the face of his maneuvering to conceal from her and her lawyer his substantial assets. Gloria is the owner of a successful beauty salon and the single parent of a teenage son. By the end of the novel her son Tarik has made a successful break with his mother, and Gloria has become romantically involved with her new neighbor, a kind, intelligent, and caring individual. At the outset of the novel, Savannah, who works in the publicity department of a local TV station, moves to Phoenix but is unsuccessful in her search for a mate. She does advance in her career, however. She will become a producer rather than a publicist at the TV station. Robin is single, an underwriter in an insurance company, who deludes herself that her relationship with Russell, a n'er-do-well, will result in marriage and children. At the end of the novel she becomes pregnant with Russell's child but has freed herself of him. All four women find ways to mitigate stress in their lives, to end relationships that are destructive, and to create lifestyles that are more fulfilling than their previous ones.

The plot of *The Color Purple* is well known. Set in rural Georgia in the pre–Civil Rights South, the central character is Celie, a woman who is raped by her stepfather. She has two children by him, both of whom are forcibly removed from her at birth. The only light in her life is her love for Nettie, her sister, and for Shug, a successful blues singer and her husband's long-time lover. For much of the novel, though, she has lost contact with Nettie, who has become a missionary in Africa because Celie's husband, Albert, has hidden Nettie's letters to her. Shug's love, however, enables her to leave Albert, embark on a business that provides her a means of support, and become reconnected with Nettie and her children, whom Nettie has helped raise.

Jacqueline Bobo's *Black Women as Cultural Readers* provides interpretations of the two novels, of the film version of *The Color Purple*, and of the reactions of two groups of Black women to these works. In Bobo's theoretical introduction to her book, she situates her work within film studies, cultural studies, and feminist studies. Her audience is clearly other academics or graduate students with specializations in these three area rather than undergraduates. I have had success with the book in the past, though, because Bobo writes clearly and accessibly and because I spend class time explaining difficult concepts and passages.

Peter Elbow's *What is English?* is a description and a discussion of the 1987 English Coalition Conference, a three-week meeting of teachers on the elementary level, the secondary level, and the university level designed to reflect on the teaching of English and on English as a profession. Although written for an audience of teachers or college professors, the book is reasonably accessible, especially given that Elbow intersperses his observations with narratives provided by the conference participants themselves. Elbow discusses themes such as democracy through language, taking a theoretical stance, the relationship between composition and literature, and assessment practices and pitfalls. Elbow avoids answering the question of what English is but does conclude that we need to try to persuade society to value teachers more and treat them better (219). Students have little difficulty with the narrative portions of the book, though they sometimes find Elbow's discussions of issues within English studies a bit challenging. By the end, though, they almost always like the book and can always connect with it given that they are students and are not that far removed from their high school or even grade school experiences.

I designed the midterm assignment to enable students to better understand and appreciate *Waiting to Exhale* and *The Color Purple* and hence better understand racial and sexual oppression and inequality. One student did research on the pre–Civil Rights South, providing a sociological and historical context for *The Color Purple*. A collaborative pair that did research on Terry McMillan's biography informed us that she is from Port Huron, Michigan, was raised by her mother, and had an alcoholic father. They also provided us descriptions of McMillan's other novels, works which represent the struggles of African Americans from a variety of social classes, and in numerous contexts. Another woman provided information about the migration of Blacks to the West and Southwest. Another researched the relationship between dual-career families and the divorce rate. Students became better informed about the situation of women, especially African American women, and provided helpful background material that illuminated course texts.

I designed the course as an act of strategic resistance and was generally pleased with the results. A number of students in their final papers chose to focus on racial or gender issues, and their papers provided evidence that the course had enabled them to think about racial and gender problems in new and productive ways. One student, for instance, surveyed views of the film *A Time to Kill* to see if prejudicial attitudes toward Blacks exhibited before watching the film made a difference in viewing the film. The movie is the story of a Black girl who is raped by two white men. The father of the girl then shoots the men and is arrested for murder. His lawyer, arguing against the death penalty, makes a moving final plea that is effective in persuading the jury. Much to the student's surprise, she found commonalties in the responses of the students regardless of their predisposition toward racial matters. Students, regardless of predisposition to be prejudiced, tended to identify with the murdered girl's father. The students concluded that the film itself, especially the lawyer's powerful closing statement, was compelling enough to override preconceptions about race.

The Black student in the class wrote about the differences between the reactions of what she called a non-Black-cultured group and a Black-cultured group to the film *The Player's Club*. The movie is about a young pregnant woman who moves out of her home because her father wants her to go to a white university, whereas she wants to attend an historically Black college. The woman works to support herself through college but is persuaded, as she is approaching graduation, to take a job as a stripper in a night club, a job that results in a brutal rape by a client. In analyzing the responses of a non-Black-cultured group and the Black-cultured group, the student in the class found that cultural background can strongly influence the interpretive process of understanding a film. She found differences in the responses of the non-Black-cultured group and the Black-cultured group. For instance, the students in the Black-cultured group tended to have greater sympathy for the protagonist's goal of attending an all-Black college than did the students in the non-Black-cultured group. I was encouraged by the categories the student created. She avoided essentialized conceptions of race by focusing on cultural attitudes rather than racial identity. Her Black-cultured group, for instance, included a white person who had been raised in urban areas and was immersed in Black culture.

These successes may have been enabled, to an extent at least, by the reactive resistance of some of the students in the class. Early in the term, for instance, when students were beginning to identify topics for their midterm papers, one student made the somewhat surprising comment that she was interested in exploring the racism of the characters is *Waiting to Exhale*. She was apparently bothered by the fact that the Black women protagonists seemed to socialize exclusively with Blacks and do not condone the marriage of Black men to white women. I responded to the student's statement by reminding her that the assignment required that she provide background information that would shed light on the novel. She needed to find a topic that was researchable. I was obviously not alone in taking note of the comment because the Black student in the class, who collaborated with another classmate on her paper, made clear in her presentation of their research findings that she was motivated to explore the issue of interracial marriage by the comment about the racism of the characters in the book. Using the work of Eldridge Cleaver, she and her classmate argued that there were good reasons why

Black women, such as those in *Waiting to Exhale*, are often resentful of the attentions paid to white women by Black males. The student who made the original comment also did extensive research and in her presentation provided demographic information that demonstrated that there is indeed a shortage of eligible Black males for college-educated Black women. The only moment when we were reminded of the original comment about the racism of the characters was the student's conclusion in which she used a quote to emphasize that a disproportionate number of Black males are now or have been in jail. The original outburst, then, the impulsive reaction to what was perceived as racism on the part of the Black protagonists in *Waiting to Exhale*, ultimately became a productive one.

The resistant student's final paper is further evidence that the outburst was productive. She chose to do extensive research on Alice Walker and learned that Walker's writing was greatly influenced by her views about the environment and feminism and that her ideals culminated in a womanist theology. She also wrote an e-mail message to the class toward the end of the term expressing her enthusiasm for the course and assigning it an "A." And after class one day she asked me what courses I was teaching in the future that she might take. Her initial resistance contributed her own learning and motivated others to prepare a response.

A second outburst may not have been as productive. A male student posted to the class e-mail list a denunciation of Bobo's book, finding particular fault with her critique of Steven Spielberg's film version of *The Color Purple*, especially her claim that many of the characters' actions were stereotypical. His resistant comment was a complaint that Bobo portrayed some whites as ignorant, redneck Southerners. Although he sent his message to the entire class via the e-mail list, no one responded to it. And in his final paper, an analysis of the reactions of fans of the film *The Rocky Horror Picture Show* as expressed by individuals in a news group, he avoided the theme of race entirely. In his paper he did make a positive reference to Bobo's book, though, quoting a passage from it—an excerpt from John Fiske's *Understanding Popular Culture*. And his final observation about the class was positive in that he found the presentations to be informative. The ones he found to be especially effective, though, were ones that did not deal with racial issues explicitly.

We do not usually have to deal with counter-strategic resistance in our classes. Student resistance to our pedagogies of resistance is usually fairly innocent in that students are not usually members of organized groups set on subverting feminist goals. Reactive resistance, however, can be destructive if it gets out of hand or if it takes the form of negative evaluations of teachers by students that faculty have no opportunity to respond to. In what Bauer and Rhoades call a dialogic classroom, however, reactive resistance can be productive because it can stimulate thought and lead to further clarification of liberatory strategies and goals. I would even go so far as to say that reactive resistance in its positive manifestations is necessary for successful teaching. If a course did not present ideas and values that clashed, to an extent at least, with those that students bring to it, little learning would occur. I have found that students who resist my pedagogical goals are often amendable to change, and their comments frequently provide opportunities for thoughtful responses from others. It is important, however, that their reactions be taken seriously rather than dismissed. In an atmosphere in which a variety of perspectives is encouraged, reactive resistance is inevitable and sometimes even desirable.

NOTE

1. My discussion of resistance differs in some ways with conceptions of resistance as articulated in Ernesto Laclau and Chantel Mouffe's *Hegemony and Socialist Strategy*, Henry Giroux's *Theory and Resistance in Education: A Pedagogy for the Opposition*, and Kathleen Weiler's *Women Teaching for Change: Gender, Class and Power*, which I discuss in my essay "Feminism and Scientism." In *Hegemony and Socialist Strategy*, Laclau and Mouffe emphasize that relations of oppression are characterized by antagonism and awareness of inequality. Resistance becomes possible when individuals become aware that their relationships with others are unequal. Democratic discourse makes resistance possible. In Giroux's terms, resistance, "contains the possibility" of galvanizing political struggle, but is still only a state of awareness that precedes change. In *Women Teaching for Change: Gender, Class and Power*, Weiler draws on the work of Antonio Gramsci and others to distinguish between counter-hegemony and resistance. According to Weiler, counter-hegemony implies that critical theoretical understanding is expressed in organized and active political opposition (54). Resistance, in contrast, is usually informal, disorganized, and apolitical (54).

WORKS CITED

Anderson, Jacqueline. "Essays That Never Were: Deaf Identity and Resistance in the Mainstream Classroom." Dixon, 66–86.

Bauer, Dale, and Katherine Rhoades. "The Meanings and Metaphors of Student Resistance." Clark, Garner, Higonnet, and Katrak, 95–113.

Bloom, Allan. *The Closing of the American Mind*. New York: Simon & Schuster, 1987.

Bobo, Jacqueline. *Black Women as Cultural Readers*. New York: Columbia UP, 1995.

Bourdieu, Pierre. *Acts of Resistance: Against the Tyranny of the Market*. New York: The New P, 1998.

Clark, VéVé, Shirley Nelson Garner, Margaret Higgonet, and Ketu H. Katrak. Introduction. *Antifeminism in the Academy*. Ed. VéVé Clark, Shirley Nelson Garner, Margaret Higgonet, and Ketu H. Katrak. New York: Routledge, 1996. ix–xix.

———. *Antifeminism in the Academy*, eds. New York: Routledge, 1996.

Dixon, Kathleen, ed. *Outbursts in Academe: Multiculturalism and Other Sources of Conflict*. Portsmouth: Boynton/Cook, 1998.

———. "Revisiting White Feminist Authority, or Gang Life in the University Classroom." Dixon, 48–65.

Elbow, Peter. *What is English?* New York: Modern Language Association of America, 1990.

Faludi, Susan. *Backlash: The Undeclared War Against American Women*. New York: Crown P, 1991.

Ferguson, Moira, Ketu H. Katrak, and Valerie Miner. "Feminism and Antifeminism: From Civil Rights to Culture Wars." Clark, Garner, Higonnet, and Katrak, 35–66.

Fetterley, Judith. Foreward. *Composition and Resistance*. Ed. C. Mark Hurlbert and Michael Blitz. Portsmouth: Boynton/Cook, 1991. ix–xii.

———. *The Resisting Reader: A Feminist Approach to American Fiction*. Bloomington: Indiana UP, 1978.

Flynn, Elizabeth. "Feminism and Scientism." *College Composition and Communication* 46 (October 1995): 353–68.

Giroux, Henry A. *Theory and Resistance in Education: A Pedagogy for the Opposition*. New York: Bergin, 1983.

Kristeva, Julia. "A New Type of Intellectual: The Dissident." *The Kristeva Reader*. Ed. Toril Moi. New York: Columbia UP, 1986. 292–300.

Laclau, Ernesto and Chantal Mouffe. *Hegemony and Socialist Strategy: Toward a Radical Democratic Politics*. London: Verso, 1985.

Lyons, Scott. "A Captivity Narrative: Indians, Mixedbloods, and 'White' Academe." Dixon, 87–108.

McMillan, Terry. *Waiting to Exhale*. New York: Pocket Books, 1992. New Haven: Yale UP, 1985.

Scott, James C. *Weapons of the Weak: Everyday Forms of Peasant Resistance*. New Haven: Yale UP, 1985.

Starke-Meyerring, Doreen. "Lost and Melted in the Pot: Multicultural Literacy in Predominantly White Classrooms." Dixon, 135–57.

Walker, Alice. *The Color Purple*. New York: Washington Square P, 1982.

Weiler, Kathleen. *Women Teaching for Change: Gender, Class and Power*. New York: Bergin and Garvey, 1988.

Winkelman, Carol. "Cyborg Bodies: Race, Class, Gender, and Communications Technology." Dixon, 2–22.

PART 2

Race and the Politics of Literacy

CHAPTER 3

Students' Right to Possibility: Basic Writing and African American Rhetoric

Keith Gilyard
and
Elaine Richardson

This essay aims to contribute to the strands of inquiry and practice sparked by the "Students' Right to Their Own Language" (SRTOL) resolution. While we unwaveringly endorse the linguistic principles contained in that watershed document and also recognize the need for continued critical speculation about the overall tenets of the tract, we believe that insufficient space has been given to empirical or practical responses to the theoretical call. We begin by briefly referencing the major ideas evinced in the SRTOL resolution and providing a glimpse into some of the related political issues. We then report on a study conducted by one of the authors that was designed to assess the practicality of implementing the principles of the SRTOL with respect to the development of academic writing among African American students. We close by reflecting upon the implications of our work for future theory and research.

BACKGROUND

In 1974, a special issue of *College Composition and Communication* contained both a resolution asserting students' right to their own language and attendant explanations of the sociolinguistic and pedagogical premises that shaped the resolution. The combined statement, revolving around a core concept of linguistic equality, supported certain progressive work around questions of language, identity, hegemony, and inclusion—with much of the focus on African American students—that was unfolding inside composition studies generally and the basic writing wing in particular. Although the document and sentiment behind it have remained important, especially during the latest publicized skirmish in the decades-old Ebonics controversy, the SRTOL is still controversial.

Predictably, conservatives have never embraced it and seek to undermine its expression whenever it appears to threaten their sense of order and, perhaps, control. For example, in an attempt to maintain the status quo, they discourage vernacular usage in schools, usually with an argument that they are preparing so-called minority students for success in the market place, all while many of the most successful people in the market place are running off with fresh stacks of pretty little green ones accumulated to the advertising beat of hip hop.

Even some on the other end of the political spectrum, who support the document, criticize its framers and others who have since defended it. Patrick Bruch and Richard Marback, for instance, do seek to "reinvigorate the statement's hope for democratic literacy instruction and democratic social transformation" (269). They are, however, disappointed with talk of repertoire expansion and code-switching that derives from the SRTOL, considering such discussion to be merely liberal, overly restrictive, and indicative of some unwillingness to link questions of literacy to specific social justice efforts. However, they have no way to prove this alleged political bashfulness (backwardness?) because they offer no assessment of practices that derive from the discussions of which they are critical. One would have to explore the educational context in which code-switching is employed to make an informed judgment as to whether it is simply a ploy of liberal pluralism or truly a radical stratagem. Cornel West certainly employs a good measure of code-switching during his public articulations of prophetic pragmatism, the philosophical premise that undergirds Bruch and Marback's work.

But there is no need for too big a fight here. The left has perhaps proved as adept at squabbling among itself as anything else. We are actually supportive of a platform more radical than liberal, but we would have everyone be wary of making totalizing statements relative to SRTOL and its aftermath. We should bear in mind that collaboration on a document like SRTOL does not necessarily mean that its composers were of identical theoretical persuasion, nor does the existence of SRTOL imply that strict uniformity exists among the practitioners supportive of the manifesto. Both of these points, as Steve Parks notes in his historical study, are sometimes obscured. While some originators and subsequent advocates have been content simply to articulate and pro-mote goals of bidialectalism and assimilation, other central figures, such as Geneva Smitherman, have embraced a greater activism. As Smither-man reminds us, putting standard speech in the mouth of Black students "ain done nothin to address the crises in the Black community." Fur-thermore, in *Black English*, one of the key texts informing the SRTOL resolution, J. L. Dillard argued that English departments accept quality work in African American Vernacular English (AAVE), a proposal that also ranges beyond simplistic notions of code-switching (278–79).

There was never a shortage of ideas about how SRTOL could be implemented beyond a liberal pluralist paradigm, just a shortage of empirical models. We thus offer one. In doing so we shift the terms of engagement somewhat; we extend the notion of "Students Right to Their Own Language" to a question of "Students' Right to Possibility." We acknowledge language rights at the outset, and this allows us to place our emphasis on the ways of knowing and becoming that our stu-dents exhibit—and that we help them exhibit—as they negotiate the structures of academic schooling.

A curriculum designed to implement the principles of the SRTOL as it concerns the teaching of writing to African American students obvi-ously needs to address the central question of to what extent African American speech styles can be instrumental to the development of criti-cal academic writing. Attempting to answer this question takes us beyond appreciation of AAVE and recognition of its equality to other language varieties to a consideration of AAVE's role in a creative, intel-lectually engaging, persuasive, and at times revolutionary discourse.

THE STUDY[1]

The research reported here derives from four basic writing classes taught at two major universities spanning winter 1996 to winter 1998. Essays were collected from fifty-two students. Because of limited access to African American students in the institutions in which this work was car-ried out, the same course was taught repeatedly over several semesters, using the same course materials and research procedures. Students were solicited through campus advertisements that announced a writing course featuring Afrocentric topics. When students inquired about signing up for the course, the researcher explained course objectives, gave students syl-labi, and obtained permission to use their writing in any report of the research done on the course. The student-subjects received writing instruction over a one-quarter, ten-week time frame, or a fifteen-week semester, using African-centered materials and instructional stimuli.

THE STUDENTS

The subjects of this study were fifty-two African American first-year students—thirty females and twenty-two males—who placed into basic writing. For purposes of this research, any student of African descent living in America for at least ten years was considered a member of AAVE culture. In line with the emphasis on possibilities that extend beyond rights associated with surface features, AAVE discourse is given precedence over syntax, with "discourse" being employed to suggest units of meaning beyond the sentence level. In addition, AAVE discourse is defined here as the language practices that have been largely used and developed by people of African descent in the United States as a survival and self-advancement strategy. We think of discourse, therefore, in the sense that Jim Gee does:

> All school activities, and thus all literacy activities, are bound to particular Discourses. There is no such thing as 'reading' or 'writing', only reading or writing *something* (a text of a certain type) in a certain way with certain values, while at least appearing to think and feel in certain ways. We read and write only within a Discourse, never outside all of them. (xviii)

A main focus of this experimental curriculum is for African American students to identify themselves as being situated within African American Vernacular discourse. They certainly are members of other discourse communities as well, but none speaks to their African Americaness as directly. Confronted with a pervasive racism, which is embedded in dominant texts or official discourses, most African Americans feel a need to reaffirm their African American selves, individually and collectively. This is often accomplished primarily through language, as is evident in the rich tradition of African American literacy. Hence, students are being asked to see themselves in this tradition as a means of developing their critical consciousness and literacy skills.

INSTRUMENTATION

Seven instruments were used to collect the data: (1) a holistic assessment scale; (2) a demographic questionnaire; (3) a language/writing attitude questionnaire; (4) the African Self-Consciousness Scale (ASC); (5) an AAVE Syntax Scale, (6) a Black Discourse Scale, and (7) field notes. The data reported here do not deal with ASC or AAVE Syntax scales so they will not be discussed any further. The present analyses deal most directly with the assessment of the students' writing and use of Black discourse features in the writing. These Black discourse patterns were also used to determine the level of AAVE in the students' writing samples. The primary data reported here focus on discourse and rhetorical analyses of an out-of-class essay, non-impromptu, where students had time to work outside of class on the essays for at least two weeks. This set of essays has been subjected to discourse/rhetorical analysis and compared with other studies of culturally different student writing with respect to the presence or absence of selected discourse features. Black discourse was assessed by measuring the frequency and distribution of such features as they occurred in students' texts. Discourse features were coded based on a modified version of Smitherman's (1994) typology. The researcher and an assistant independently coded essays and then met to compare and synthesize their findings. Forty-seven essays were given a discourse rating from five to one on a continuum from Black to European-styled discourse, with five representing a highly Black discourse-styled essay and one a European discourse-styled essay. Features of Black discourse that occurred in the data from this study are the following:

1. Rhythmic, dramatic, evocative language. Use of metaphors, significations, vivid imagery. Example: "Our history through the eyes of white America after it has been cut, massacured and censored is pushed down Blacks throath."

2. Proverbs, aphorisms, Biblical verses. Employment of familiar maxims or Biblical verses. Example: ". . . there is a time and place for everything."

3. Sermonic tone reminiscent of traditional Black church rhetoric, especially in vocabulary, imagery, metaphor. Example: "The man should once again be the leader of the household as God intended and the female . . . the helpmate."

4. Direct address, conversational tone. These two are not necessarily the same, but often co-occur. Speaking directly to audience. Also, can be a kind of call/response. Example: "Would you rather be respected as Aunt Jemima and Sambo or Queen Nzinga . . . ? As yourself or someone else . . . ?"

5. Cultural references. Reference to cultural items/icons that usually carry symbolic meaning in the AAVE communities. Example: "There are still those Uncle Toms . . . out to get you."

6. Ethnolinguistic idioms. Use of language that bears particular meaning in Black communities. Example: ". . . Black english is a 'Black Thang' you wouldn't understand. . . . That's on the real!"

7. Verbal inventiveness, unique nomenclature. Example: ". . . [W]e will begin dealing with this deep seeded self-destruction and self-hate. . . ."

8. Cultural values, community consciousness. Expressions of concern for the development of African Americans; concern for welfare of entire community, not just individuals. Example: "Before Blacks can come together in racial harmony they need to strengthen their own people. Trying to unite . . . will only cause more problems if we have not taken care of our own business."

9. Field dependency. Involvement with and immersion in events and situations; personalizing phenomena; lack of distance from topics and subjects. Example: ". . . [w]e should first try to accomplish better race matters within ourselves. We can do this by patronizing and supporting our Black community."

10. Narrative sequencing. Dramatic retelling of a story implicitly linked to topic, to make a point. Reporting of events dramatically acted out and narrated. Relating the facts and personal sociopsychological perspective on them. Example: "I have learned . . . some things that never crossed my path in thirteen years of miseducation. . . . This was very important for me because I . . . felt that [my] writing was wrong and far beyond improving. . . ."

11. Tonal semantics (repetition of sounds or structures to emphasize meaning). Example: "European views are the rules. . . ." "We are victimized . . ." [structure repeated four times in subsequent sentences].

12. Signifying. Use of indirection to make points. May employ oppositional logic, overstatement, understatement, and/or reliance on reader's knowledge of implicit assumption that is taken to be common knowledge (shared worldview). Example: "In light of having limited means of getting first hand information we then have had to rely on books and the media to provide us with an unbiased account of information . . . we know how honest the media is."

13. Call/response (structural). Writer returns repetitiously to the prompt as a structural device, checking for constant connection with the question or text at hand. A repeated invocation of the language from the prompt, manifested as a refrain. Example: ". . . to be a member of the AAVE Culture and literate. . . ." "Black and literate. . . ." ". . . Blacks being literate" (repeated four times).

14. Testifying. Telling the truth through story. Bearing witness to the righteousness of a condition or situation. Example: "I use [the works of Angelou and Douglass] to liberate myself from my hardships to come."

15. Topic association. A series of associated segments that may seem anecdotal in character, linked implicitly to a particular topical event or theme, but with no explicit statement of the overall theme (Ball 1992).

Essays were analyzed for actual occurrences of the above-mentioned features and given an overall rating. The typology above is based on Smitherman (1994), except where indicated. All of the examples, however, were gleaned from students' essays.

Quantitative analyses focused on correlation of writing assessment scores and Black discourse scores. The demographic and language attitude questionnaires along with field notes are used to supplement analyses of texts and students' experiences in the course.

PROCEDURES

The research population of African American college students received training that involved four components: (a) instruction in academic writing/rhetorical practices incorporating rhetorical and discursive practices of African American Vernacular English (AAVE) culture, (b) examination of the African American literacy tradition through exploration of values, beliefs, and history as presented in African American texts and media, (c) the writing process (prewriting, drafting, revising, editing, etc.), and (d) writing workshops. A fundamental aspect of the course was introducing students to Black discourse patterns from an analytical point of view. Students studied excerpts from Smitherman's *Talking and Testifying*, especially the section on Black modes of discourse. They also studied examples from Smitherman's typology and other articles; they analyzed rap lyrics and studied various media and texts that exemplified Black discourse styles. Rhetorical devices were examined in several enslavement narratives and other literature by African Americans such as Sister Souljah's *No Disrespect*. Activities and assignments were developed which encouraged students to experiment with these Black discourse and rhetorical patterns.

HOLISTIC WRITING ASSESSMENT, DEMOGRAPHIC, AND LANGUAGE ATTITUDES SCALES

The holistic writing assessment scale consists of eight categories, with 4.0 representing a well-developed and well-written essay that successfully attempted a thorough response to the prompt, moving to various scores, 3.5, 3.0, etc., representing different levels of idea development and command of the written code, ending at 0.0, which represents a poorly written response that did not address the task. AAVE was not specifically mentioned on the scoring rubrics. The demographic/informative questionnaire functioned to provide socio-cultural information. The language/writing attitude questionnaire was used to uncover the subjects' perceptions of themselves as writers and to obtain subjects' language attitudes, the writing process, and the course experience and was administered pre and post curriculum.

RATER INFORMATION

For each student in the research population, a panel of experts assessed writing samples. Each essay received two ratings using the holistic writing assessment scale. The ratings were averaged. The raters were experienced composition professionals who regularly taught college-level writing both to students of color and others. All were members of the National Council of Teachers of English (NCTE) or the Conference on College Composition and Communication (CCCC). Twenty raters participated in this study, twelve women and eight men. Two of the women were of European American descent. Nine of the women were African American. One woman was of Asian descent. There were four European American male raters, three African American male raters, and one Latino male rater. The average level of teaching experience for the raters was 18.2 years of college-level instruction. The least experienced rater had taught writing for four years. The most experienced rater had taught writing for forty-nine years.

PROMPT

Students were asked to compose an essay in response to a prompt that revolved around the African American rhetorical tradition, as discussed in Bormann (1971):

> Perhaps the greatest distinction between current Black rhetorics and the rhetoric of abolition is that the main audience for the latter had to be the white community, because in the 1830s and the 1840s the great bulk of the Blacks were slaves and could not be reached by the words of the speakers and writers. Today a rhetorician planning a persuasive campaign for reform of race relations can decide to adopt a strategy of unity with the entire society, white and nonwhite, as did Martin Luther King and his followers and as did some leaders of the biracial Congress of Racial Equality (CORE), or they may choose to adopt a strategy of divisiveness and appeal primarily to the Black audience.

Students were asked to interpret the passage by Bormann, certainly controversial in and of itself, and explain a contemporary approach to a persuasive campaign to reform race relations in this country. They were encouraged to use whatever sources from the course readings they needed to support their arguments and to incorporate Black discourse and rhetorical patterns. Students specifically were asked to compose college-level responses, using their best prose, including Black discourse styles.

QUANTITATIVE ANALYSIS

One of the tenets of the African-centered writing curriculum is that form and content are inseparable. In other words, language use reflects ideology. African Americans often write from a deeply felt sense of what their experiences as African Americans has revealed to them, and they frequently feel compelled to employ Black discursive and rhetorical strategies. One of Smitherman's (1994) findings was that African American students who used more Black discourse scored higher than those students who did not. Following Smitherman's lead, an analysis was conducted to determine whether essays received higher essay scores with greater use of Black discourse features. In order to examine the relationship of AAVE discourse use and essay ratings, a bivariate analysis was conducted using essay mean scores and Black discourse mean scores. The results, shown in the table below, are statistically significant.

The Relationship between
Black Discourse Usage and Essay Scores

Essay (Admin 2) Rhetorical / Argumentative	Scoring Method	R-Value	P-Value
Argumentative	Holistic	.85	.000*

*Statistically significant at .01 or lower

As was found in Smitherman (1994), there was a positive correlation between the use of Black discourse and higher scoring essays. In other words, student texts were not down-graded because of the use of Black discourse features, a fact that suggests that teaching African American students—especially or including basic writers—to develop their voices within the context of their own literacy and rhetorical traditions can help them to avoid the tangled discourses famously alluded to by Mina Shaughnessy in *Errors and Expectations.*

The most frequently used Black discourse features were "cultural values," "community consciousness" and "field dependency." The nature of the prompt, its basis in the Black experience, seems to have influenced the students' heightened involvement. Among the many Black discourse features, it is interesting to note the employment of field dependency. Generally, field dependency functions in opposition to the "objectivity" and "neutrality" that characterize academic discourse. Field dependency is the hallmark of the Black style, a signature feature. It is as salient a Black discourse feature as "zero copula" is for AAVE syntax.

QUALITATIVE ANALYSIS

Instead of analyzing a single text or concentrating on a single student, we will look here at several samples from various students' texts in order to convey a feel for the Black discourse-styled texts produced.

Student #1 Winter 97

By feeding into the stereotypes that America has created the African American race will never advance being ignorant, militant, and extremely violent because all that is just adding fuel to the fire. Instead we need to take that same energy and convert it into something positive and productive for the upliftment of our race. By creating wise, well researched criticism America will [have] no choice but to listen especially if the information that is being presented is reaching through to miseducated Americans, (not only the African-Americans) and is *turning them on to the light*. Causing positive ruckus is far more beneficial than negative ruckus and you can't go to prison for speaking the truth. That's a right we are protected under by the Constitution. *By enlightening the darkened* we will be threatening the "secure" establishments America has created to prolong oppression.

There are several Black discourse patterns that can be discerned above. One pattern above is rhythmic, dramatic, evocative/imagistic language use. Notice the play above on "light." The "miseducated Americans" are those Blacks and non-Blacks who have bought into racial stereotypes. The rhetor has turned this stereotype upside down and inside out, revealing another Black language pattern, signifying. The "darkened" or the "miseducated" will be "en*light*ened." The quality of light has been traditionally associated with "knowledge," "goodness," and, hence White folks. Darkness has traditionally been associated with a "state of ignorance," or "evil," and consequently, Black folks. But here, the Blacks possess or will possess the qualities of knowledge and light. This is an instance of signifying, also known as semantic inversion.

Student #2 Winter 97

Unity consists of several movements that need to take place within the African American community. I believe first and foremost we, as a people, must deal with the disease of Black on Black crime. We must cry out to our young brothers out there who are destroying themselves, and everyone around them, by murdering one another. I remember very recently hear a quote on the radio stating that the number one killer of young, Black men today is young, Black men. When we begin to really take militant steps in an effort to stop the murder rate in our communities, then we will begin dealing with this deep seeded self-destruction and self-hate that has planted its poisons into the hearts and souls of our young adults. . . .

There are several Black discourse patterns that can be identified from the above essay excerpt. This essay demonstrates "direct address/conversational tone," in that it assumes an immediacy with the audience. The rhetoric is directed toward Black people. For this reason, the writer uses the pronoun "we" and the ethnolinguistic idiom "brothers," which is a lexical item for Black men. Also interesting is the rhetor/writer's incorporation of a narrative interspersion as a testimony to Black-on-Black crime. The most interesting Black discourse pattern here though is the use of rhythmic dramatic, evocative/imagistic language: ". . . [W]hen we begin dealing with this deep seeded self-destruction and self-hate that has planted its poisons into the hearts and souls of our young adults. . . ." "Deep seeded" is itself an instance of "verbal inventiveness." The standard term that this item brings to mind is "deep seated." However, the writer here creates "deep seeded" as it is more in line with the writer's meaning expressed through the metaphor of poison garden. This garden has been grown through the seeds of "self-hate" and "self-destruction" that have been planted in Black communities.

Student #3 Winter 97

Trust and honor make up the soul of African-Americans. Is that trust and honor still with us? Where did it go? During a time when we were lost in a strange land some four centuries ago the only face to bring comfort was that of another African lost in the same wilderness far from home, far from our roots. Within those last four hundred years we have struggled to gain our freedom and our African hearts. The price we paid for this American freedom was our ability to trust and the fire to come together as one. Our satisfaction with freedom in America overshadowed our dream to be Africans again. Four hundred years of losing our languages, morals, and originality has reduced us to rearrange our ways to seek the same gods that caused Europeans to bring us to this country, such as money, cars, and a million dollar home. I say, head for the underground railroad one more time African, because you are not free if you can't love your brother.

The above writer/rhetor is clearly adopting the rhetorical strategy of directing his/her rhetoric to a Black audience. The discourse evidences no nonstandard Black vernacular syntax but is yet styled in AAVE discourse. Notice the conversational tone/direct address, the use of the questions, and the admonition, "I say, head for the underground railroad one more time African, because you are not free if you cannot love your brother." This sentence contains evocative-imagistic, ideographic language use in its employment of the "underground railroad" symbol. The underground railroad symbolizes a freedom from thinking of oneself in terms of European ideals. Further, the essay uses the common Black discourse pattern of cultural values/community consciousness.

Student #6 Winter 97

> To me this [the rhetoric of divisiveness—focus on a Black audience] sounds like a wonderful rhetorical strategy. Unfortunately, this strategy will only take us so far. I believe Blacks in this nation will not come together because there is too much jealousy and greed between our people.
>
> Our people struggle with the concept of working together and having unity. The economic situation has most of the money in the hands of white people. The only way to solve problems we have between various cultural backgrounds is to work with other whites.
>
> Divisive rhetoric is like a bunch of Black people knocking on the door of the White house. On the other side of the door, are a bunch of white people. The scenario becomes that you will never get in no matter how much you knock unless the white person on the other side of the door opens it. My point is that divisive rhetoric will get Blacks to the door, but not inside the door.

The above writer/rhetor is arguing for and employing the rhetoric of unity which in Bormann's terms is directing his/her rhetoric to a racially mixed (White, Black, multicultural) audience and is styling her/his discourse to reflect this. This essay, however, is very problematic because of its inherent contradictory premises. The writer argued against Black unity (divisiveness rhetoric), but at the same time used an analogy with Black people united. "Divisive rhetoric is like a bunch of Black people knocking on the door of the White house. . . ." In any case, the writer employs a conversational tone and a familiarity with his/her audience.

Student #7 Winter 97

> The diverseness rhetoric would not work for this plan of action, because the decisions needed to be made would have to be made with all Americans in mind. I'm not saying that diverseness would not work in easing race relations, But it is not the means I would choose to fix whats been brokien for so long. Race, Race is a term a ignorant word, it has nothing to do with people it was [a] term used for seperating people, and I think this is what caused all of this trouble in the first place. Let me explain, if you use race to catagorize someone, there must be a dominant race of people. A white person made up race so who do you think thinks they're the dominant race, that's right you

guessed it. Unity is the key, once White America is turned into everybody America, this place will finally be what everybody makes it out to be, a great country.

This writer/rhetor is arguing for the rhetoric of unity, directing his/her rhetoric to a racially mixed (White, Black, multicultural) audience. The writer seeks to deracialize the problem while at the same time showing that the problem is white domination of America. The writer employs conversational tone as a rhetorical strategy to create credibility with his/her reader, hoping to persuade readers to his/her point of view.

The above excerpts from students' papers demonstrate various levels of written literacy development. Not all of the student writers had realized their writing potential, but they certainly were on their way, spurred on by Black discourse strategies such as field dependency. To report on the students' long-term gains is beyond the scope of this essay, but further data, which will be reported in subsequent publications, does exist to support the instructional design implemented. Black discursive style, rather than a quality to be merely appreciated, is essential to the development of a Black, formal, public voice.

To get a sense of the students' perception of the curriculum, it may be helpful to look at student reflections on ways in which the learning about AAVE and the Black literacy tradition was beneficial to them:

Student # 20 Fall 96

It helped me develop a better understanding of our language and possibly why other people may not get it. I was exposed to some excellent literature.

Student #15 Fall 96

The course helped me understand more about the AAVE culture and language.

Student #21 Fall 96

This course has helped me to recognize the difference between standard english and Black english and to be able to write according to my audience.

Student #3 Fall 96

This course has helped me to identify my weakness in writing. I also feel more comfortable about my writing style and the Black discourse I use because now I have control over it.

Student #14 Fall 96

I have become more aware about the language of my people. I learned that to talk Black is not to talk improper; it is just a different way of talking. I learned to take more pride in my people and my ancestors.

Student #6 Fall 96

It has opened my eyes to the struggles of African Americans. I learned to write in the language of Wider Communication and Black English at the same time. It has been very useful, and will continue to be as I pursue my English degree.

Student #12 Fall 96

I have learned to coincide my voice with the voice of the work I am critiquing to come up with a proper analysis of the subject.

Student #19 Fall 96

I honestly feel that I learn and comprehended so much information because I was learning about my people. In addition I was learning with my peers. I am happy that Sister [. . .] was the instructor of this course. She knew the course material very well therefore it was easier for the class to learn. She was able to teach from her heart and soul. You don't find many instructors like that. This class has not only given me the opportunity to learn more about my culture, I have also had more confidence towards all my classes because of my new found identity.

CONCLUSION

By making the African American rhetorical tradition the centerpiece of attempts to teach academic prose to African American students, especially those characterized as basic writers, we believe that we increase the likelihood that they will develop into careful, competent, critical practitioners of the written word. Such students seem to become more vested in improving their writing when it is directly and functionally connected in this manner to issues and exercises that are of immediate concern to them. This approach does not "essentialize" Black students, to anticipate a criticism that always seems just around the corner these days when ethnic identity is discussed. Neither is it an argument for limiting the enormous benefits of studying African American rhetoric to a strictly African American population. Rather, this method serves as recognition that the path to broad articulations for those who have generally been alienated from the so-called mainstream often runs through intensive valuing of and practice in the particular. Nor, obviously, do we suggest that African American students be allowed to settle for texts that are inaccessible to the larger community. The point is to pursue our best chance of placing greater numbers of strong, critical Black voices in dialogue with each other and the larger community, resulting—potentially at least—in better political possibilities. For writing teachers in their roles as teachers, the best opportunity to contribute to this process involves both embracing the doctrine of "students' right," still one of our most important statements related to concerns of grammar, *and* making curricular use of the political tensions and expressive traditions inherent in overall Black discourse.

NOTE

1. The quasi-experimental teaching was performed by Elaine Richardson.

WORKS CITED

Ball, Arnetha. "Cultural Preference and the Expository Writing of African-American Adolescents." *Written Communication* 9.4 (1992): 501–32.

Bormann, Ernest, ed. *Forerunners of Black Power: The Rhetoric of Abolition.* Englewood Cliffs, NJ: Prentice-Hall, 1971.

Shaughnessy, Mina. P. *Errors and Expectations.* New York: Oxford UP, 1977.

Smitherman, Geneva. *Talkin' and Testifyin: The Language of Black America.* Boston: Houghton Mifflin, 1977. Detroit: Wayne State UP, 1986.

———. "'The Blacker the Berry, the Sweeter the Juice': African American Student Writers." *The Need for Story: Cultural Diversity in Classroom and Community.* Ed. Anne Hass Dyson and Celia Genishi. Urbana, IL: National Council of Teachers of English, 1994. 80–101.

Souljah, Sister. *No Disrespect.* New York: Times/Random House, 1994.

CHAPTER 4

Orphans of Oppression: The Passive Resistance of Bicultural Alienation

Stephen Brown

Where there is power, there is resistance.

—Foucault 93

Alienation in school is the number one problem, depressing academic performance and elevating student resistance.

—Shor 14

If there is one thing I learned teaching on an Athabascan Indian Reservation in Alaska it is this: resistance in the borderland classroom assumes many guises. Alaska has been described as a place of extremes. Geographically, it is situated at the extreme ends of the North American continent. Culturally, it is situated at the extreme ends of Empire. Temperatures, likewise, can range from one extreme to the other, from ninety above zero in Fairbanks in June to seventy below in Barrow in December. Daylight similarly fluctuates between extremes, lasting until three A.M. in the summer, no longer than the length of a composition class in winter. It should come as no great surprise then that the behaviors, discourses, and personalities of native students in these bicultural borderlands should exhibit extreme traits: ranging from hostility and nihilism on the one hand, to apathy and ambivalence, confusion and withdrawal on the other. When marginalized students cross the threshold into the classroom they are experiencing a violent rupture with their home culture and an equally violent "initiation" into the dominant culture. Feelings of shock, uncertainty, insecurity, alienation, confusion, and homesickness are often the norm. Though I faced many problems as a bush teacher in Alaska, by far the most ubiquitous, enduring, and challenging were those associated with the adverse effects of deracination and pseudo-assimilation: with what Irving Howe terms the "tensions of biculturalism" (110), with what Edward Said calls the "mutilations of exile" (51). The end result of these dual processes is often a condition of bicultural estrangement in which students occupy a variety of subject positions relative to the dominant culture and the indigenous subculture, each enacting its own resistance. Whereas some may identify more closely with the dominant, Euro-American culture, and evince a strong hostility toward their own indigenous subculture, for others the precise opposite is the case: they may identify more strongly with their indigenous culture while resisting assimilation into the Euro-American culture, as well as pedagogies that foreground such assimilation. Further, differences may emerge among the members within each of these two polar extremes of identity: for example, some students may identify more closely with the traditional elements of their native culture while resisting its more contemporary discourses, attitudes, and behaviors; for others, the reverse may be the case. This is useful to know for borderland practitioners wanting to radically alter the content of assimilationist-oriented pedagogies, foregrounding instead traditional and/or contemporary aspects of the indigenous subculture.

Further, in between these two polarities of identification was yet another group of students who identified closely with neither culture, who were alienated from both, drifting in an acultural limbo, the students whom today would be labeled most "at risk," who evinced a good deal of apathy, confusion, ambivalence, introversion, or nihilism within the classroom, as well as self-destructive behavior outside it—alcoholism, vandalism, drug abuse, and suicide, to name a few. An entirely different species of resistance emerged among these students: the passive resistance of not belonging, of bicultural alienation—a resistance whose primary effects were not open hostility, unsolicited profanity, "sly civility," or even a menacing mimicry (as evinced by their peers) but invisibility, silence, and absence. The "passive" resistance of these students (its causes, effects, and pedagogical implications) comprises the primary focus of this inquiry.

BICULTURAL ESTRANGEMENT AND PASSIVE RESISTANCE

> But one may fail because of overwhelming circumstances . . . and, at the worst, the defeated may fall to a level where effort ceases. (Adams 278)

While a few Athabascan students identified strongly with either the Euro-American culture or with the indigenous subculture, a significant number of their peers appeared to identify closely with neither culture. This is not to imply that their situation was the result of choices freely arrived at; rather, their bicultural estrangement was an unforeseen by-product of the voracious processes of deracination and pseudo-assimilation, of cultural bleaching on the one hand and of cultural ostracization on the other, of deracination without full or meaningful assimilation. The genocidal tendencies of the dominant culture (including its educational apparatus) had succeeded in bleaching their Indianness out of them, while its discriminatory practices denied them entry into the Euro-American culture.[1] They were the victims of a dual alienation that left them without any identity, without a home in either the physical or the psychic sense—suffering the debilitating effects of an Athabascan diaspora rendered all the more ironic by the fact that it was played out on the very landscape that was once theirs, within sight and sound of the very peaks and coastlines, lakes and woods with which their very identity as a people had once been inseparable. Lewis and Jungman write, "At some point during this process, however, there seems to occur a kind of crisis of personality, or identity, a period when the individual feels poised precariously over the abyss that seems to separate the two cultures. . . . It is at this point that all life can seem artificial and pointless" (xix).

For many weeks all I saw of these native students was the tops of their heads, which were bowed in seeming contemplation of their desktops, but which were in reality filled with paralyzing thoughts of their own inadequacies as writers, readers, and speakers of standard English. For weeks at a time I neither heard their voices nor saw their faces. Like the immigrants of whom Adams writes, they too were seemingly overwhelmed by their singular circumstances, paralyzed by the debilitating effects of deracination and marginalization that had bleached their subculture out of them while denying them full membership in the dominant culture—producing a bicultural alienation that was evidenced by a myriad of debilitating effects: confusion, apathy, ambivalence, anger, nihilism, shame, and silence, to name just a few.

All were seemingly overwhelmed into silence by a collective awareness of their academic inadequacies: of their thick native accents, of their poor command of standard English, of its written and spoken codes, of their inability to process the Word as written in academic English, of their illegible penmanship, poor spelling, fifth-grade reading level, of their "deficient" comprehension skills and their "poor" aptitude on tests. Every time they opened their mouths to speak, these "inadequacies" were exposed. Therefore, if given the choice, they remained silent.

Silence was the shroud that concealed a paralyzing awareness of their own "deficiencies," the operatic mask that hid their intellectual disfigurements. For these Athabascan students, schooling meant a painful encounter with these realities on a weekly, daily, and an hourly basis. Schooling, therefore, intensified their need to escape such a painful, self-conscious "reality check" through a variety of self-destructive behaviors: absenteeism, alcoholism, drug abuse, and even suicide in extreme cases. The preponderance of small tombstones on the hillside south of the reservation was a poignant reminder of the lives that had come to an end as tragic as it was premature. Overwhelmed by the circumstances of their alienation, by the jibes of their Athabascan classmates, by the racial slurs of the white timber camp students, by the reproaches of some teachers who regarded them as so much "dead wood" in the classroom, and finally by circumstances beyond their control—given all of this, is it any wonder that these students "fall to a level where effort ceases." Paulo Freire provides a compelling portrait of the alienated borderland learners, whose development is arrested by the intractable nature of the conflict that divides not only their loyalties but also their soul:

> The oppressed suffer from the duality, which has established itself in their inmost being. They discover that without freedom they cannot exist authentically . . . they are at one and the same time themselves and the oppressor whose consciousness they have internalized. The conflict lies in the choice between being wholly themselves or being divided; between ejecting the oppressor within or not ejecting him; between human solidarity or alienation; between following prescriptions or having choices; between being spectators or actors . . . between speaking out or being silent, castrated in their power to create and recreate, in their power to transform the world. This is the tragic dilemma of the oppressed which education must take into account. (32–33)

These silent students, whose presence was in reality an absence, who were in reality "absent" from the learning process even when "present," manifested their difference from their more acculturated peers not only in spelling and penmanship, in reading and writing, but in dress, discourse, and behavior as well. As with many of their Athabascan classmates, the process of deracination had left them alienated from their indigenous subculture. Unlike most of their peers, however, the complementary process of acculturation had been arrested at a more superficial stage. If they had assimilated the dominant culture's technologies (its two-thousand dollar snowmobiles, its two-hundred dollar boom-boxes, its chainsaws and high-powered rifles) they had not assimilated its modes of dress or speech. In contradistinction to their classmates, who wore Brittanias, Dockers, and Nikes, and who spoke standard English with little or no Athabascan accent, these students dressed in the same monochromatic, functional uniform as the older generation of Athabascans: heavy work boots, woolen work shirts, and jeans. They tended to drop out of school in greater numbers and to engage in nihilistic patterns of behavior. Observes Adams, "more than the others they are found in the prisons and jails, and in an exceptionally high degree they depend on the agencies of charity" (290). The aborted careers of this group are what produce the negative stereotype of the dumb, lazy, good-for-nuthin' "injun," whose marginalization is mistakenly assumed to be the inevitable result of these traits when in reality it is the cause of them.

Traditionally, subcultures like the Athabascan's exerted a great degree of "moral control" over its members. When that culture is suppressed, when it is "bleached out" of its members through the dual processes of deracination and quasi-acculturation into the dominant culture, those controls disappear, producing a "decadence of special group morale," one of whose by-products is an "increase in anti-social conduct" (Adams 305). These are the students that have been labeled the most "at risk," the most likely to "fail," or drop out. They are left to dwell on the fringes of both cultures, on the extreme margins of the contact zone where presence mutates into eternal absence and agency degenerates into apathy. They comprise the borderland classroom's counterpart to the silent majority for whom the silence of the Far North constitutes a bitterly ironic backdrop to their own cultural silencing. Lacking membership in either culture, they are abandoned to the open orphanage of their bicultural alienation—like the students shipwrecked on the shores of an acultural island in *Lord of the Flies*—a fitting trope for the dehumanizing effects of marginalization among teenagers reduced to the most atavistic struggle for survival.

Is it any wonder that such circumstances produce what we would term "abnormal," "anti-social," or "nihilistic" behavior? Such students have been cast off by both cultures, inhabiting an island of exile within the contact zone—a veritable wilderness of alienation that poses challenges to survival most are ill-equipped to confront, much less surmount. Is it any wonder then that so many succumb to the "beast" of drug or alcohol addiction in order to escape the even darker "beast" of isolation—an isolation made all the more unbearable given their communal heritage? Lacking a language to describe their oppressive experience, to name their world, is it any wonder that they remain silent, that they are held captive in silence because they lack the "signs" for making such a confusing world intelligible to themselves, much less to anyone else? And if they are ever to escape this island of isolation in the heart of their native darkness they must do what the boys in *Flies* did: discover a means for signaling their presence to the world. This is what pedagogy can, and must do, for borderland learners: give them the means of signing themselves into existence, of signing their presence to the world, so that each might sing the song of a native self. As Maya Angelou observes, the caged bird sings with a freedom it doesn't possess, sings of the freedom it has never known, and in singing surmounts its captivity. Here is an audience of captives whose captivity teachers unwittingly prolong and intensify by prolonging and intensifying their bicultural alienation through a pedagogy of assimilation predicated on the concomitant process of cultural genocide. Canonical texts like *Flies* and noncanonical works such as *Caged Bird* can provide borderland students with a language for enunciating their exilic careers, with the signs that enable them to sing the song of themselves.[2]

Unlike their noisier, more assimilated classmates, these students spoke rarely, if at all, in the classroom. Of the multiple discourses enunciated by native students within the classroom, theirs was the most marginalized for the simple reason it was rarely if ever heard. At first I assumed they were merely shy or behaving in accordance with Athabascan customs that mandated indirectness in the presence of a white stranger. However, when their silence persisted through the autumn and into the winter, I began to wonder if it might be the by-product of a deeper "block," of a more paralyzing check on their spirits—the result, for example, of a debilitating sense of shame, arising from a self-conscious conviction of their own academic inadequacies—of the type so eloquently described by Angelou in *Caged Bird*: "If growing up is painful for the Southern Black girl, being aware of her displacement is the rust on the razor that threatens the throat" (3). Like Angelou's narrator, these students had imposed silence upon themselves as a means of coping with the traumatic effects of their own difference, with the amputations of deracination and the mutilations of marginalization, with the "otherness" of their Otherness. The trauma-induced muteness of Angelou's narrator is an apt trope for the cultural silencing of these students, and thus a useful text to "read" in such a topos. Thus, noncanonical as well as canonical texts comprise useful vehicles for conducting an inquiry into the debilitating effects of marginalization, deracination, and acculturation.

Learning how to interpret their silence is a critical lesson for the practitioner whose own attitude toward, and understanding of, the seeming "apathy" or "indifference" of these students must itself undergo a transformation if meaningful interaction and active learning are to occur—if the passive absence of such students is be transformed into an active presence. Learning how to "read" their silence is the first step to liberating the voices caged within it, to transforming the winter of their silent discontent into a spring chorus of reemergence.

Though marginalized to the point of invisibility within the class-room, the conduct of these students was not in the least disruptive. Indeed, it was almost as if they would do anything so as not to be noticed—as if their overriding aim was to blend into the walls and the desks, was to disappear, to escape from this confined space of academic mirrors that was forever confronting them with unpleasant images of their own inadequacies as learners. Their silence was a form of disap-pearing from an oppressive situation, a guise of invisibility they assumed in order to survive in a hostile, threatening environment. The attendance sheet might indicate that these students were "present" on a daily basis, but they were present in name only.

When they did speak English, it was with the thick, glottal accents of Dena'ina, their mother tongue. Thus, speech itself intensified their sense of difference, impeding their assimilation inasmuch as the freedom to form social relations in the dominant culture is impaired by any dif-ference, whether in complexion or accent, as the result of a code of race relations that privileges "sameness" and marginalizes "difference." As Adams asserts, "'language deficiencies tend to limit social contact and the lack of contact means the lack of opportunity for acculturation" (284). These students, consequently, become ghettoized within their own culture, and particularly within the classroom, where "sameness" or approximation to an American ideal, to norms and standard codes of speech, dress, behavior, is the harsh measuring stick to which all stu-dents are held—the great "ruler" by which all are measured. Those who don't measure up to the codes of "sameness" are found wanting, and thus marginalized, by natives as well as whites, by students as well as teachers.

For these students, coming to class entailed a painful encounter with their own "shortcomings" relative to the putative "norms"—a demoral-izing "reality-check" that operates as a check on their self-esteem, as if their personalities were being graded by teachers and even worse by their peers, native as well as white, and given a big, black check mark, connoting failure not just on a grammatical exam, on a composition quiz, or on a reading comprehension test, but on the more totalizing plane of personality and acculturation. They have not only "failed" the test of penmanship, grammar, and reading, but even worse they have failed the test of assimilation that their peers have passed with flying col-ors. And of this they are reminded every time they cross the academic threshold with its rigid and ubiquitous standards of measurement. For these students, entering a reservation classroom entails as much culture shock as Ellis Island entailed for European immigrants a century ago.

It behooves the borderland practitioner to learn how to "walk in the moccasins" of these students, to see the experience of schooling from their perspective, to open his or her eyes to the mutilations of marginalization these students are experiencing on a daily basis. Every waking moment in class is for these students a harsh reminder that they do not measure up to the colonizer's standards of "sameness" across a broad spectrum of criteria. The pejorative terms used to describe these students by teachers ("dead wood") reinforces the perception that not only have they "fallen to a level where effort ceases," but that their teachers' misperceptions about them have fallen to a similar level: believing such students to be beyond academic redemption, they cease to make the effort to reach them, much less to understand the causes of their alienation, apathy, ambivalence, confusion, and conflict. The apathy that is the primary effect of a traditional pedagogy becomes the goal of it as well: "I don't care if they fail, as long as they don't disrupt the class while failing." The problem, in short, is assumed to lie with the student and not with a pedagogy that fails to take any account of their lived realities, or to manifest any interest in exploring useful alter/natives designed to counter the adverse effects of bicultural marginalization.

To the eye untutored in the underlying causes of these effects, as was I when I first arrived in the village, the behavior, personalities, and discourse of these students seem to validate the negative stereotype of the "bad" Other: of the stupid, slow, lazy, drunken, nihilistic, good-for-nuthin' injun. Those who subscribe to this stereotype commit the egregious error of mistaking the effects of marginalization for its causes. As Adams contends, these students fail not from any inherent defect in their character or in their heredity, but simply from "overwhelming circumstances" that reduce them to a state "where effort ceases" (278). The apathy induced by their oppression is often mistaken by the colonizer as an inherent docility, when in reality it is an outward manifestation of an extreme fatalism sired by the emasculating effects of their colonization. Again, Freire's observations are to the point: "They nearly always express fatalistic attitudes toward their situation. When superficially analyzed, this fatalism is sometimes interpreted as a docility that is a trait of national character. Fatalism in the guise of docility is the fruit of an historical or social situation, not an essential characteristic of a people's behavior. It is almost always related to the power of destiny or fate or fortune" (47–48).

This fatalism manifests itself as well in their reluctance to join the resistance struggle of their people outside the classroom, and of their peers inside it. As Freire observes, "as long as their ambiguity persists, the oppressed are reluctant to resist, and totally lack confidence in themselves. They have a diffuse, magical belief in the invulnerability and power of the oppressor" (50).

Thus, the negative effects associated with their cultural disorganization (apathy, confusion, ambivalence, nihilism, shame, alienation, withdrawal, docility, low self-esteem, drug abuse, alcoholism, crime sprees) are the direct result of their marginalization, not the causes of it. How can such students manifest the traits privileged by the dominant culture (initiative, resourcefulness, ambition) if never given the opportunity in the culture at large to practice them? What worth do these traits have if they are never to be utilized?

Yet, these students are represented by whites as if the reverse was true: the apathy and nihilism generated by their exclusion from the dominant culture are posited as the cause of that exclusion. As Freire attests, "by his accusation the colonizer establishes the colonized as being lazy. He decides the laziness is constitutional in the very nature of the colonized" (136). Thus, the personality traits produced by his or her marginalization are assumed to be proof positive that the native inherently and hereditarily lacks the "right stuff" for full participation in the American materialist dream. Hereditary differences in skin color are augmented by a host of other differences in personality traits, which are erroneously assumed to be hereditary as well. The colonizer's racial intolerance thus produces the very traits that the colonizer then uses in order to rationalize his or her racial intolerance of the native. This cause-and-effect relationship between discrimination and personality development is then inverted by the colonizer to justify the further oppression of the native. Observes Adams, "in many cases the inferiority of social status contributes to the development of personality traits that tend to justify the exclusion of hybrids from the society of the race of 'superior' status" (310). Freire similarly observes that the "professionals, in order to justify their failure, say that the members of the invaded group are 'inferior' because they are 'ingrates,' 'shiftless,' 'diseased,' or of 'mixed blood'" (154). These marginalized learners had been reduced to a state of apathy in the classroom by the process of deracination without acculturation, by the irrelevancy of a college-prep curriculum to their lived realities and future plans, and by the standards of measurement associated with that curriculum which were forever exposing their "deficiencies." Their classroom apathy was compounded by the alcohol they drank and the drugs they consumed to cope with the confusions, contradictions, and ambiguities of their bicultural, or rather acultural, existence.

Their assimilation was impeded by other factors as well: by the great disparity between their indigenous subculture and the dominant Euro-American culture. This also reinforces negative stereotypes of the native. "If there is a great disparity of cultures," as Adams observes, "the people will advance slowly and they will seem to be stupid, and no matter whether it is true or not, they will be considered to have innate inferiority or biological inheritance"(254). Acculturation is thus slowed by the great abyss between the two cultures, making the native appear to be slow-witted, which in turn is seized upon by whites to further justify his or her marginalization. As Adams notes, "the inter-mediate status conditions their personality traits in such a way as to justify the status they actually have" (238).

With little or no opportunity to exercise the traits privileged in the Euro-American culture, many native students cease cultivating them. Two factors make the acquisition of such traits, and of literacy itself, irrelevant to their lived realties: the unequal code of race relations that deny them full access to the dominant culture and the cash allotments they receive from various transnational corporations and government agencies for the rights to the natural resources on their land, if not to the land itself. These monthly cash payments were like an opiate the dominant culture administers to the natives to dull the pain of their bicultural alienation, to repress the impulse to insurrection, to perpetuate the status quo. Thus, the various neocolonial apparatuses of the dominant culture, including schools, corporations, and churches, succeed in addicting the native to a cash-based economy while denying him or her full and equal participation in that economy—an addiction which sounded the death-knell of their own subsistence lifestyle. Cash, of which these corporations and government subsidized institutions had plenty, is no less a destructive agent than the alcohol they drink and the drugs they consume, with respect to its corrosive impact on their subsistence lifestyle. This further reinforces the negative stereotype of the lazy injun' on the dole—again as if it was a cause, instead of an effect of an inability to freely form social contacts in the dominant culture. As Adams states, "commonly they do not feel it is important to keep on working when they have enough for the near future. They are willing to work some of the time for a living, but they want to take some of it to live—some time for activities that are valued for their own sake" (243).

Other personality traits that reinforce the colonizer's negative stereotype of the native are derivative of the subculture. Individual competition for material gain, whether in the form of a raise at work or a grade in class, conflicts with the communal ideology of the Athabascan. Like their Hawaiian counterparts, an Athabascan "cannot make even a start toward economic competence because if he accumulates some property his moral standards compel him to share it with his needy relatives and friends" (Adams 244). The situation is compounded by the disparity between each culture's definition of "family." The Athabascan traditionally has no conception of the term "nuclear family." For the Athabascan, the family includes all relatives, and to a certain extent, every member of the tribe, making it an extended family. This has important implications, for status in such a community is not based on individual material gain, as in Euro-American culture; indeed, it is a function of the precise opposite: of the individual's tendency to share the wealth with other members of the community. This communal code of living was still in evidence in the village, not only in the extended families to which my students belonged, but in the preservation of such traditions as the potlatch, or give-away, which was held on an annual basis in the school gymnasium.

Not surprisingly, the effects engendered by these "tensions of biculturalism"—the great disparity between the codes privileged in the two cultures—negatively affects their acquisition of literacy. As Michael Holzman affirms, "the contrast between the culture of the school and that of the community creates an interference pattern . . . more and more successfully blocking the communication, the teaching and learning, of skills and knowledge" (164–65). For these students, the disparity between cultures often proves too great to overcome. Already faced with a difficult task in negotiating this cultural disjunction, they are now told they are too slow to manage the transition, that they lack the requisite intelligence to fully assimilate into the dominant culture. Once again, they are victimized by assumptions that misconstrue effects for causes, victimized by a bicultural catch twenty-two.

Metaphorically speaking, these "inherent" traits (slowness, lethargy, stupidity) are the "negative" image of the personality traits produced in the colonizer (initiative, ambition, resourcefulness) by his or her legitimate social status and full assimilation. In other words, the agency manifested by Euro-Americans relative to the native Other produces all the attributes they manifest. The ability to freely form social contacts, to attain goals, the "zest for power, initiative, resourcefulness come with the exercise of authority," even as apathy, indolence, and nihilistic behavior are generated by the denial of authority (Adams 249). Of what use to the Other is a zest for power that has no realistic chance of ever being actualized? Of what practical value is ambition if the Other is denied access to the dominant culture as a consequence of an asymmetrical code of race relations that isolates and devalues difference? Of what practical value to the Athabascan is a post-secondary education if he or she is denied access to the marketplace beyond the academy because of discriminatory hiring practices? Of what practical value to the native are initiative and ingenuity, if these likewise are destined to die on their indigenous vine? Of what worth is a facility for forming social relations in the dominant culture, if the native is denied the equal opportunity for doing so? These dominant traits of the Euro-American personality perish in the harsh context of alienation, marginalization, and discrimination. For the native Other these attributes have negative survival value. Adams describes their predicament with succinct eloquence: "without authority, they manifest those traits dictated by the situation: apathy, indolence, a sense of inferiority, and these effects are pointed to by those in authority as the cause of their condition when they are in fact the effect of it" (249).

Now descendants of European immigrants might very well assert that their forebears overcame similar discriminatory practices though initiative, ambition, hard work, and ingenuity. However, a critical difference distinguishes the careers of these immigrants from their Native American counterparts, and it is this: the disjunction between the two cultures was not nearly as great for the European immigrant as it is for the Native American. European immigrants were coming from a culture that similarly privileged a cash-based economy, an individualistic work ethic. They already possessed many of the attributes that favored assimilation into the dominant culture because they had the opportunity to exercise those traits in their home culture. Thus, the degree of cross-cultural disparity was nowhere nearly as severe for these immigrants as it is for the Native American, and as Adams's research shows, one of the primary factors affecting the rate of assimilation is the degree of difference between the two cultures.

The violence of the effects produced by this dual alienation, by this fragmenting of the native personality, has induced Rodanzo Adams and Patrick Colm Hogan to describe the end result as a state of "cultural disorganization" or "cultural disintegration" respectively (277, 88). Hogan writes,

> Cultural disintegration involves a sense of alienation from all cultures, being "no longer at ease" (in Chinua Achebe's phrase) in any culture, finding a home neither in indigenous tradition nor in Europeanization. Clearly, alienation is not in itself an experience one chooses to have; it is rather an inability to enact any choice . . . frequently associated with emotional and mental disintegration. (88)

In contradistinction to their peers who identified more strongly with one or the other culture, these students identified strongly with neither culture. Lacking a culture that conferred membership, they comprised as it were a community unto themselves: a community of exiles among exiles. Hogan's comments are instructive not only because they provide a working definition for "cultural disintegration," but because they underscore the determined nature of such experience—an experience that is not the result of free choice but of "overwhelming circumstances."

The experience of bicultural alienation for such students is a difficult one. As Adams affirms,

[T]heir lot is a hard one, for they are marginal not only in respect to their positions in relations to two peoples and two cultures, but also in respect to their personality traits. . . . Owing loyalty to two peoples and to more or less conflicting organizations of customs and standards, the marginal man [and woman] does not yield full allegiance to either. . . . The conflict inherent in this situation gives rise to inner conflict and behavior tends to be disorganized. (277)

In their silent passivity and dual alienation from dominant culture and indigenous subculture, these alienated students resembled Tayo, the protagonist in Leslie Silko's *Ceremony*, of whom Paul Gunn Allen says, "invisible and stilled, like an embryo, he floats, helpless and voiceless, on the current of duality, his being torn by grief and anger" (128). The double alienation of these borderland learners also reminded me of the ptarmigan, an indigenous game bird, whose autumn plumage became a motley mixture of brown and white, of summer and winter markings— a half molted condition which left them ill-adapted to the colors of either season, to either the brown leaves of a dying summer or to the white snows of the impending winter. Trinh Minh-ha succinctly voices the bicultural alienation experienced by students like the Female Other: "Not quite the Same, not quite the Other, she stands in the undetermined threshold place where she constantly drifts in and out" (218). The conflict-ridden topos such students occupy "is the perilous territory of not-belonging. This is where in primitive times, people were banished, and where in the modern era, aggregates of humanity loiter as refugees and displaced persons" (Said 51). Freire's analysis of the effects of colonization upon the Other reinscribes the observations of Silko, Gunn-Allen, Minh-Ha, and Said insofar as it also attests to the dual, conflict-ridden world that the oppressed inherits:

There is also an unnatural living death: life which is denied its fullness. Oppression dualizes the "I" of the oppressed. Thereby making him ambiguous, emotionally unstable, and fearful of freedom. Part of the oppressed "I" is located in the reality to which he adheres; part is located outside himself, in the mysterious forces which he regards as responsible for a reality about which he can do nothing. He is divided between an identical past and present, and a future without hope. (173)

Freire's observations here are significant inasmuch as they "unveil," if only partially, the underlying causes of the apathy manifested in these borderland learners. His observations echo as well the findings of Adams and Hogan with respect to the cultural disorganization or disintegration experienced in this extremity of bicultural alienation. The extent to which the psychic and emotional world of the Other is destabilized by the experience of marginalization depends on the degree to which identity remains rooted in one culture or the other; its most debilitating effects, however, are evidenced in those students for whom identity is rooted in neither culture.

As evidenced by these writers, these tropes of disenfranchisement—of invisibility, exile, duality, alienation, not-belonging, in-betweeness, and marginality—recur across boundaries of ethnicity, nationality, and gender, signifying a shared experience of marginalization, raising hopes of finding common ground and waging resistance struggle across boundaries. This has important implications for borderland pedagogy as well, for it holds forth the hope that narratives by the Other from diverse cultural contexts might inform one another.

As a place, the reservation is characterized not by a presence, but by an absence—specifically, by the absence of home and self. It is not a real home, but a permanent holding area created by whites in which the Athabascan is not a true self-determining subject, but an object articulated, contained, and controlled by whites—articulated in realist novels such as *Call of the Wild* and *Last of the Mohicans*. The Athabascan has been displaced from his or her true home, is in actuality a refugee on her own reservation, homeless in his own home. Native students, some more than others, have a deeply felt sense of loss, of being lost, or of not-belonging. Again, Said's observations are instructive:

> One enormous difficulty in describing this no-man's land is that nationalisms are about groups, whereas exile is about the absence of an organic group situated in a native place. . . . For exile is fundamentally a discontinuous state of being. Exiles are cut off from their roots, their land, their past. (51)

The grim irony for the Athabascans is that, unlike the Saidean exile displaced from Palestine, their exile and alienation occurs within sight of, if not actually upon, the very land once associated with their roots, their past, their cultural integrity.

THE "SIGN" AS BRIDGE TO TOMORROW: THE INDIGENIZATION OF SIGNIFICATION

In a sense, the borderland classroom resembles a battlefield ward in which the casualties of this violent cross-cultural conflict are gathered, each suffering the "mutilations" of exile, some in silence, others in rage, some with a pleasant smile and a sardonic jest, others with an angry word and a profane gesture. The bush teacher who ventures into this cross-cultural contact zone can expect to be confronted with the myriad effects of marginalization, whether moderate or extreme. Somehow, pedagogy must account for the violence of the effects manifested in those we are charged with teaching; somehow, it must make the healing of those wounds a primary objective; somehow, it must purge from itself those practices which only exacerbate these wounds, which add the insult of pseudo-acculturation to the injury of deracination, which add the insult of neocolonialism to the injury of colonialism.

And so I began to wonder if there might not be some way of combining these two disjointed realms of literacy, the birch forest and the borderland classroom, some way of linking learning to the native landscape, and the conflicts being waged over it between Athabascans and whites, some way of foregrounding what many of these Athabascan students already knew, some way of emphasizing these alter/native "texts" whose contents they already knew by heart and could "read" at a glance, some way of not only teaching in the bush, but *to* the bush, some way of putting the "bush" back into bush teaching.[3]

By bringing borderland students into "contact" with their native landscape and the conflicts immanent in it, we are in effect bringing them back into contact with lost, uncolonized realms of the indigenous Self, which was historically inseparable from the land. We are in effect fostering the reemergence of an old/new Native American subjectivity from the indigenous ground in which the Tree of Knowledge has been rerooted. The earth at the foot of this Tree of Knowledge is the site for the emergence of this new, radical red subjectivity—a spawning ground as red as the native rivers teeming with salmon. And like the hook-nosed Chinook, not until the Athabascans return to their origins will they too be able to reproduce themselves. Return and reproduction are inseparable processes for the exile, which is why preservation of the originary habitat is essential for the survival of the Athabascan, as it is for all Native Americans. The ground under the native tree of knowledge is as fecund as the soil under the wooden scaffold from which sprang the mythical mandrake, nourished on the blood of sacrificial victims.

To facilitate the rebirth of this radical red subjectivity, the Athabascan must first recolonize the Tree of Knowledge: those sites where knowledge is made and disseminated. They must take this tree, uproot it from the colonized terrain in which it is now situated, and replant in the good red earth of their own subculture. To regain the paradise he or she has lost, the Athabascan must first regain the signs that name that paradise. To recover the World they must first recover the Word, and those topoi where it is used to oppress them, including the borderland classroom. Only then will the Athabascan be able to make the word flesh—as red as the meat of the hook-nosed salmon, as red as the snows of a December dawn unfolding from the heart of the Athabascan's darkness.

Words, signification, representation when restored to the native are what allow him or her to escape this nightmarish no-man's land of nonexistence, in which they are formed, reformed and deformed as objects to be acted upon, unless and until they can effect their liberation through signification, radically reconstitute themselves as subjects, reclaim their World with the Word, and reestablish the harmony between native signs and the things they signify, between their language and their lived reality. Only then might their alienation give way to reconnection, their disintegration to reintegration, their dismemberment to re-memberment.[4]

NOTES

1. See my article, "The Bush Teacher as Cultural Thief," for an interrogation of the genocidal effects of traditional borderland pedagogy. *The Review of Education* 20.2: 121–39.

2. For a detailed discussion of the genocidal effects of canonical works and the usefulness of noncanonical texts in the borderland classroom see my article, "De-Composing the Canon: Alter/Native Narratives from the Borderlands." *College Literature* 25.2 (Spring 98): 30–44.

3. See my article, "Composing the Eco Wars: Toward a Literacy of Resistance," for a more detailed discussion of the constructive uses of environmental conflicts in the borderland classroom. *JAC: A Journal of Composition Theory* (April 1999).

4. For a more detailed inquiry into classroom resistance and other issues related to borderland pedagogy see my book, *Words in the Wilderness: Critical Literacy in the Borderlands*. Albany, NY: State U of New York P, 2000.

WORKS CITED

Adams, Rodanzo. *Interracial Marriage in Hawaii: A Study of the Mutually Conditioned Processes of Acculturation and Amalgamation*. New York: MacMillan, 1937.

Allen, Paula Gunn. "The Feminine Landscape of Leslie Marmon Silko's *Ceremony*." *Studies in American Indian Literature*. Ed. Paula Gunn Allen. New York: MLA, 1983.

Angelou, Maya. *I Know Why the Caged Bird Sings*. New York: Bantam, 1969.

Foucault, Michael. "Two Lectures." *Power/Knowledge: Selected Interviews and Other Writings*. New York: Pantheon, 1980. 78–108.

Freire, Paulo. *Pedagogy of the Oppressed*. Trans. Myra Bergman Ramos. New York: Continuum, 1989.

Hogan, Patrick Colm. "The Gender of Tradition: Ideologies of Character in Post-Colonization Anglophone Literature." *Order and Partialities: Theory, Pedagogy, and the 'Post-Colonial.'* Ed. Kostas Myrsaides and Jerry McGuire. New York: State U of New York P, 1995. 87–110.

Holtzman, Michael. "Nominal and Active Literacy." *Writing as Social Action.* Ed. Marilyn M. Cooper and Michael Holzman. Portsmouth, NH: Boynton/Cook, 1989. 157–173.

Howe, Irving. "Living with Kampf and Schlaff: Literary Tradition and Mass Education." *The American Scholar* 43 (1973–1974): 107–12.

Lewis, Tom J., and Robert E. Jungman, eds. *On Being Foreign: Culture Shock in Short Fiction.* Yarmouth, ME: Intercultural P, 1986.

Minh-ha, Trinh T. "No Master Territories." *Where the Moon Waxes Red: Representation, Gender and Cultural Politics.* New York: Routledge, 1991.

Said, Edward W. "The Mind of Winter: Reflections on Life in Exile." *Harper's* (Sept 1984): 49–55.

Shor, Ira. "Educating the Educators: A Freirean Approach to the Crisis in Teacher Education." *Freire for the Classroom: A Sourcebook for Liberatory Learning.* Ed. Ira Shor. Portsmouth, NH: Boynton/Cook, 1987. 7–32.

Silko, Leslie Marmon. *Ceremony.* New York: Viking, 1977.

CHAPTER 5

Race and Collective Resistance

Tom Fox

This essay combines two interests of mine: the effects of racism on student writing and the field of critical pedagogy. As I worked on this essay, however, I realized that critical pedagogy's term "resistance," both informally and in scholarly research, does not describe the relationships African American students forge with me and our composition program. I don't have many examples of classroom "refusals" that I could analyze to undercover the politically progressive sources, nor do I have many examples of student silence or disruptions. Instead, I have a rather long list of students who are quite successful and a shorter list of students who did not complete their studies for a variety of nonacademic reasons. It strikes me that the group of successful African American students (from the very urban areas most publicized by the media) on a mostly white campus were not much written about. I want to write about these students because I admire them and learn from their perspectives on the academy. I also see them as engaged in political action—resistance to white supremacy—*and* engaged in successful academic writing. In "resisting" white supremacy, they do not involve themselves in isolated acts of refusal, but instead ally themselves with traditions of resistance exemplified by historical and contemporary African American intellectuals. These traditions are present within my class curriculum. Student "resistance," aligned with traditions of political resistance, can manifest itself as alliances, alliances with writers who have resisted similar or related facts of American life, alliances with progressive segments of the academy, with people of all colors who also wish to resist white supremacy, and even alliances across boundaries: Black and white, teacher and student, etc. These alliances are not friendships; they are strategic, purposeful, and political connections with educators and writers.

EARLY RESISTANCE STUDIES

There aren't many examples of this kind of collective resistance in the
discussions of resistance in composition studies. This may be because
the concept of resistance in the field of critical pedagogy was shaped by
studies that examined working-class culture within oppressive school
settings. Paul Willis's *Learning to Labour,* a classic, influenced much of
the scholarship. Willis's frame—that schools reproduce class divisions
but that students are agents within that process—is politically clear and
consonant with a cultural studies agenda. The strength of Willis's text is
that the specifics of his ethnographic research do not become limiting:
he does not circumscribe the context too tightly. Willis steadfastly
asserts a dialogic relationships between "structural factors" and the
experiences of the "lads" in and out of school. Willis's refusal to isolate
either "structural factors" or "experience" argues for fairly precise
political consequences. He even names them—in a list—in the final
chapter of the book. The specifics of those suggestions are less important than the fact that Willis's concept of resistance, arising from the
particular setting in working-class Britain, is embedded in political
action.

Of course there are many limitations in Willis's study, most of them
identified by Willis himself. The five pages on racism, for instance, seem
insufficient to account for comments like the following from the "lads":

SPANSKY: We had a go at the Jamaicans, 'cos you know, we outnumber
them. We dayn't want to fight them when they was all together. We out-
numbered them.

SPIKE: They was all there though.

SPANSKY: They was all there, but half of them walked off, dayn't they, there
was only a couple left. About four of us got this one.

JOEY: Not one of us was marked . . . that was really super. (48)

Given Willis's insistence on the importance and political potential of a
cultural level somewhat independent of the economic, Willis's quick dis-
pensation on racism seems like a missed opportunity.

Willis's achievement in *Learning to Labour* was to identify and
describe the agency that characterized the working class students of his
study. While Willis's descriptions of the students seem fully realized, the
school and teachers suffer from a more one-dimensional portrayal.
Though Willis convincingly shows the ways in which the "lads" are not
completely part of a deterministic system, teachers and schools, it seems,
have only one role to play. On the first page of the ethnography, teachers are portrayed by the "lads" as being "able to punish," and they

hardly ever escape this one role. Teachers as disciplinarians continues throughout the book, even in Willis's extended discussion of teachers in the section of *Learning to Labour* entitled "Differentiation and the Teaching Paradigm." The entire range of teaching practices is defined by the ways in which it disciplines students. Even the "relevant" curriculum, which is the most liberal, is seen by the "lads" and analyzed by Willis as only a more elaborate way to gain consent in this hegemony of school power.

In this study, agency is granted to students, but teachers are entirely determined by their function in schools' role as reproductive institutions. Resistance, for Willis, means simultaneously resistance to dominant culture and resistance to teachers, with added irony that such resistance also leads to reproduction. Willis, of course, historicizes class relations, but not resistance. The "lads" are tied to contemporary working-class culture, but not to any historical resistance.

Henry Giroux, heavily influenced by Paulo Freire's *Pedagogy of the Oppressed*, began to examine this one-dimensional understanding of teachers in his early work on reproduction and resistance, but more fully in the 1988 collection *Teachers as Intellectuals*. Here teachers are seen not necessarily as part of an oppressive school, but inhabitants of a contested terrain, full of "contradictions, spaces, and tensions" that offer potential for social and educational transformation (xxxi). He criticizes radical theories of education that often portray teachers "as being trapped in an apparatus of domination that works with all the certainty of a Swiss watch" (xxxi). Giroux's argument for what he calls the "language of possibility" was instrumental in the field of critical pedagogy, articulating a radical position for teachers to work within institutions. Resistance, after Giroux, could be expanded to account for teachers, too. Like Willis before him, Giroux focuses on large-scale political implications. He hesitates using the term resistance, noting that resistance refers to practices that "are informal, disorganized, apolitical, and atheoretical in nature" (162). The term he prefers is "counterhegemonic" because it "implies a more political, theoretical, and critical understanding of the nature of domination" (162).

RESISTANCE/RESISTANCE/RESISTANCE
IN COMPOSITION STUDIES

Giroux's ideas and the terminology associated with critical pedagogy became influential in composition studies. Geoffrey Chase's article "Accommodation, Resistance, and the Politics of Student Writing" bravely attempts to both apply Giroux's ideas to composition and to more certainly define the terms. He defines "accommodation" as "the process by which students learn to accept conventions without necessarily questioning how those conventions privilege some forms of knowledge at the expense of others" (14). He defines "opposition" as "student behavior which runs against the grain and which interrupts what we usually think of as the normal progression of learning" (15). Finally, "resistance" is defined as "students' refusal to learn in those cases in which the refusal grows out of a larger sense of the individual's relationship to liberation" (15). Chase, who is extraordinarily clear in this article, then makes distinct the difference between "opposition" and "resistance":

> Although resistance is a movement against dominant ideology, it is a movement towards emancipation. Opposition, on the other hand, is also movement against the dominant ideology, but it does not lead toward anything else, and because it does not lead to a transformation of any kind, it serves ultimately only to reinforce the dominant ideology. (15)

Chase goes on to give concrete student examples of all three behaviors. Of particular importance to my argument is the example of Karen, whose "sustained refusal" to follow the guidelines for her senior project was bound up with her belief that history is tied to her life and the lives around her, and that her account of a radical feminist historian had to be written against the formal guidelines in order to be politically effective. Chase doesn't explicitly discuss his own pedagogy in this struggle, though obviously he privileges Karen's choices above the oppositional and accommodating students.

In the early nineties, critical pedagogy defined resistance as both resistance against the assignments and resistance against dominant ideology. What if one is a critical teacher teaching children of privilege? That question is C. H. Knoblauch's in "Critical Literacy and Dominant Culture." He notes that the model of critical pedagogy developed through Freire, Giroux, and Ira Shor is based on working with underprivileged students, whereas he works, as do many researchers in composition studies, primarily with students of privilege. "Resistance" in this context gets all turned around: students with values that maintain dominant culture resist teachers whose critical pedagogy seeks to dislodge those values and culture. Knoblauch's analysis leads to a whirl of questions:

> Can the university really serve as a site for radical teaching? What is the meaning of "radical teachers" for faculty in such privileged institutions—paid by the capitalist state, protected from many of the obligations as well as consequences of social action by the speculativeness

of academic commitment, engaged in a seemingly trivial dramatization of utopian thought, which the university itself blandly sponsors as satisfying testimony to its own open-mindedness? (15–16)

Knoblauch's questions disturbed whatever stability of the term "resistance" had. In the collection in which "Critical Thinking and Dominant Culture" appears, *Composition and Resistance*, the terminological slippage of "resistance" becomes, well, terminal. James Zebroski, like Chase before him, begins promisingly by trying to restrict the use of "resistance" to the meaning that Giroux applies to "counterhegemonic":

> I want to save "resistance" for some very specific uses. I don't want to use it when I talk about students not wanting to do something or myself not wanting to do something. I don't want to use it when I am talking about local conditions. I want to use it when I'm talking about social structures and their effect all across discourse. And I want to use that specifically in terms of, well, reigning social structures. (8)

But a scant thirty-four pages later, Donna Singleton summarizes the confusion around the term: "Are we meaning by "resistance" taking a critical look at anything, everything? Is that what we mean?" (42). And then, Knoblauch, using the non-restrictive, colloquial sense, says, "We start challenging FAO Schwartz as a cultural sign, and they begin to realize what's at stake for them in that challenge, and then you get real resistance, talk about *resistance*" (125). Knoblauch, referring to his analysis of his students in "Critical Literacy and Dominant Culture" simply means, students do not want to do the analysis that critical pedagogy requires of them.

What a mess! What's happened is that, in the circulation of the term "resistance," it has increasingly been narrowed down to classroom behavior and, thus, depoliticized. Knoblauch intended to widen the applications of critical teaching to contexts where students are privileged, but in the bargain, and in the wide-ranging discussions that mark *Composition and Resistance*, the term has nearly lost its political utility. Since Willis, then, resistance studies have attempted to accommodate broader contexts, noting that not all teachers and schools are oppressive and not all students are oppressed. In the process of broadening "resistance," however, the precision and usefulness of the term for political purposes has been reduced.

I had thought, at this point in my essay, that I would attempt, then, like Zebroski to legislate a particular use of the term, or to write a caveat of some type that says, "for the purposes of this essay, I define resistance as. . . ." But, as everyone except the Academie Francaise knows, efforts to legislate language use always fail. Additionally, one of the lessons of the above survey of resistance is that researchers struggle with varied meanings because they work in widely differing contexts. The main reason that "resistance" is imprecise is that the contexts in which it is used "resist" restriction.

RACE, RESISTANCE, AND SCHOOL FAILURE

What's this got to do with race? In some ways, it's easier to be precise: for most of the African American students that I teach, resistance means resistance to the various and multiple means of maintaining white supremacy. This resistance can take all kinds of forms, from various refusals in racist classrooms to highly engaged participation in academic discourse. I am obligated to state the obvious first. Outside of historically Black colleges and universities, I believe that the academy is in general hostile to students of color. In the field of composition in particular, writing tests (such as California State System's EPT) regularly select African American students for basic writing, putting them into non-baccalaureate credit classes, for sometimes more than a year. While I won't condemn all basic writing classes indiscriminately, I will say that many basic writing programs are positioned as academic purgatories, and without a doubt, the sinners are more likely to be students of color than not. Basic writing often functions, as Ira Shor argues, as "Our Apartheid."

The explanations for the higher percentage of students of color in remedial classes vary. One school believes that it's a question primarily of language. Speakers of African American Vernacular English, this explanation claims, get marked down for deviations from standard English or by the fact that students of color use rhetorical strategies that are unfamiliar to the graders of the essay. Geneva Smitherman's important article, "The Blacker the Berry, the Sweeter the Juice," problematizes these claims. Studying the NAEP tests of seventeen year old African American boys—a population likely to use AAVE—Smitherman found two surprising and salient facts: (1) the significance of syntactical features of AAVE in student writing is declining, and at present is barely statistically significant. To those familiar with the literature, this finding is not terribly surprising; it is supported by other researchers, such as Jane Zeni and Joan Krater Thomas. The conclusion one draws here is that most speakers of AAVE, at least by the time they are seventeen, also have a good understanding of standard English. These conclusions are often met with vigorous resistance. I can only report what highly respectable researchers have found, and what my experience is working with African American students from

Richmond, Oakland, and South Central Los Angeles. While I work with students who are college bound, many are specially admitted, and most have not passed the placement test in English. Smitherman's primary finding, however, is even more controversial. (2) She found that students who adopted a rhetorical strategy that seemed to come from a repertoire of African American discourses scored *higher* on the NAEP exam. In other words, when African American students drew from traditions of African American discourse, their essays were judged to be more powerful: *"The more discernibly African American the discourse, the higher the primary trait and holistic scores; the less discernibly African American the discourses, the lower the primary trait and holistic scores"* (93). What this means to me is that African American students are neither hampered by language nor by rhetoric when they come to do college writing. This conclusion bothers people because it is undeniable that success in higher education for African Americans is a problem. Good people wish, therefore, to find something concrete to teach—like language or the rhetoric of academic writing (if we could define that precisely enough to do it) to solve the problem. But that is Harvey Graff's literacy myth exactly: that mastery of a specific discourse results in access. If only working-class students or African American students spoke middle-class English, then class and race boundaries would disappear. Yes, of course, language is a convenient marker of class, race, and gender, but its convenience does not make it a cause of inequality.

So if we can dismiss language and rhetoric as primarily causes, schools' failure to educate African American students is a far more complicated story—one that replaces a single explanation (language deficiency) with a complex array of "forces" that discourage success for African American students: testing, social lives, housing concerns, job availability, classroom discourse, all the points of contact between an African American student and the institutions and cultures shaped by white supremacy. So while I have had many African American students fail my classes, I can think of only one who failed (and she later passed) because of lack of skills. The others failed usually because of housing difficulties, profound senses of anomie, poverty, homelessness, those "stares" they receive as they walk across a mostly white campus; they fail because they are such a profound minority, because they are followed around at the Safeway store, or because they are routinely stopped by the police without cause. In short, most "failure" is caused by the ordinary, poisonous racism. Those students who suspected the academy might constitute a "safe house" are profoundly reminded that few institutions in America are free from white supremacy.

RACE AND COLLECTIVE RESISTANCE

In a recent *College Composition and Communication* article, "History in the Spaces Left," Jacqueline Royster and Jean Williams argue that scholars of color and students of color alike have been consistently portrayed in composition research as secondary, marginal, and out of the mainstream, despite the fact that African American scholars have played a central role in higher education for two hundred years. For instance, they cite Sheryl Fontaine and Susan Hunter's discussion of why no scholars of color contributed articles to their collection, *Writing Ourselves into the Story: Unheard Voices in Composition Studies*. In discussing this issue, Fontaine and Hunter refer to a conversation with one scholar of color where the scholar said that she did not have much to say about basic writing and did not wish to contribute to their collection. Royster and Williams argue that perhaps scholars of color do not wish to be seen as "unheard," having participated so long and vigorously in the field. They wonder: "Is it possible that they [Fontaine and Hunter] were conflating ethnicity in higher education with powerlessness and basic writing and assuming that her [the scholar's] viewpoint, her place for writing herself into the story as an ethnic minority, would be the same as the one they imagined for her?" (567). Royster and Williams critique composition studies for the fact the "in officialized narratives, the viewpoints of African Americans are typically invisible, or misrepresented, or dealt with either prescriptively, referentially, or by other techniques that in effect circumscribe their participation and achievements" (579). Royster and Williams conclude with three implications:

- An historical view of African Americans in higher education that begins in the nineteenth century, not the twentieth century.

- Representations of students that are not keyed by the metaphor "basic writer."

- A recovery of specific contributions that suggest a history of scholarship and a tradition of professional engagement. (579)

In short, Royster and Williams argue for an end to narratives about Black students and scholars that reinforce what they call the "negative effects of primacy" (581), that is, an end to narratives that ignore the historical and central presence of African Americans in higher education for two centuries.

Royster and Williams are, in the main, writing about scholarship. I would like to translate their claims into pedagogy. The best pedagogy of race is an in-your-face-anti-deficit theory pedagogy, one that makes sure that African American contributions to intellectual history are palpable presences, obvious shoulders for students of color to stand on. This pedagogy rests on the following assumptions:

- Resisting white supremacy is a collective responsibility that requires alliances across racial boundaries.

- The academy is designed to maintain homogeniety and resist students of color, but this maintenance is hegemonic.

- It is possible to resist because the institution is contested, and has been contested for two hundred years.

- African Americans, in particular and for historical reasons, have seen literacy as a means of gaining freedom, and there is a rich record of writing that is stunningly appropriate for supporting collective resistance and teaching academic discourse.

African American teachers have the valuable advantage of being a role-model-in-the-room, especially if they are academic writers themselves, but white teachers are not therefore at a loss. As Beverly Daniel Tatum reminds us, "slaveowner" is not the only tradition with which white teachers can align themselves; there "is a history of white protest against racism, a history of whites who have been allies to people of color" (62). Not only that, if one accepts the fact that critical pedagogy is not necessarily centered on the single presence of the teacher, that texts can teach, programs can teach, and students can teach, too, then the limitations of the absence of a role-model-in-the-room can be ameliorated.

RACE, RESISTANCE, AND THE GOOD STUDENT

"Resistance," in the somewhat unconventional way that I am using it, is illustrated, perhaps ironically, by William, whose classroom demeanor was entirely respectful and whose academic work, in my judgment, was superior. I have discussed his work for different purposes in my book, *Defining Access*. In this essay, I want focus on the concept of resistance. Reading and rereading his work, his writing in the first-year course seemed to support his ongoing and determined resistance to racism. The course that he took used a cultural studies approach and taught students to write critiques of various cultural sites. The readings were, as one would expect with such an approach, academic theorists. I chose mainly scholars of color: Ralph Cintron, Patricia J. Williams, bell hooks, Cornel West, and others. Additionally, I constantly referred to nineteenth-century writers of color who also wrote "critiques" such as David Walker, Ida B. Wells, W. E. B. DuBois, and others.

In William's class, the first assigned reading was from Ralph Cintron's ethnography, *Angel's Town: Chero Ways, Gang Life, and the Rhetorics of the Everyday.* The selection was chapter four of that book, "A Boy and His Wall." Cintron's aim in his book is to understand the everyday rhetorics of a Mexican American community, and in this chapter he reads and interprets the wall of a fourteen-year-old boy. The chapter describes a cramped urban apartment, Valerio's difficulties in school, and the meaning of the items Valerio puts on his wall. Cintron, however, concentrates not on so much on how social and economic conditions limit the family, but on their response to these conditions, on how people "create respect within conditions of little or no respect" (109). In an early reader-response assignment, William immediately picked up on this theme, arguing that the line "but people find ways to subvert" was the most important sentence in the chapter. The following is the first formal assignment I gave:

> For the past week, we have read and analyzed Ralph Cintron's "A Boy and His Wall." In the class discussions and in your reader responses, we noted that Cintron's interesting idea is that Valerio's wall goes beyond personal taste or individual impulse. The images on the wall represent Valerio's involvement in other systems—religious, economic, and cultural. Cintron especially focuses his interpretation on "the deep fissuring that separates those who have more power and socioeconomic standing from those who have less" (99).
>
> In your paper, I want you to look at your own wall. Describe the items on the wall, as Cintron does, and then, in the meat of the paper, show their significance. The best analyses will move outward from the wall and the individual to show how the wall represents your involvement in the social systems that Cintron discusses. Additionally, I want you to compare your analysis to Cintron's by referring to his text in your paper. Quote his work carefully in your paper to either work with your ideas (by comparison) or against them (by contrast).

William's essay begins by critiquing social stereotypes of African American athletes and then describes his wall: "playing three years of varsity football, my walls are filled with pictures, newspaper write-ups, plaques, and my game jersey." Following this description is William's analysis of his college scouting letters:

> The most damaging evidence of that claim is my "collection" of college scouting letters. . . . These letters should be compared to a slap in the face. I was probably more excited than anyone to know that colleges wanted me to play for them, but those letters just add to that

stereotype. It's almost like they are saying that sports is all that I am good for. As Valerio's wall was almost making the same statement. All he was good for is to fix up cars. . . . One perspective is not all that my wall holds. Stating a stereotype, yet showing my dreams is what my wall is all about. At one point in my life, I wanted to participate in sports beyond the collegiate level. With the letters I received, my dreams seemed to be within reach. "But people find ways to subvert," and upon my reception of my first letter of academic acceptance to a university, I slowly broke away from that dream.

The final paragraph resists reducing even the concept of dream:

In society, almost everything has two views about it. My wall is no different. Neither is Valerio's. Our walls share similar qualities, the stereotype of our people being only "one-dimensional," that our minds will not be the tool to aid us in building a good future. Only my athletic ability, and Valerio's way with cars will be the way for him and me to make it. Our walls harbor much of what society thinks of us that for a split second, we might believe what we are told. But then I think that is when dreams come in. I dream of doing much more than what society tells me I can do, or could do. My dreams are the way for me to subvert these stereotypes and accomplish my goals.

I would like to consider what kind of social action this writing is, what William is up to in this essay. First and foremost I would like to honor the fact that William's analysis of his wall demonstrates a remarkable, strong person. He is a talented football player, loves the game, has potential, and received several scholarships to attend college and play college ball. Of importance to his story is the fact that CSU, Chico cancelled their entire football program two years before William entered. He entered a school with *no* football program. Yet because of his desire not to contribute to the stereotype foisted upon him (elsewhere he writes, "being big, bald, and Black helps to set stereotypes on me, most of which I don't want"), he considers the athletic recruitment letters to be "insults." Yet he keeps them on his wall. The one *academic* acceptance was Chico, the university that he chose to attend. Aside from the remarkable person that he is, William's engagement in Cintron's essay, his efforts to make it relevant to his concerns, is complex and important. If we conceive of resistance in a broad, collective way, not just in terms of classroom refusals, then one role that our teaching and composition classes can do is invite students into the community of scholars who similarly reject and resist white supremacy. The weaving in and out of Cintron's language with William's ideas is more than William following orders to quote Cintron, more than the acquisition of academic conventions. It's a possible alignment of concerns and tactics.

Such conscious use of scholars of color by William contrasts with the representation of student in the resistance studies of the 1980s and 1990s. They describe a relationship where students refuse or disrupt the pedagogy of the teacher, often without conscious intention. Scholars, then, interpret the refusals or disruptions as political or proto-political action. What's missing, or less emphasized, in these accounts is the students' political identifications outside the classroom. Perhaps because most resistance studies have dealt with class, and because class is often represented as fluid, students' political identifications are not fully developed or evident to the researcher. I have not found this to be the case with African American students, who, though they have the same range of political views as any group, are usually quite aware of where they stand on race issues. That's not to say that all African American students have the same opinion; it is to say that as far as race goes, their political identifications are clear.

So, William, for instance, identifies with African American male athletes and with African American intellectuals. What's different about this situation from either *Learning to Labour* or the students in Knoblauch's study is that those students' identification with resistance outside the classroom or in history is vague. William's sense of resistance comes from an identification with African Americans, who, together, seek to make life more tolerable. William doesn't need to resist me or my assignments in the classroom. Frankly, although William found value and support in my classroom, as an individual, I'm not that important. So while I have been arguing, and many others, too, that the classroom is a highly political arena, that doesn't mean that "politics" as we construct them outside the classroom—Willis's "structural" battles—are reproduced with exactitude in the classroom.

The main difference is that the classroom's location within institutions that have the supposed power to admit or reject young people to or from cultures of power makes all the relationships within them tainted. For instance, another way to read William's work would be to say he was the obedient student who deftly read the context and wrote just what the teacher wanted. His purpose would be to get "certified" by the first-year writing course and then continue to make a career that would break stereotypes. This reading is supported by William's description of his work in the class in his portfolio cover letter: "With revising I tried my hardest to do exactly what you said. I would go back and read the comments that you made and try to do exactly what was asked." Hardly the picture of a "resistant" student, yet his texts, particularly a revision of a paper analyzing *The Jaime Foxx Show*, show me that, despite "following" a white teacher's direction, William connected the accommodating posture of good student in my class with a deeper, more critical, more *resistant* position in his *Jaime Foxx* paper. Compare the two endings:

Unrevised:

> For some people it is hard to see Blacks making it without being an Athlete. To see Blacks that own their own hotel business, that is something that goes completely against the norm. This is where popular culture can be tied in. Popular culture in ways shows you the idea of where your culture fits in. Like that all Blacks are naturally gifted athletes. People automatically assume that is true. But what if they changed that stereotype? That Asians were the gifted athletes, and that Blacks were the naturally smart people. How do you think the world would look? The "Jaime Foxx Show" goes against what popular culture says. We are watching a show that doesn't depict Blacks in a negative way. They are shown in a respectable manner, as with Seinfeld and E.R., and the rest of those type of shows.
>
> I have a void in my life. A small one that every week or so needs to be filled. This void is somewhat small, but has a big impact on some decisions that I make in everyday life. This void is filled with a false reality. A reality that shows that we are more than athletes. More than gang members. We can achieve a status much higher than what the dominant society has taught us. The reality that is shown helps us to realize that there is much more out there for us to grab. The "Jaime Foxx Show" proves that there are intelligent role models out there. Even though there characters are fictional they still offer a rare but true picture of the Black Race.

Now the revised two paragraphs:

> How does one subvert confinement particularly when it takes on multiple shapes and each shape feels like an insult skillfully manipulated by some overwhelming bad luck or American culture or something? (Cintron 2). Right there. Right where it says American culture. American culture has confined certain races and ethnic groups to certain roles. Those role almost seem almost inescapable. That is why there is a need for this show. It shows different people in roles that have been occupied by others for years. It gives relief to those that otherwise wouldn't dream of occupying those roles. "The Jaime Foxx Show" breaks away from the norms that popular culture, the *American* culture, gives you. Popular culture is *supposed* to guide you, as Fiske says, "The aim of this productivity is, therefore, to produce meanings that are relevant to everyday life" (Fiske 6). In some cases that statement is true, and other cases it is false. "The Jaime Foxx Show" shows Black Americans who subverted American culture. But is also shows Black Americans in roles that aren't found too many times in the *real* world. But this is why we tune in. This *oddity* is enjoyable to see.
>
> When we watch television, we are looking for something. Looking for that needed laugh, or a shoulder to cry on, or just to see who is sleeping with Brooke this week. All is all, we are looking for pleasure. We all have a void in our lives that somehow needs to be filled. When

I watch "The Jaime Foxx Show," I am filling that void. I need to see that false reality. I need to see positive images of people just like me, people who have been through the same things that I have, making it in this world. I need to be influenced by success, not by negatively shown imagines of Black Americans. "The Jaime Foxx Show" is a relief. Proving that not all people of color are into trouble; that there are positive role models (even though they are made up) and that we can be intelligent people; it shows everyone a rare, but true picture of the Black race.

Here is the commentary that preceded William's revision:

William—this is excellent work, probably your best during this semester. I would like to enter it into the English 1 essay contest, but you'll have to revise. Here's where I would work: first of all, think through all that we have read, discussed, and written this semester, and bring anything relevant to bear on your analysis of *The Jaime Foxx Show*. The essay judges are impressed by students' abilities to bring together sources to help make an argument. I also want you to think about your argument at the end. I really like your image of the "void" and thought it worked well. I wondered, though whether your use of "false" and "true" at the end of your paper was effective. Think about it. Be sure to edit perfectly and cite your sources carefully.

I take William sincerely when he says, "I tried my hardest to do exactly what you said." He did review the work of the semester, and perhaps the most visible change—not insignificant at all—is the inclusion of two of the authors we worked with (revisions earlier in the paper also included the addition of Michael Dyson and Sut Jhally). I like to think that William saw himself as speaking to those published authors and there is evidence for that when he comments on the Fiske quotation, "In some cases that statement is true, and in other cases it is false." And of course, he edits well and cites his sources. But the most remarkable parts of the revision don't seem to stem from anything that I wrote. For instance, calling *The Jaime Foxx Show* an "oddity." Or the stylistic bravado of "Right there. Right where it says American culture." Or the new clarity of the lines right after that: "American culture has confined certain races and ethnic groups to certain roles. That is why there is a need for this show. . . . It gives relief to those who wouldn't otherwise dream of occupying those roles." He didn't change the "false reality" and "true picture."

I want to close with some doubts. During the last several years, I have worked hard at teaching students to write critiques like the one William wrote about *The Jaime Foxx Show*. I have learned to be fairly explicit about teaching the genre, very explicit about citing and using sources, and helping students to edit their work. I have found that my students can do very well what I'm teaching them. I want to believe that it's more than an elaborate doggy trick, an invitation to friendly accommodation. I want to believe that by the palpable presence of historical and contemporary scholars of color, students are forging alliances with those who have used writing to resist White supremacy, that they are deepening their understandings of the various forms and means that reproduce racism, and deepening their understandings of the various forms and means that scholars of color have used to resist it. I don't know for sure.

Even with these doubts, I will argue for the urgency of revising our sense of resistance, particularly with students of color. The most obvious way to change institutions is to change the people who inhabit them. Pedagogy that limits resistance to behaviors that result in failure in higher education seem to limit both our students' future and our possible roles in radical action.

WORKS CITED

Chase, Geoffrey. "Accommodation, Resistance, and the Politics of Student Writing." *College Composition and Communication* 39 (1988): 13–22.

Cintron, Ralph. *Angels' Town: Chero Ways, Gang Life, and the Rhetorics of the Everyday*. Boston: Beacon, 1997.

Fontaine, Sheryl I., and Susan Hunter. *Writing Ourselves into the Story: Unheard Voices in Composition Studies*. Carbondale, IL: Southern Illinois, 1993.

Fox, Tom. *Defending Access*. Portsmouth, NH: Boynton/Cook, 1999.

Freire, Paulo. *Pedagogy of the Oppressed*. Trans. Myra Bergman Ramos. London: Penguin, 1972.

Giroux, Henry A. *Teachers as Intellectuals*. Boston: Bergin and Garvey, 1988.

Graff, Harvey. *The Literacy Myth*. New Brunswick, NJ: Transaction, 1991.

Hulbert, Mark C., and Michael Blitz. *Composition and Resistance*. Portsmouth, NH: Boynton/Cook, 1991.

Knoblauch, C. H. "Critical Teaching and Dominant Culture." *Composition and Resistance*. Ed. Mark C. Hulbert and Michael Blitz. Portsmouth, NH: Boynton/Cook, 1991.

Royster, Jacqueline Jones, and Jean C. Williams. "History in the Spaces Left: African American Presence and Narratives of Composition Studies." *College Composition and Communication* 50 (1999): 563–84.

Shor, Ira. *Critical Teaching and Everyday Life*. Chicago: U of Chicago P, 1980.

———. "Our Apartheid: Writing Instruction and Inequality." *Journal of Basic Writing* 16 (1997): 91–104.

Smitherman, Geneva. "'The Blacker the Berry, The Sweeter the Juice': African American Student Writers." *The Need For Story*. Ed. Anne Haas Dyson and Celia Genishi. Urbana, IL: National Council of Teachers of English, 1994.

Tatum, Beverly Daniel. "Teaching White Students About Racism: The Search for Allies and the Restoration of Hope." *Critical Literacy in Action*. Ed. Ira Shor and Caroline Pari. Portsmouth, NH: Boynton/Cook, 1999.

Willis, Paul. *Learning to Labour: How Working Class Kids Get Working Class Jobs*. New York: Columbia, 1997.

PART 3

Technology and Rhetoric

CHAPTER 6

Fa(c)ulty Wiring?
Energy, Power, Work,
and Resistance to Technology

Ellen Strenski

> Complex circuits . . . use special passive components referred to as
> resistors. . . . These items restrict the flow of current. . . . Energy is
> dissipated in a resistor when current flows through it. The amount
> of energy dissipated each second is power. A resistor is rated by
> the amount of power it can dissipate. . . . Now suppose you have
> a complex circuit with resistors and a power supply.
> —Manny Horowitz
> *Elementary Electricity and Electronics* (73)

The computer is a writing instrument: to use one is to write. The Internet is a new hybrid communication medium, part speech, part print,
part video, which in turn demands a new digital literacy. Composition
pedagogy is accordingly being transformed as many instructors claim

I presented a version of this chapter at the Western Humanities Conference on
Information, Technology, and the Humanities, October 17–19, 1997, at UC
Riverside, on a panel entitled "Composing Technology: Teaching, Texts, and the
Lure of the Digital," sponsored by the Electronic Text Collective at UC Irvine,
to whom I am indebted for the formulation of various ideas in this chapter. Ver-
sions of other material included in this chapter were presented as "Electronic
Episolarity" at the Fourth Annual Cultural Studies Symposium at Kansas State
University in 1995, and "Teach a Man (or Woman) to Fish (or Use the Inter-
net)" at the 1996 conference of the Association for Computers and Writing in
Logan, Utah.

electronic textuality and online rhetoricity to be an autonomous professional field, and as such, develop a corresponding pedagogy for on-
screen reading and online writing,[1] but not without contention. Some
enthusiasts are single-minded and strident "techno-giddies," as Jean
Baudrillard portrays them in *The Ecstasy of Communication*. They pro-
voke among their colleagues an equally dogmatic opposition to any use
of computer technology beyond word processing, part threat response
to change and an ominous redivision of academic labor, and part revul-
sion at a perceived demeaning of traditional literacy and a perceived
professional degradation of faculty status and individual scholarly
expertise. Still other instructors, many of them graduate students or
temporary lecturers, struggle uncertainly to apply an ever-increasing
number of ever-changing "tools" within an educational-administrative
environment that increasingly views technology in terms of efficiency
and economy. Pulled away from information technology by some (typically more senior) colleagues who disdain technology, these instructors
are drawn toward computers both by curiosity and a strong cultural and
institutional imperative to get online fast. However, they too often produce superficial applications designed to impress but not to teach, which
in turn fuel the skeptics' fears in a spiraling cycle of ever-increasing general frustration. The result is an increasingly polarized discussion
plagued by hype: corporate-induced administrative euphoria heralds a
brave new world of unlimited personal growth and commercial profitability, while a more skeptical view is frequently just as hyperbolic in
its jeremiads against the pernicious influence of technology.

Compositionists ignore this contentious battle over educational uses
of computer technology to our collective peril. However distasteful, and
at whatever initial risk of complicity, we must associate ourselves publicly with information technology and align the required, general-educa-
tion breadth courses we teach with the new digital literacy demanded by
online reading and writing. Cultural uses of information technology in
general, and educational ones in particular, are textual as well as technical processes. As specialists in the interpretation, critical analysis, and
manipulation of various kind of texts, on screen as well as on paper,
composition instructors are already specialists in the basic principles of
inference and interpretation that govern the use of information technology in the classroom. If we do not assert this claim and our professional
right to make it, then others will gladly take our place: librarians
(Thompson) on the one hand, and computer scientists (Cunningham) on
the other. To these others will go the spoils, that is, the FTEs and other
campus resources now following information technology as institutions
scramble to integrate it into the curriculum, and we will have missed our
chance to shape the development of these tools for humanistic use, per-

haps even to ensure our own enduring professional presence on campus.

Untangling the hype from the hope may clarify ways in which information technology can help composition instructors work together to help students become better writers. Reminded by Rey Chow that we are wordsmiths, and that "the battles we fight are battles of words" (17), we can engage the fray on this linguistic terrain. Terminological screens and filters determine our sense of this contentious opposition between the "techno-giddies" and the contemptuous: "much that we take as observations about 'reality' may be but the spinning out of possibilities implicit in our particular choice of terms" (Burke 46). A way of seeing is also a way of not seeing. Metaphors are not just stylistic decorations. "True metaphor, so far from being an ornament, has very little to do even with an act of comparison. . . . [It] becomes almost a mode of apprehension" (Murray 11). Metaphors have consequences, a point established by, among many others, Lakoff and Johnson in *Metaphors We Live By*. But metaphors are often imperceptible, and when they are imperceptible, they are even more influential.

The set of metaphors now comprising the dominant model of online experience derives from biology. Juxtaposing to it an alternative model can serve to demonstrate its constructed nature, and thereby begin to dissolve the impasse of our professional antagonism by revealing alternative explanations and making possible a different reception of computer technology in the composition classroom.

This chapter first acknowledges the reigning biological model of information technology, one so accepted in discourse about computers that it is typically not even noticed. Then, for the sake of argument, the text shifts metaphorical perspective to another model of information technology, one based on electronic circuitry. This alternative electronic model emphasizes control and understands power as energy rather than domination, and can be applied to portray faculty functioning as resistors in an institutional mechanism. As such, faculty resistors protect the mechanism: they channel energy; they make work possible; they neither stall the functional operations of their institutions, nor do they allow their colleges and universities to run out of control, overheat, or self-destruct. This faculty resistance is valuable, but it must be calibrated appropriately in order for the circuitry—and accordingly, the mechanism—to function properly: some resistance is essential, but not too much. Calibration comes from critique and from professional development: educating the educators. How to offer faculty appropriate assistance with information technology so that they can function at optimum levels—incorporating new computing resources into their work—comprises an unprecedented practical, institutional challenge.

One of the tenets of this chapter is that the computer is a communication tool, and that digital literacy is appropriately situated with other kinds of traditional literacy within English departments and composition programs. So, too, planning for a new kind of faculty development to enhance instructors' technological command over potential pedagogical resources can benefit from collective experience with an older form of faculty-development initiative emerging in the same place from the same impulse for pedagogical reform: writing across the curriculum. Writing Across the Curriculum (WAC), as it has been refined over the last quarter century, aims to involve faculty from all academic departments in the effort to improve student writing and thinking. Information Technology (IT) aims to encourage faculty to exploit computer technology in order to create new teaching and discussion spaces on course listservs, new archival spaces on the World Wide Web for course curriculum materials, and new kinds of open-ended, often collaborative and interactive electronic assignments that enhance critical learning. This chapter compares these two kinds of instructional development along four dimensions: the content to be learned, the learning environment, the developers, and the learning process. Once the special features of these two kinds of faculty development have been revealed by this comparison, special tactics for IT can be envisioned to accommodate them.

The chapter then identifies six specific sites in composition studies where faculty resistors are especially important, in order to raise and direct discussion, make work happen productively, and prevent disaster. As such, this section builds on and extends the excellent, but more general, analysis by Lankshear, Peters, and Knobel in "Critical Pedagogy and Cyberspace," tailoring it specifically to composition studies. These sites include the unique opportunities offered by this "velcro" medium for groupwork; the stylistic debate over "plain English"; the need for composition classes to include formal instruction in online critical reading; the need for them to include instruction in online writing; "off-loading" "remedial" writing instruction to the Internet antipodes; and labor implications for the many graduate students, part-time instructors, and temporary lecturers who teach composition.

The chapter ends with a celebration of the unique opportunity opened up by this new medium for pleasure and for dreaming, and therewith portrays it as a profound source of hope.

FROM BIOLOGY TO CIRCUITRY

Consider some of the component metaphors embedded in these common words and phrases:

- the *growth* of the Internet (not the expansion or increase)
- the *cyborg* image in film and fiction—a symbiotic interdependence of the individual human organism and machine, for instance, the human writer and word processor
- *VE*, the virtual environment, that is, the online environment (not context)
- computer *viruses* (not, for instance, counterfeiting or sabotage)
- the *life-cycle* of listservs and news groups (not rise and fall)
- electronic *communities* like the Well (not collections, collectivities, or groups)
- technological *developments* (not innovations)

Howard Rheingold typically sums up "cyberspace as a social petri dish, the Net as the agar medium, and virtual communities, in all their diversity, as the colonies of microorganisms that grow in petri dishes" (6). These metaphors are so common because they have such effective explanatory power, but they inevitably carry with them, and indeed determine, a variety of attitudes and beliefs. For example, according to biologist Garrett Hardin, the word "development" derives from embryology. A fertilized organism "develops" and eventually, inevitably, hatches or otherwise emerges, unless it is hurt or eaten or damaged in some other way. Attempts to thwart or resist this developmental process are "bad." Essentially biological, the metaphor of "development" automatically carries associations of "good" and "inevitable." However, considered dispassionately, technological innovations—technological "developments"—may be good or bad, inevitable or not. The American SST (Super Sonic Transport) was defeated; nuclear power plants do not really have to be built, etc.

Where do faculty, especially faculty who oppose computer technology, fit in this online environment? This includes faculty who refuse to use e-mail, join professional electronic discussion groups, conduct scholarly research on the Internet, or make web pages for their courses. From the biological perspective, they look either like predators or, more plausibly, nonadaptive organisms destined to evolutionary extinction. Their resistance to technology appears thanaturgical, a poisonous death force that stunts the development of technological life. This biological model is individualistic: the independent organism struggling for survival in a competitive environment where technological competence and cyborg adaptations are assets.

But might these reluctant, suspicious faculty who at least drag their feet, if not actively prevent change, be something other than obstacles?

Might their behavior be understood as a more complex professionally informed response? Might the dynamic of faculty opposition to technology, especially on the part of humanists, and among them compositionists, have merit? Is it possible to go farther than the position of *comprendre c'est tout pardonner*, and to see faculty resistors as other than pig-headed obstructionists, indeed, with unique institutional value?

For the sake of discussion, let them be perceived as "resistors" in the electronic sense, as components in a complex circuit board analogy. Such an electronic model is above all a systems model, an institutional model of educational components that work or don't work together—that overheat, run out of control, blow up, or break down.

To propose this alternative perception is not to suggest an exclusive dualism: biological or electronic. Burke's dramatistic model, for instance, would map on to the "roles" that faculty play and their various rhetorical and other kinds of online "performances," as indeed Greg Ulmer has demonstrated in his *Teletheory*. Michael Joyce has pointed to yet another, hydraulic model of fluidity, flow, and water imagery to describe online readers and writers. In principle, the chemical model of agents and reagents might fit to some extent, too. However, teasing out some of the implications and unacknowledged assumptions in these other two sets of metaphors, the biological and the electronic, reveals technologically challenged colleagues as something other than just irritating—if not debilitating—obstacles, a perception urgently needed.

THE ELECTRONIC CIRCUIT MODEL

If faculty are resistors in this alternative model, how does the analogy map on to the other components and processes in this educational system? Consider, first, how some educational activities are more powerful than others. Some kinds of teaching, some learning, some writing, some reading, are more efficient than other kinds. Some institutions work better at getting instructors to work better at teaching in order to get some students to work better at learning better. Is more efficient work accomplished in those particular colleges and classes? How is this work accomplished efficiently? Where does the energy come from? And how is this energy dissipated efficiently through these institutional components without causing damage or breakdown? Note the number of metaphorical terms derived from the electronic model that are insinuated into these introductory questions: *efficiency, work, energy, power, dissipation*. Two more would be *pressure* and *force*.

Consider, second, how change is inevitable. Where are these pressures on educational institutions and their instructors for change coming from? In addition to internal faculty critique and self-correction, such pressures are being exerted from innumerable external sources— taxpayers, students, alumni, legislators. The efforts of colleges to attract students, faculty, and resources are being galvanized not just by competition from other similar accredited educational institutions, but increasingly by competition from the private industry and the bureaucracy that hires their graduates. Increasingly, these employers find that they must supplement their new hires' preparation. Increasingly, these employers are regularizing their own instruction. Increasingly, this instruction is coming to look like courses and programs. For example, a recent national Census Bureau survey of hiring, training, and management practices in American business (Applebome) reported that 81 percent of employers surveyed provided or paid for their workers' continuing training (1). Many employers now rely, not on the preparation offered by conventional educational institutions, but on commercial suppliers, outside consultants, and their own in-house training programs to maximize their employees' job effectiveness. At the same time, traditional educational boundaries are dissolving through business partnerships with university extension departments and through distance education, while talk increases about "privatizing" our public colleges and universities. For example, University of California President Richard Atkinson has publicly exhorted UC faculty to consider the online University of Phoenix as our most serious competition, an organization tellingly described in James Traub's "Drive-Through U: Higher Education for People Who Mean Business." Regardless, innumerable "campuses," like that of Microsoft in Washington State, are emerging with their own educational apparatus: trainers, trainees, classrooms, publications comprising an entire parallel educational establishment.

The organizations on these other campuses, in turn, are being driven by the external pressures exerted on them. One major pressure is technological innovation, including information technology. For example, this same Census Bureau survey found increasing skill requirements everywhere in the workplace, even in low-level jobs: "about 2 of 5 production and non-supervisory employees used computers in their jobs" (Applebome A11), a finding about the institutional pressures of computer technology on employees' proficiency and productivity that is confirmed by other studies, notably, for instance, that of Shoshana Zuboff.

These associated characteristics of competition, change, and information technology are noteworthy because they are part of the pressure on industry right now, which in turn is competitively exerted on colleges and universities. They also deserve attention because they evoke a legitimate fear in certain faculty who sense, however dimly, a professional threat to their scholarly lives and livelihoods.

Some instructors, of course, fear the possibility that one day they may be physically replaced by an actor reading lectures prepared by some award-winning scholar for videotape or video conference. But also disturbing to others, if less tangible, is the simplistic, reductive challenge of information technology to the value of original, creative critique. This critique, to continue the circuitry analogy, is the equivalent internal pressure forcing current through the humanities undertaking, a pressure equivalent to that driving research in the sciences.

Work is accomplished through electronic circuitry because various components regulate the flow of electricity. Among the most important of these components are resistors. Some resistance in electronic circuitry is essential. Without it, the machine would overheat and self-destruct. A good educational example of such self-destruction, occasioned by the absence of enough regulation by appropriately calibrated resistance, is the six-year experiment in universal, secular, public education established in France during the Revolution. A prototype of our own curriculum today, this system collapsed internally from a lack of direction, that is, a lack of regulating control or resistance. There were few—certainly not enough—competent teachers to organize and teach the new secular scientific subjects that were mandated by the revolutionary government. As a result, the whole system ran out of control and broke down, and Bonaparte restored the *lycée* system of the *ancien regime* as soon as possible (Durkheim 304–5).

But too much resistance impedes the mechanism's ability to function efficiently, if at all. The history of European educational theory and practice again provides a good example of this process of impedance. For a thousand years, from the eighth century to the French Revolution, through various versions of scholasticism, humanism, and the Jesuit educational campaign, the fit subject of institutional study was an abstraction: humankind, with or without God. This formalism deliberately excluded history, other than ancient history, and all natural and social science. Such curricular resistance is astonishing given the developments of the Renaissance and subsequent scientific development outside these ivory towers. However, until the French Revolution, students at all levels still studied the primarily literary trivium: grammar, dialectic, and rhetoric. Meanwhile, all around the schools and universities gifted amateurs were recording and applying useful scientific advances, among other things, the printing press, an appliance much beloved by many of today's resistant faculty (Durkheim 279–80).

Faculty today function quite properly as resistors in their institutions. They behave accordingly by controlling the pressures applied to these institutions. They direct, restrict, and regulate the flow of current; they create power ("the rate at which work is done") by dissipating the institution's energy which, in turn, is driven primarily by externally applied pressure to compete. The point is that much wringing of hands over faculty resistance to information technology portrays it as a relatively simple, stubborn resistance to any change. So it can be; but so, too, it can be valuable. However, faculty resistance must be calibrated appropriately in order for the circuitry—and accordingly for the mechanism—to function properly: some resistance is essential, but not too much.

A good example of this kind of valuable resistance is provided by UC Irvine's School of Humanities Computing Policy Committee and the committee's response to a campus "Informatics" initiative <http://www. rgs.uci.edu/informatics/>. The UC Irvine Chancellor wanted the university to prepare its graduates with "21st century information skills." Thus, a combined faculty/administrative task force (with not a single representative from the humanities departments) recently made a number of recommendations, one of which—a breadth requirement in informatics—would displace presently required humanities courses. The School of Humanities Computing Policy Committee, composed primarily of faculty, responded to the report by appropriately resisting and impeding this surge of energy, and doing so as professional experts in the humanities. Here are some of the resistant observations, glossed below: "The Committee was troubled by the report's failure to communicate clearly the content of the field of informatics. Informatics is a term widely used (especially in Europe) to mean what at UCI is called Information and Computer Science." Indeed, it has been elsewhere bruited that the UC Irvine Department of Information and Computer Science aspires to become a School of Informatics. This linguistic observation by a group of wordsmiths about definition exposes an attempted campus land grab and thereby becomes a useful impedance.

> The Task Force failed to adequately represent or consult the various communities on campus. The membership of the committee did not effectively represent the interests of several crucial groups, among them humanists, social scientists, and students. This, we think, is responsible for the narrow and reductive vision of informatics that emerges from the report. The report seems to conceive of informatics primarily in a skill-oriented fashion; it fails to address the full significance of information technologies in intellectual work and social relations.

This reminder that knowledge is socially constructed emphasizes the need for democratic participation by all affected. Such a contextualization of the system and its consequent responsibilities—beyond a reductive tune-up of individual students—is also a valuable, impeding observation.

> Third, it is not at all clear to us what the process will be now that the report has appeared. . . . The proposal for a new breadth requirement in our opinion requires more discussion and deliberation. The Task Force's proposals would entail radical change in the way we deal with and develop breadth courses. Such change should only be undertaken after the most careful and thorough review.

This caution and claim for time to exercise professional judgment offers more good resistance: a kind of surge protection.

> Finally, the committee claims its own right to participate in this process of working to bring about change in the system, and to contribute productively to this process, thereby generating power, exerting pressure on the institution, and channeling it in a certain direction:

> The Committee wishes to emphasize that it does see information technology as a very important subject, one that is vital for the future of the university. Indeed, it is already being explored in the School of Humanities in practical forms, including the development of instructional techniques, as well as in analytic ways, including courses and seminars devoted to interrogating the historical, social, cultural, political, and philosophical effects and roles of electronic communications technology.

A revealing postscript to this exchange of documents comes in the form of a response from UC Irvine's Executive Vice Chancellor: "Having discussed this issue with many community supporters and business people, I am impressed with the possibilities they see for humanities students who are comfortable in the electronic work place of the future. I know this approach can have great advantages for the humanities." Notice how he contextualizes all this in terms of the work place, thereby returning this chapter's analysis to its beginning, completing the circuitry.

FACULTY DEVELOPMENT: WAC VS. IT

Although educational institutions are not circuit boards, certain similarities are suggestive, particularly the role played by one kind of electronic component—faculty resistors. At the risk of being misleading, these similarities nonetheless point beyond the simplistic reductionism that can stall instructional development and debilitate it. They reveal one way of appreciating faculty work, and, on the basis of this analysis, imply ways that an institution can strategically arrange to enhance this work. Institutional inertia and faculty resistance are not necessarily or always bad. Countless historical examples of academic resistance, which range, for instance, from criticism of the McCarthy Senate hearings to repudiation of Lysenko's crackpot biology, attest to the value of academic inertia. However, some change is both inevitable and desirable. Institutions must create ways of encouraging this change and channeling instructors' resistance productively. Hence the need for appropriate faculty development in information technology—to increase instructors' computer competence and to encourage them to enlarge their pedagogical repertoires accordingly.

How, then, to develop the right kind of faculty resistance to Information Technology (IT)? Only when they are properly prepared can faculty generate appropriate, critical resistance. One appropriately humanistic answer is to be guided by successful past experience, in particular, by the practice of Writing Across the Curriculum (WAC). These two kinds of instructional development can first be compared along four dimensions: the content to be learned, the learning environment, the developers, and the learning process. Once this comparison has revealed their particular features, special tactics can be envisioned for accommodating IT.

CONTENT TO BE LEARNED

The Problem

The content of WAC workshops is familiar. All instructors have some idea about creating assignments, and commenting on and assessing student papers. The worst that can be said about WAC is that it involves much hard work. Given the academic reward system, it is easily perceived as drudgery.

IT, on the other hand, is *not* familiar. The content is perceived as a displacement and a devaluation. The medium is displaced—from the tangible solidity of print to fluid, unstable, electronic bits. Consider faculty publications. Value accrues to them from competitive exchange in an academic marketplace through refereed publication and subsequent citation. Faculty are engaged in a prestige contest of creating valuable, original intellectual property that circulates in an academic market controlled by professional organizations to guarantee scarcity, for example, a limited number of refereed journals (Strenski "Writing Across the Curriculum").

The computer does more than simply disrupt this familiar process. It destabilizes, devalues, and inflates this currency market. This perceived disintegration of standards is much worse than the drudgery associated with WAC. It is no wonder, then, that many faculty recoil from becoming acquainted with the technology's implications for scholarly production, even if it is only at the undergraduate level of assigned papers. The technology is dangerous, possibly infectious, and therefore best kept at a distance.

One telling example of such faculty fear is the graffiti that appeared on an instructional development flyer from UC Irvine advertising a faculty panel on "Pedagogical Uses of the Internet." A very distinguished professor, not knowing he was being observed, annotated this flyer in red pen with words that he added as a kind of new subtitle for the panel: "End of reading books." For him, this surely foreboded the "End of writing books" as well. Meanwhile thoughtful observers cannot help but notice the increasing consolidation of academic publishers. Consider, not to mention the "edutainment" conglomerates, how relatively few textbook publishers exist today. For example, Longman, once owned in the 1970s by Sir Harold Macmillan, was bought up in the 1980s by Addison-Wesley, which was bought up in the 1990s by HarperRow, and is now owned by the Pearson Family, which also owns various newspapers and sports organizations. Surely, if technology is implicated, as it must be, in this consolidation and consequent shrinking of possibilities of original publications, then our distinguished graffiti artist has a legitimate grievance.

A Response: Self-sufficiency, Comparison, and Spells

Self-sufficiency and the associated concept of privacy are relevant principles. The social gratification of WAC workshops is missing with IT insofar as IT involves solitary, private undertakings. Among various IT instructional development efforts at UC Irvine, the "Connecting from Home" offerings have been among the most popular. Once instructors can operate from home, they are launched. So, too, thanks to a former graduate student who now works in the campus bookstore, a friendly, inviting, useful selection of books on IT greets instructors (and others). This preselection is a very different arrangement from the one at, say, Borders, which organizes its books alphabetically or by computer application, and it allows instructors to browse for self-help material easily. This gesture toward self-sufficiency must, of course, take the form of gentle reassurance and support, not an irritated RTFM.

Specifically, a menu of various learning activities should be offered to instructors and made available at their convenience, for example, workshops, panels, individual "personal trainers," "office hour" consultations (even "house calls" in faculty housing), or series of classes amounting to "mini-courses." These activities should range from instruction in the precondition of knowing how to use e-mail, through various collaborative efforts with campus librarians on WWW research and manipulating UNIX files and creating HTML documents with various web editors, to pedagogical applications of the Internet.

Another principle that can frame much faculty discussion of IT, and that diffuses the kind of hostility illustrated in the graffiti about the end of books, is this one, taken from Elizabeth L. Eisenstein's book, *The Printing Revolution in Early Modern Europe*: "the significance of setting many different texts side by side" (257). This principle, and its associated intellectual activity, is one of comparison. Comparison—and critical thinking—can be shown to be enhanced by computer technology, for instance, as in the comparison exercise devised by a UC Irvine teaching assistant for an "Argument and Research" composition class. This exercise required students to access, read, and analyze two texts on the WWW: one ("Cyberporn") that originally appeared in *Time*; and the other, an academic critique of the *Time* article. This assignment, exercising students' critical thinking capacities in an extremely efficient, focused way, can be said to be inspired, knowingly or not, by Eisenstein's observation about the value of comparing texts, in print or electronically. This and similar exercises—about, and necessarily using, computer technology—are ones that almost all instructors recognize immediately as valuable, and it thereby simultaneously demonstrates and justifies IT.

The third suggestion here pertains to the value of academic incantations, that is, the strategic use of powerful quotations—like the one from Eisenstein above. For example, a handout or report about IT faculty development might suitably start with a quotation from a source such as Alan T. McKenzie's chapter, "The Academic On Line." That very useful chapter itself starts with two such incantations, one from Samuel Johnson's *Dictionary* and one from Lyotard's *The Postmodern Condition*.

The point of all these activities is to domesticate IT and to lead faculty to see that the computer is a communication tool being reclaimed for humanistic purposes through an emerging scholarly effort—research, teaching, reading, and writing.

THE LEARNING ENVIRONMENT

The Problem

WAC workshops are variations on the typical faculty committee meeting. Instructors sit around tables and examine papers. What is discussed is loosely defined by sets of sample assignments, student papers, handouts on principles of grading, etc. Instructors often write to immerse themselves in the feel of journals or drafts. They sometimes learn new terms, like "prewriting," but the physical scene—where they sit, what they see, what they hear, what they do—is familiar.

Not so with a workshop on IT. To function best, it will be conducted "hands on" in a computer lab—a cyborg space. Instructors will sit next to a machine, not a colleague, thus confronted by an ominous and expensive apparatus that threatens to break down. Control over the proceedings is also taken out of workshop leaders' hands. Instructors and students seem equally vulnerable to the whims of their machines. Such interdependency with machines is unsettling, and can be easily resented as a territorial intrusion on the humanities by the sciences, in which faculty seem to be, as one UC Irvine instructor in an IT workshop complained, "selling our souls."

If the IT workshop is staged as a demonstration in a conventional room, there will still be obtrusive carts of equipment, cords and wires, media personnel, etc. It will look and sound different. It will be a new universe of discourse—not for a few neologisms like "prewriting," but strange, alien terms such as "URL," "FTP," "HTML," that jar in their ugliness and violate in their syntax, like the use of "subscribe" with a direct object: "subscribe yourself" to a listserv. Moreover, the workshop activities are not creatively messy in the way that many humanities undertakings are, but follow rigorous algorithmic procedures for login to accounts, changing permissions and passwords, etc.

A Response: Formality

Few would dare disclose publicly that they can't do times tables, but some instructors still seem proud of their technological incompetence. This leads to an academic version of learned helplessness and hostile, whining infantilism. One way to inhibit this destructive behavior is to observe a strategic, ritual decorum. For example, any IT workshop should be quite formal. Although this recommendation is perhaps counter-intuitive, it should *not* aim at being friendly. It should aim at being formal. This is not the place for cool T-shirts—anything but.

THE DEVELOPERS

The Problem

WAC workshops are conducted by faculty peers. If the workshop leaders are not members of the participants' departments, they are consultants from an English department or from a writing program. If their specialized knowledge is unfamiliar, it is at least certified by familiar academic procedures conferring rank and qualification, and by a recognizable research tradition in the academic peer-reviewed journals sponsored by professional associations.

IT workshops, on the other hand, are conducted by two kinds of alien beings. Leaders can be, first of all, consultants from an Office of Academic Computing. These functionaries are administrators, a lesser kind of being in relation to academic faculty. They are tolerable, but only barely: however technologically competent they may be, they are not always good teachers. Because the alien discourse about URLs, FTP, HTML, etc. issues from their second-class mouths, they are perceived as contaminating presences, and often disparaged out of hand by faculty participants.

Worse, the leaders can be graduate student underlings. Many graduate students arrive on campus already technologically proficient and computer literate. They are the "shock troops," the ones at the frontier who become department sysops and webmasters—an available, relatively inexpensive source of expertise. Never before have graduate students possessed valuable information—the currency of a new realm—that their mentors did not also possess. This situation reverses the centuries-old academic apprentice-master relationship and jeopardizes it.

Exacerbating the irritation occasioned by the presence of such unorthodox instructors is the recognition on the part of regular rank faculty that their own self-governing status is changing for other reasons having nothing to do with technology. For instance, at the University of California, only half—and in some departments considerably less—of all instruction is performed by regular, tenured or tenurable faculty. The rest is in the hands of these more technologically knowledgeable graduate student TAs and temporary and part-time lecturers working on short-term contracts. Adding these two other kinds of IT instructors—graduate students not assigned as teaching assistants for small sections of large lecture classes taught by professors, but teaching their own workshop equivalents of classes, and technical administrators—can only be perceived as an affront by "regular" faculty.

A Response

The leaders must behave formally in every way. For example, the same group of basically graduate student instructors at UC Irvine became more effective after changing their name from "Techno-Teachers" to "The School of Humanities Internet Resource Group." So, too, any consecration is useful. At UC Irvine, the Chancellor has gone on record as promoting our undergraduates' command of "21st century information skills." This manifesto can be appropriated as a blessing. The School of

Humanities Internet Resource Group has claimed—correctly, although somewhat indirectly—to be working for her and for the Executive Vice Chancellor in charge of academic computing on campus, not for a low-status operation like the humanities computing lab.

THE PROCESS

The Problem

The faculty development model for WAC workshops is the assembly line, where individual instructors are developed in a predictable sequence. They are "developed," like photographic film, to invoke yet another metaphor, and then move back to their home departments, where, operating autonomously, they assign more drafts, write more comments on papers, etc., and a new batch of instructors comes to the next series of WAC workshops.

The emerging model of effective IT faculty development is different. In the same way that reading teachers talk about reading "readiness," so, too, with computer literacy. Faculty are "ready" (or not) for IT at different times and in different ways. It simply does not work to collect them together in workshops, even if that were possible, and teach them the computer equivalent of phonics. Nor can institutions legislate computer-enriched classes in the same way that they can do with writing instruction by, for instance, mandating an upper division writing requirement to be satisfied by writing intensive courses requiring assignments of 4,000 words, as at UC Irvine, where this faculty obligation is shared (if not equally willingly) by the members of various academic departments. An unwilling instructor assigned to teach in a computer lab can simply lecture to students who peer over the tops of their dark monitors.

A Response

Here, several more metaphors are introduced: leverage and a water image of cascading and trickling. IT faculty development is more akin to the "each one teach one" mentoring model of adult literacy. Moreover, IT faculty development is money that is well spent on composition instructors, often graduate student TAs. It is while they are graduate students that these future faculty develop the teaching skills and attitudes—the intellectual tool kit—that they will carry with them for the rest of their careers. Preparing these apprentice instructors, while they are still young and still forming their teaching practices and expectations, is a very cost-effective investment. As composition instructors, they are gatekeepers teaching general education breadth requirements (primarily to first-year students, another kind of pedagogical investment)—both "leverage." Moreover, these TAs already share a common culture and opportunities to talk to, influence, and teach one another—a "cascading" mentoring model. They can also influence their faculty mentors in a "trickle-up" process when they TA for large lectures.

Part of faculty resistance to technology is a recognition of shifting power on both sides of the teacher-learner relationship. Those who know about computers must use their new power so they do not alienate their colleagues, and so that they do help them, and in turn, help their students. The alternative—reinforcing this opposition rather than trying to dismantle it—seems both self-indulgent and professionally suicidal.

SITES IN COMPOSITION STUDIES

Encouraged to speak up about issues of information technology and computers in the composition classroom, what should faculty resistors say? They can, of course, echo arguments about the influence of computers on pedagogy more generally. One of the more important of these general claims observes that computer-assisted teaching is not so much an "enhancement" as a fundamental disruption of the conventional teacher-student relationship. It is not cheaper and it does not take less time:

> . . . contrary to an expectation that the role of the teacher will diminish with Internet or computer-based course delivery, the demands on the teacher's time remain the same and may increase. However, the types of demand change. This is where the teacher must change in order to provide a service to learners. One of the initial changes is that the teacher becomes a monitor and mentor. The teacher's role becomes less instructive and more supportive. At the same time the Internet changes the role of the learner from one of recipient to participant. (Forsyth 31)

But faculty resistors who teach composition can also function within their programs, departments, and schools of humanities to draw attention to, explain the complexity of, and argue for time and resources to address properly the following six issues of more local professional concern.

The Internet as a "Velcro" Medium for Groupwork

The electronic medium inexorably exerts pressures on writers to combine, amalgamate, and merge voices and texts. The file sharing and the commenting capabilities of commercial software like Daedalus Interchange or Sixth Floor Media's ConmmonSpace, not to mention the hypertextual creations of Storyspace or HyperStudio, can enhance the instructional potential of peer editing and other kinds of student collaboration. Moreover, a special "velcro" quality of the Internet makes it easy for student writers to "glue" bits of text together—hypertextually or not, their own texts or those of others. The resulting coauthorship can be a rich textual tapestry; it can also be problematic, if not dishonest.

The easy cut-and-paste capability of computers makes illegitimate borrowing easy, as it does distorted editing and attribution. Moreover, the Internet seems to provide an endless, public source of information to be plundered. A recent report in the *Los Angeles Times*, "Redefining Research, Plagiarism" (Fritz A1), explains, "Going online to get homework isn't a novel thing. To some students, it's not even cheating. It's just evolved into an institution; a big study group of sorts." Consider, for example, the outrage of this student, whose name is deliberately withheld but who is quite real, when she was confronted with a curious similarity between parts of a paper she had submitted to an instructor at UC Irvine and parts of a paper submitted to an English instructor at a college in Texas that was published on that instructor's class web page. The UC Irvine student was furious, indignantly denying that she had ever seen the other student's paper, and in her defense produced the web source she had copied, claiming that the Texas student must have copied it too, also without attribution. Because what she had copied from the Web and inserted in her paper, and then submitted as her own work, was not another student's paper, but rather the electronic work of some anonymous journalist, she believed her action was legitimate opportunism. Instructors' responses must be twofold: first, to let students know that we are aware of online paper mills like The Evil House of Cheat, *www.schoolsucks.com*, among others, and, second, to work even harder to instill in students a sense of respect for other people's intellectual property rights, even as we encourage cooperation.

From the instructor's viewpoint, this hybrid medium also invites faculty collaboration—if not team teaching, then consultation. Because Internet information is so heavily dependent on graphics, composition instructors must become minimally familiar with graphic design and interpretation. For help, we can turn not only to our colleagues in Art departments but to the readily available curriculum materials created to help students respond to print advertisements, which can be easily adapted to analyzing web pages, for example, Cynthia L. Selfe and Diana George's useful list of questions (Appendix A: How to Look at an

Image) that students can ask in order to analyze a web graphic (*Literacy, Technology, and Society* 579–80).

Compositionist resistors, then, will raise these issues of groupwork and collaboration for discussion with their students and with their colleagues, and will channel energy to work on modifying their curricula accordingly.

The Need to Develop and to Include Instruction in the Critical Thinking Skills of On-screen Reading

Students are increasingly turning to the World Wide Web for all kinds of information, and there they are snowed in several senses by a blizzard of undifferentiated data that combines entertainment, commerce, and politics with various kinds of research reports and academic as well as professional editorials. For some sense of the extent of this information, consider, for example, that American tobacco companies last year were legally required to post twenty-seven million documents on the WWW, the exact same number, twenty-seven million, of volumes contained in the University of California library, one of the largest libraries in the world. Presented literally out of the ether by mindless search engines, this overwhelmingly immense, decontextualized mass of Internet information encourages the accelerated processing of a speedy reading: a quick glance, search for clues, and then on to another link. Quantity assumes more importance than quality, which, in turn, is hard to assess.

Consider this experience of a UC Irvine student enrolled in the second of two lower-division ("Argument and Research") composition courses requiring freshmen to select as the basis of their coursework a controversial public policy issue. This student chose the issue of STDs, for example, AIDS research and government policy about experimental drugs. What happened when he ventured onto the Internet looking for information? The first link recommended by a search-engine's robot algorithm took him to The Sexual Health Information Center Main Menu (<*http://www.apgo.com/health/infomenu.htm*>), which turned out to be hosted by the Adult Playground Group, "Canada's largest, highest-quality, online provider of TOTALLY FREE XXX Hardcore adult related pictures and entertainment services; with an educational aspect as well" (<*http://www.apgo.com/advertising/adinfo.htm*>). There this inquiring freshman did find, among other links, a useful one to the respected organization of Planned Parenthood and to its own database of medical information about STDs and to its links, in turn, to other credible medical sources. This process of trail blazing through highly diverse and branching levels of data of varying quality and credibility is a different process from turning the pages of a printed source, and it requires appropriate instruction for students to develop the ability to do so wisely and efficiently.

If this were not bad enough, blatant commercial sponsorship is yet another trap for the unprepared undergraduate. Research universities are under increasing attack (Shenk) for academic-corporate cooperation that may affect the integrity of scientific research, but this kind of cooperation, if not collusion, is typical on the WWW. For example, another foray onto the Web took the student to the pharmaceutical company of Glaxo Wellcome, which makes the AIDS antiviral drug AZT, denounced by several AIDS activist groups on their web sites as poison. Glaxo Wellcome not only sponsors research into anti-HIV drugs, but publicizes this research. A recent posting, titled "New Chomekine Holds Hope for HIV Treatment," on the Glaxo Wellcome corporate site (http://www.glaxowellcome.co.uk/science/molecular_piracy.html) announces, "Full details of the research, carried out in . . . collaboration with . . . Glaxo Wellcome, are reported in the September 12th issue of *Science* (<http://www.glaxowellome.co.uk/science/molecular_piracy. html>). To begin to appreciate the significance of this research in order to use and cite it, the UC Irvine undergraduate should at a minimum be guided by an instructor through a preliminary exercise that would prepare him to compare this corporate site's public relations posting, an activist site's criticism, a *Los Angeles Times* report about it, and the *Science* article—sources that are all available on the WWW or college online databases.

Composition instructors, whose essential job is to teach close reading and its associated critical thinking skills, are ideally situated to help students learn these new survival skills of "quality filtering," as librarians refer to this process, by consciously transferring their practice of reading literary texts to reading on screen. If teaching digital literacy is essentially nothing new, however, the eruption of technological change is nonetheless confusing as the Internet explodes the traditional definitions of "the library" and "information source" and "classroom" far beyond concrete objects and physical spaces, and as institutions challenge their various departments and programs to develop and provide correspondingly appropriate instruction. Composition resistors must help students, in turn, resist the appeal of quickly scanning miscellaneous on-screen information. Instead, we must teach these skills of careful, efficient searching, possibly channeling energy into collaborations with our librarian colleagues. Concurrently, we must teach the interpretive skills of skeptical scrutiny so that these can be applied to online information.

The Need to Develop and to Include
Instruction in Online Writing

Effective online writing, created to be read on-screen, reflects the hybrid nature of electronic textuality and differs from writing for print. At the very least, the emotional volatility of the medium demands that any online instruction include Netiquette, as attested by the unfortunate case of a UC Irvine student's racist, emailed death threats that went all the way to the U.S. Supreme Court (Hua).

Moreover, emerging research confirms the common experience of "How Users Read on the Web" (Nielsen 1997). The result is that "They don't." Nielsen's study determined that only 16 percent of online readers read each word; the others scan quickly for conspicuous clues such as bullets, headings, colorful images, and highlighted keywords. Moreover, they will not read more than one or two screens down into a document. Although in 1996 a commentator could claim, "There are no good books about writing specifically for the Web" ("Writing for the Web"), since that time, several have appeared and various design principles are emerging.

Apart from the arrangement of graphic elements for ease of reading, for example restricting the number of characters on each line to a maximum of fifty-five, or the judicious inclusion of credible hyperlinks, the major change in web writing affects the sequence and organization of information. Most belletristic essays—the mainstay of first-year composition courses—follow an inductive pattern that leads up, finally, to a conclusion based on evidence earlier displayed. Not so on the WWW. According to Nielsen ("Inverted Pyramids in Cyberspace"), "We know from several user studies that *users don't scroll.*" Since most read only one screen, web information must be presented in the "inverted pyramid" taught in journalism courses. For quick scanning, the central points must be listed quickly and simply as if for a flyer or a poster.

Such observations raise provocative questions for the writing instructor. If a web page is more akin to a poster than any other textual genre, with only so much time available in our curricula, do we want to spend it teaching students how to create posters, even if we can learn the HTML and Javascript enhancements ourselves to do so, first? Is, indeed, the kind of journalistic telegraphese of bulleted lists and highlighted headings appropriate for college instruction in an English department or writing program within a school of humanities, as opposed, say, to marketing or commercial art? Does such simplistic formatting automatically degrade ideas, deform them into stereotypes, and thereby restrict a range of expression and experience? Faculty resistors must claim time to have considered these questions adequately. Meanwhile, electives in web writing can be piloted to determine whether such fears are real or not.

THE STYLISTIC DEBATE OVER "PLAIN ENGLISH"

Writing instructors, if not acting as arbiters of it, at least include as part of their curriculum the issue of style. They assign George Orwell's essay "Politics and the English Language," and their handbooks include exhortations to clarity. But style is a problematic issue for critical educators, as, for example, Henry A. Giroux has conveniently outlined in "Language, Power and Clarity or 'Does Plain Prose Cheat?'" The presence of web telegraphese exacerbates this contention over the use of plain language in theoretical analysis. If the online medium exerts pressures to frame ordinary information in such poster fashion, what then happens to theoretical discourse? Can complex analysis of conflated assumptions and inferences be translated to bullets and headings and inverted pyramids? Critical pedagogues are accustomed to being criticized for unnecessarily obscure, inaccessible, undemocratic diction and overly complicated syntax. But composition instructors, located at the very production site for principles of discourse, are inextricably implicated in this quarrel.

One of the best ripostes to this demand for what Richard Lanham has called a CBS style (Clarity, Brevity, Sincerity) is the explanation of French sociologist, Pierre Bourdieu:

> If you accept the fact that, in order to make yourself understood, you have to work at using words in such a way that they say just what you wanted them to say, you can see that the best way of talking clearly consists in talking in a complicated way, in an attempt to transmit simultaneously what you are saying and your relationship to what you are saying, and in avoiding saying, against your will, something more than and different from what you thought you were saying (*In Other Words* 52–53).

A bulleted list—flattening levels of generality—may be easier to construct than a paragraph including compound-complex sentences that exploit syntax in order to express logical relationships, and may appeal to those students who are unsure about grammar and feel vulnerable to error. But, *pace* George Orwell, composition instructors must resist the fetishism of correctness and easy readability at the expense of accurate complexity, and must defend necessary ambiguity against the many modern Mrs. Gradgrinds in our profession.

Moreover, the Internet itself can help promulgate progressive ideas.

Alan Heaps's "The Web-Based Syllabus: Rethinking the Politics of Initial Classroom Documents" illustrates both the value of an appropriately nuanced analysis of a theoretical issue, and the logistical convenience of the WWW as a means of disseminating it.

"Off-loading" "Remedial" Writing
Instruction to the Internet Antipodes

Universities accept responsibility for the "underprepared" students that they admit (when they do accept it) uneasily, as attested by the history of Subject A instruction in the University of California system, or the recent controversy over "remedial" education in the CUNY system. Increasingly, colleges and universities are turning to cyberspace as a place to send these students. Otherwise regular University of California Subject A students (students who failed a composition placement exam) are increasingly being taught by community college instructors for community college transfer credit, and community college students are being taught by commercial educators on the WWW. For example, Santa Monica College students can now take courses from a company called EducationToGo <http://www.educationtogo.com>. Tuition for these Internet courses is paid to Santa Monica College, which presumably reimburses EducationToGo for their students' participation in this venture.

These courses may be good; they may be bad. But the need for faculty scrutiny would seem obvious to a faculty resistor.

Labor Implications for the
Graduate Students, Part-time Instructors,
and Temporary Lecturers Who Teach Composition

With our job market already in such peril, and possibly over a third of compositionists holding part-time positions (Faigley 34), faculty resistors need to be alert to technology that flouts our humanistic goals. For example, software has been peddled throughout the University of California system, called "Remote TA," the "TA" signifying not a graduate student, but rather the "technical assistance" of the computer. At the UC Irvine teaching colloquy where this program was introduced as a great "innovation" in pedagogy, administrators were enthralled by its cost-cutting potential; because of its tutorial interface and "expert" TA (a software module), only one "assistant" is required to run this service for multiple course sections. Although developed by a professor of computer science, Dick Walters, Remote TA is already being used for various humanities courses (Spanish, Japanese, Russian) at beta sites, and has been funded for three years, beginning October

1997, by the Fund for the Improvement of Post-Secondary Education.

While certainly "efficient" and seemingly economical, such technology may be less than humane in its deletion of a segment of the aspiring or current work force of lecturers, coordinators, and graduate students. Not under coercion, but out of professional pride and responsibility, faculty resistors must adopt a sense of "virtual ethics" that brings together humanistic critical self-reflection, technical awareness, and an acknowledgment of institutional responsibility. We also must remain aware that to use technology as a pedagogical enhancement is potentially, in turn, to be used by the institution providing this infrastructure and service and seemingly buying us off with purchases of PowerMacs and new PCs.

CONCLUSION

Mobilizing composition faculty to take responsibility for engaging in the current campus discussion about information technology so they can function appropriately as resistors in their institutions is partly a day-to-day working duty. But beyond our professional responsibilities, the effects of computers on writers also offer a unique pleasure and a unique source of political hope. This chapter ends with a celebration of electronic writing, especially the common worldware application of e-mail. E-mail correspondence between teacher and students in electronic office hours, and among and between teacher and students in the extended discussion space of class listservs is not just another technical transaction, like using an automated teller machine. Rather, however rudimentary, it is epistolary art, akin to conversation, and it derives its power as art from gift exchange. However modest, e-mail releases a new academic resource for "dreaming" while opening a new pedagogical space for critical teaching and learning.

To summarize this argument, first, the "chatty" (Shapiro and Anderson 23) and "conversational" (Duranti 65) quality of electronic correspondence encourages e-mailers, as many observe themselves doing, to "ramble on." More is going on than the lifting of logistical constraints; inhibitions, too, are circumvented. According to Sara Kiesler and others, people are up to five times more likely to engage in emotionally revealing behavior in computer-mediated communication than in face-to-face interactions. E-mailers value spontaneity. They do not want to revise. The result is associative, open-ended discourse that prompts self-disclosure. Moreover, e-mailers' messages are often emotionally engaging, full of play with personae, puns, humor, self-deprecation, ingratiation, or, on the other hand, flames. Although e-mail is definitely not utopia, and although it brings its own special problems to the classroom, once they start composing, most students write a lot of words; they enjoy the process. Before e-mail, most students wrote nothing that was not required. Now they write a great deal and enjoy doing so.

Unlike most other kinds of texts, e-mail automatically evokes a response in kind: more mail. This dynamic of "epistolarity" explains the prolixity of e-mail messages, while the association with art and artistic exchange accounts for the quality of emotional disclosure in them. This particular kind of art, necessarily framed by the letter or message format, also automatically provides opportunities for irony and play through these juxtapositions. When Derrida writes in *The Post Card: From Socrates to Freud and Beyond*, "In the last analysis I do nothing that does not have some interest in seducing you," his poetic license exaggerates (69). However, he does get at an important emotional dimension that characterizes e-mail especially well, what Altman refers to as "the interpersonal bond basic to the very language of the letter (I-you) [which] necessarily structures meaning in letter narratives" (118).

The result is post-print text. If "Narrative is the native form of oral culture, [and] exposition is the native form of alphabetic literacy (in the sense that scientific writing is the privileged discourse of the print apparatus)," then according to Gregory L. Ulmer, "collage pattern is the native form of electronics" ("Grammatology" 163). Ulmer explains: "Logically, the electronic apparatus does not come 'after' print but 'between' print and oral 'literacy.'" (Heuretics, xi). Following McLuhan and others, Ulmer claims that this new electronic form of collaborative collage has its own, correspondingly distinctive, "conductive (dream-work) logic" ("Grammatology" 161). Ulmer is referring specifically to the electronic communication of hypertext, but his comments fit equally well a typical extended e-mail conversation in a thread on a listserv or a group web project hyperlinking individual students' contributions. The result is a multivocal, fragmented text in process, starting with an original message sent, responded to, snipped, requoted, all the while accumulating associative exegesis from other writers along with modifications and increasing columns of arrows to indicate copying and recopying.

This new, powerful form of communication is a resource for all teachers. Not only does it come with its own built-in incentive (students want to use it), but it is also profoundly democratic in principle. Troubling material obstacles, especially more difficult access to the machines for poorer students, aside, many differences—age, gender, class, accent, race—that mark and disqualify or discourage people from engaging in some real life encounters do disappear in e-mail.

How, then, does dreaming fit in here? The medium is very generative: e-mailers like to ramble on, to try out new personae, to get attention, to make emotional connections. The logic that gives meaning to their new, post-print, electronically produced texts—if Gregory Ulmer is correct—is conductive, associative, dreamlike. Everyone agrees that we need alternative scenarios of what life could be like to counter despair and paralysis. They do not have to be nightmares. In its modest, quotidian way, e-mail endows us all with just such a powerful resource for imaginative, inventive, artistic expression in multiple public spheres.

Communicating via e-mail, teachers and students can escape some of the classroom constraints, roles, and expectations by emerging in this new electronic social space and forum. Henry A. Giroux, writing recently in the *Harvard Educational Review*, comments on how "Communities that have been refigured as space and time mutate into multiple overlapping cyberspace networks." Referring to the postmodern culture of youth, Giroux writes: "They reorder their imaginations through connections to virtual reality technologies and produce forms of exchange through texts and images that have the potential to wage a war on traditional meaning, but also run the risk of reducing critical understanding to the endless play of random access spectacle" (288). Faculty resistors must act to tap and channel these new energies, to get the work of learning to write well accomplished.

Andee Rubin and Bertram Bruce remind us, "an innovation is not an object that can be packed inside a box but rather a set of practices that emerges from the social setting of its use. Thus, in a sense, teachers do not accept or reject an innovation; instead they *create* it" (262; emphasis in original). The creation of a set of pedagogical practices involving the use of computers to improve students' reading, writing, and thinking is a worthy goal, as is faculty development to encourage them to aspire to such creation. A precondition is readying composition instructors to be good faculty resistors and to get wired the right way.

NOTE

1. See, for instance, "*Computers and Composition* Comprehensive Bibliography," the online index to all works, and works cited, in *C&C*.

WORKS CITED

Altman, Janet. *Epistolarity: Approaches to a Form.* Columbus, OH: Ohio State UP, 1982.

Applebome, Peter. "Employers Wary of School System." *New York Times* 20 Feb. 1995: A1, A11.

Atkinson, Richard C. "Welcome and Opening Remarks," March 26, 1997, UCLA. All-University Conference on Teaching and Learning Technologies and the Present and Future of the University of California.

Baudrillard, Jean. *The Ecstasy of Communication.* Trans. Bernard and Caroline Schutze. Ed. Sylvere Lotringer. Brooklyn, NY: Autonomedia, 1988. Originally published as *L'Autre par lui-même*, 1987.

Bourdieu, Pierre. *In Other Words: Essays Toward a Reflexive Sociology.* Trans. Matthew Adams. Stanford, CA: Stanford UP, 1990.

Burke, Kenneth. *Language as Symbolic Action: Essays on Life, Literature, and Method.* London: Routledge & Kegan Paul, 1985. 1st ed. 1938.

Chow, Rey. *Writing Diasporas: Tactics of Intervention in Contemporary Cultural Studies.* Bloomington and Indianapolis, IN: Indiana UP, 1993.

Computers and Composition Comprehensive Bibliography <http://www.hu.mtu.edu/~candc/bib/>.

Cunningham, Sally Jo. "Teaching Students to Critically Evaluate the Quality of Internet Research Resources." *SIGCSE Bulletin (A Quarterly Publication of the Association for Computing Machinery Special Interest Group on Computer Science Education)* 29.2 (June 1997): 32–34, 38.

Derrida, Jacques. *The Post Card: From Socrates to Freud and Beyond.* Trans. Alan Bass. Chicago: U of Chicago P, 1987. Originally published as *Carte postale.*

Duranti, Alessandro. "Framing Discourse in a New Medium: Openings in Electronic Mail." *Quarterly Newsletter of the Laboratory of Comparative Human Cognition* 8 (April 1986): 64–71.

Durkheim, Emile. *The Evolution of Educational Thought.* Trans. Peter Collins. London: Routledge & Kegan Paul, 1985. 1st ed. 1938.

Eisenstein, Elizabeth L. *The Printing Revolution in Early Modern Europe.* New York: Cambridge UP, 1983.

Faigley, Lester. "Literacy After the Revolution." *College Composition and Communication* 48 (1997): 30–43.

Forsyth, Ian. *Teaching and Learning Materials and the Internet.* London: Kogan Page, 2nd ed., 1998.

Fritz, Mark. "Redefining Research, Plagiarism." *Los Angeles Times* 25 Feb. 1999: A1, A10.

Giroux, Henry A. "Doing Cultural Studies: Youth and the Challenge of Pedagogy." *Harvard Educational Review* 64 (1994): 278–308.

———. "Language, Power, and Clarity or 'Does Plain Prose Cheat?'" *Living Dangerously. Multiculturalism and the Politics of Difference. COUNTERPOINTS. Studies in the Postmodern Theory of Education.* Vol 1. Ed. Joe L. Kincheloe and Shirley R. Steinberg. New York: Peter Lang, 1993. 155–71.

Hardin, Garrett. *Stalking the Wild Taboo.* 2nd. ed. Los Altos, CA: W. Kaufmann, 1976.

Hawisher, Gail, and Cynthia Selfe, eds. *Literacy, Technology, and Society: Confronting the Issues.* Upper Saddle River, NJ: Prentice Hall, 1997.

Heaps, Alan. <http://www.hu.mtu.edu/~agheaps/papers/radcult.html><http://www.hu.mtu.edu/~agheaps/papers/radcult.html>.

Horowitz, Manny. *Elementary Electricity and Electronics.* Blue Ridge Summit, PA: TAB, 1986.

Hua, Thao. "Ex-Student Sentenced for Hate Email." *Los Angeles Times* 5 May 1998: A24.

Joyce, Michael. *Of Two Minds: Hypertext Pedagogy and Politics.* Ann Arbor, MI: U of Michigan P, 1995.

Kiesler, Sara, et al. "Affect in Computer-Mediated Communication." *Human-Computer Interaction* 1 (1985): 77–105.

Lakoff, George, and Mark Johnson. *Metaphors We Live By.* Chicago: U of Chicago P, 1981.

Lankshear, Colin, Michael Peters, and Michelle Knobel. "Critical Pedagogy and Cyberspace." *Counternarratives: Cultural Studies and Critical Pedagogies in Postmodern Spaces.* Eds. Henry Giroux, Colin Lankshear, Peter McLaren, and Michael Peters. New York and London: Routledge, 1996. 149–88.

Lyotard, Jean François. *The Postmodern Condition: A Report on Knowledge.* Trans. Geoff Bennington. Minneapolis: U of Minnesota P, 1984.

McKenzie, Alan T. "The Academic On Line." *The Digital Word: Text-Based Computing in the Humanities.* Ed. George P. Landow and Paul Delany. Cambridge, MA: MIT, 1993. 201–16.

Murray, J. Middleton. *The Problem of Style.* London, OUP, 1922.

Nielsen, Jakob. "Inverted Pyramids in Cyberspace." (June 1996) <http://www.useit.com/alertbox/9606.html>.

———. "How Users Read on the Web." (October 1997) <http://www.useit.com/alertbox/9710a.html>.

Orwell, George. *Politics and the English Language: An Essay.* Evansville, IN: Typophiles, 1947.

Rheingold, Howard. *The Virtual Community: Homesteading on the Electronic Frontier.* Reading, MA: Addison-Wesley, 1993.

Rubin, Andee, and Bertram Bruce. "Alternate Realizations of Purpose in Computer-Supported Writing." *Theory into Practice* 29 (1990): 256–63.

Shapiro, Norman Z., and Robert H. Anderson. *Toward an Ethics and Etiquette for Electronic Mail.* Santa Monica, CA: Rand, 1985.

Shenk, David. "Money + Science = Ethics Problems on Campus." *The Nation* 268.11 22 March 1999: 11–18.

Strenski, Ellen. "Writing Across the Curriculum at Research Universities." *Strengthening Programs for Writing across the Curriculum.* Ed. Susan H. McLeod. San Francisco: Jossey-Bass, 1988. 31–41.

Thompson, G. W. "Faculty Recalcitrance about Bibliographic Instruction." *Bibliographic Instruction in Practice: A Tribute to the Legacy of Evan Ira Farber.* Ed. L. Hardesty, J. Hastreiter, and D. Henderson. Ann Arbor, MI: Pierian Press, 1993. 103–105.

Traub, James. "Drive-Through U: Higher Education for People Who Mean Business." *The New Yorker* 73.20 (20 Oct. 1997): 114–24.

Ulmer, Gregory L. "Grammatology (in the Stacks) of Hypermedia: A 'Simulation' and 'Discussion.'" *Literacy Online. The Promise (and Peril) of Reading and Writing with Computers.* Ed. Myron C. Tuman. Pittsburgh: Pittsburgh UP, 1992. 139–164.

———. *Heuretics: The Logic of Invention.* Baltimore and London: Johns Hopkins UP, 1994.

———. *Teletheory: Grammatology in the Age of Video.* New York: Routledge, 1989.

Walters, Dick. "Remote TA." May 1999 <http://escher.cs.ucdavis.edu/>.

"Writing for the Web." <http://www.useit.com/papers/webwriting/>.

Zuboff, Shoshana. *In the Age of the Smart Machine: The Future of Work and Power.* New York: Basic Books, 1988.

CHAPTER 7

Resisting Resistance: Power and Control in the Technologized Classroom

Janice Walker

> Resistance is futile.
>
> —The Borg (*Star Trek:*
> *The Next Generation*)

James Berlin delineates three major paradigms of the "poetic-rhetoric binary" in English studies: "literacy for the scientific meritocracy," marked by current-traditional rhetoric and literary criticism as philology; the "liberal-cultural paradigm," wherein rhetoric becomes a branch of poetry, a "product of genius," with oral reading at the center of teaching literature since "to those of taste the text spoke for itself"; and the "social-democratic" that argues that "Rhetoric in college should focus on training citizens for participation in a democracy" (34). The computer classroom has often been hailed as such a social-democratic space, helping to promote a liberatory pedagogy by fostering student resistance, empowering students by decentering the classroom. For example, Lester Faigley posits that electronic discourse offers "a means of exploring how . . . agency resides in the power of connecting with others and building alliances" (199), and Richard Lanham argues, "The instructor's privileged position has been metamorphosed by electronic text. The students write to and for one another, not for the Person Up Front. The success of these classes is measured by how well the students constitute their own social and scholarly community" (xiv).

Initially, of course, computers were introduced into the classroom as

119

a way of fixing errors in writing rather than as a new medium for communicating. However, with the development of networking technologies and especially of the Internet, it soon became evident that computers could be used as more than fancy typewriters. At the same time, it has also become evident that what writing teachers are doing, or need to do, is not only about teaching students to write traditional academic papers. Although Berlin argues that "colleges ought to offer a curriculum that places preparation for work within a comprehensive range of democratic educational concerns" (51) that will both prepare students to enter the work force and prepare them as "critical citizens" (52), the reality of the classroom often works against this. With or without computers, the classroom is politically situated. Moreover, the unfamiliarity of the computer classroom in particular can work against even the most ardent proponents of liberatory pedagogy as resistance to new technologies forces us to justify its existence in traditional terms.

PROMISES AND PERILS OF THE NETWORK

Although the possibilities do exist (and are, indeed, being explored by technorhetoricians) for cyberspace to be a space for grappling with the Other, nonetheless the metaphors we use to describe it (and to justify it) also allow for it to become a space for colonization (Johnson-Eilola). One example of this is the use of English—and especially of American English—as the standard for communication in online spaces: ASCII (American Standard Code for Information Interchange), the seven-bit code that assigns numbers from 0 to 127 to the English character set, is used by many Internet and computer applications to transfer data between applications and platforms. Thus, regardless of the language we use to speak (or write), our commands to the computer must be translated into a form of American English in order for us to communicate. Internet addressing also bespeaks American colonization of electronic space, or e-space. That is, while most Internet domain names include a two-letter code designating the country of origin, the ".us" country designator is usually glaringly absent.[1] The United States thus becomes naturalized, the standard against which everything else is measured. Even the interface for the computer's operating system—for example, the Windows or Macintosh interface with graphical icons that represent a middle-class desktop (i.e., file cabinets and file folders, trash cans or recycle bins, etc.)—can be seen as a form of colonization, a way of naturalizing the world of white, middle-class, primarily male Americana. E-space also allows the user to resist such accommodation, but only so long as resistance remains within the parameters delineated by the programmers. That is, we can opt to change the appearance of the icons or even to do away with them entirely; however, they remain the default regardless of our resistance. That is, no matter how much we may resist them, they are still the norm.

The early days of computers and composition were in many ways a time of uncritical optimism. Writing teachers explored ways to use the new medium to create a more egalitarian classroom, foster a sense of community, and empower students by decentering the classroom. Faigley concludes that the networked classroom does indeed create "opportunities for resistance to the dominant discourse of the majority" (199). However, after what can only be described as a disconcerting experience in e-space, he found that it also allows students to wrest control of the conversation away from the teacher as well as from each other. Furthermore, whether we realize it or not, we may be doing more than relinquishing control of the classroom to students when we go online; in our very attempts to reassert control in the face of experiences such as Faigley's, we may also be relinquishing control to the computer interface itself. That is, the technology (or, more accurately, the developers and maintainers of the hardware and software) may ultimately be what (or who) decides how the technologized classroom is configured and, thus, to decide what is or is not allowed in these spaces. Furthermore, the same technology that allows teachers and institutions to empower students can also be used to give "universities the opportunity for more power than ever before" (Flores 108). Far from being democratizing, then, computer spaces can mirror (and thus reinforce) real-life structures of power and control online:

> Teachers of English who use computers are often involved in establishing and maintaining borders themselves—whether or not they acknowledge or support such a project—and, thus, in contributing to a larger cultural system of differential power that has resulted in the systematic domination and marginalization of certain groups of students, including among them: women, nonwhites, and individuals who speak languages other than English. (Selfe and Selfe 481)

THE COMMODIFICATION OF THE NETWORK

Even without our knowledge and consent, electronic spaces may even create new hierarchies, allowing for the imposition of control in frightening ways. A primary goal of the developers of technology is that the technology itself be transparent. But this very transparency is implicated in the "paradox of hypertext": "Whereas an overly restricted and/or difficult-to-use functional text might give users a critical position in relation to the technology . . . , a fluid, very fast functional text that appears to respond directly to the user's immediate needs constructs accommodating users" (Johnson-Eilola 63). The very act of linking thereby contributes to what Johndan Johnson-Eilola calls the "politics of amnesia" (50): hypertexts become collections of interlinked texts, assuming an appearance of infinite possibilities, while actually existing within a continually circuitous and delimited space. Continuing to envision online space as an extension of print technologies furthers this accommodation by metaphorizing it as only a "more technically efficient" distribution channel, and thus naturalizing it rather than exposing the implications behind the metaphors (87).

Seeing cyberspace as merely a translation of print space also helps to further the commodified vision of online space conceived by its creators. Theodor Nelson, often credited as the creator of hypertext, has proposed what he calls a "transcopyright," which would, he argues, allow for "broad reuse of materials" by creating a cyberworld wherein "words and ideas [are] freed from the technological limitations of paper and ink" (Epstein). However, freedom from the limitations of print is not the same as "free":

> Nelson described a world spanning network of information repositories containing all the information in the world "cross-referenced, linked and transcluded." The central tenant of his work, Transcopyright, provides unimpeded access to information to those quoting excerpts in a new context (transclusion) while *automatically providing compensation and protection to the holder of the copyright of transcluded media.* (Epstein; emphasis added)

This proposal would, in effect, "'meter' each use of a copyrighted work, and [automatically] charge a user a fee for the use" (Epstein). Evidently, the vision of cyberspace promoted by many of its developers—a pseudo-haven where race, gender, age, physical handicaps, and other markers of individuality melt away in a vast network of pseudo-equality, and where the free (and democratic) exchange of information and ideas creates a space to resist the dominant paradigm—is far different from the actualization of cyberspace as a commodified space where power (i.e., access to fast computers and faster networks) and authority (i.e., knowledge of advanced programming, for instance, as well as possession of the means to utilize it) rest in the hands of the few. Of course, commercial interests have fostered much of the technological development that has, in turn, spurred the growth of online environments. Nonetheless, the online world has rapidly been changing as a result from a forum for discussion (readily allowed by text-based interfaces) to a forum for presentation of commercial interests, requiring more and more powerful hardware and

software in order to exploit the glitzy, point-and-click graphical interfaces that, in effect, shut down communication as a two-way (or multi-
user) act (Johnson-Eilola 184).

PANOPTICONS AND POLITICS

Moreover, by allowing space for dissent and circumscribing it, online
environments may also defuse it (Johnson-Eilola; Moulthrop). Chat
rooms, hot mail, CD-ROM text books, and other programs that may
be used in the classroom to maintain order in the face of chaos can
actually work against a teacher's attempt to use computers to
empower students by erecting borders that, in effect, resist students'
attempts to resist. Rather than examining the underpinnings of technological development and its configurations, teachers and administrators often seek for a means to reinstate control by designing computerized classrooms in more and more circumscribed ways. For
example, designing the computer classroom in a panopticon arrangement, with students facing the walls of the classroom, allows teachers
to peek over students' shoulders and monitor their work in progress,
assuring that students remain on task. The teacher becomes almost
invisible, operating behind the student's back, able to oversee the student's keystrokes, correct his or her grammar, or otherwise interfere
in the writing, research, or communication process. The proscenium
classroom keeps the teacher at center stage, but it also allows students
to work without overt teacher surveillance; however, networks can be
designed that allow teachers to "snoop" into a student's ongoing
work electronically or eavesdrop on electronic conversations often
without the student's knowledge or consent. In some instances, network designs may even allow for teachers to wrest control of the computers in the classroom away from students entirely, or, in synchronous communication sites such as MOOs, to disallow the
students' very right to speak or act.

The first online dissertation defense at Lingua MOO in 1995 is a
case in point. The defense was held in a specially designed MOO
"room," called a "$classroom,"[2] which imposes certain restrictions on
participants. For example, in the case of the dissertation defense, only
panel members were allowed to pose questions; questions were mediated
by the use of a queue; and while the audience could talk amongst themselves (unless they chose to "wear" a special virtual headset which
blocked input from fellow audience members), members of the panel
were unable to hear their comments or see their emotes (Grigar and Barber). Rooms such as this can be effective, of course, by disallowing some

of the chaos that is often so much a part of synchronous, or real-time, communications. As Ken Schweller argues in "MOO Educational Tools,"

> The proper use and not the misuse of tools such as the $classroom can be liberating rather than oppressive. There is nothing so annoying as trying to follow a speaker's online argument or carry on a serious discussion and being constantly interrupted by extraneous emoting or a bystander's off-topic conversation. Moderation rooms . . . offer a way to control this conversational confusion and empower the users to dynamically select moderation levels appropriate to a room's changing activities. (94–95)

Within the confines of the composition classroom, however, this kind of control may also work against attempts to allow students the right to their own discourses. In the case of the dissertation defense, rather than exploring how new media can empower students or considering new ways to approach old tasks (or even considering whether or not the tasks themselves can or should change), it instead mirrors existing structures and thereby effectively negates even the possibility of change.

As Cynthia L. Selfe and Richard J. Selfe, Jr. note in "The Politics of the Interface: Power and its Exercise in Electronic Contact Zones," software can "enact—among other things—the gestures and deeds of colonialism, continually and with a great deal of success" (484). Limiting student access to programming or communication commands, building permissions, and so forth in MOOs or other types of online spaces, or to "inappropriate" material (i.e., pornography, sexually explicit materials, or even controversial information) on the WWW or in newsgroups can thus be seen as measures of dominance, a way to thwart attempts to resist the dominant paradigm, and thus reassert our control. In so doing, we may even be asserting more control than is possible in the traditional classroom space. Some schools ban telnet access across the board because it can be used to access MOOs and MUDs considered by many administrators to be games rather than educational spaces and, hence, considered by some to be a waste of valuable—and limited—resources. Many sites designed specifically for educational purposes may also allow teachers to control students' speech or actions, effectively squelching the normal underlife of a classroom and resisting student resistance. Firewalls and other filtering devices may be designed to ensure that access is only allowed to certain types of information or sites, and intranets and software such as WebCT or Web Course in a Box may limit admittance only to those to whom we have granted permission. (The decision to exact these measures of control, by the way, is often made by systems administrators without the input of teachers.)

Although many teachers in the computerized writing classroom believe that "The unique perspectives of computer-networked classrooms, because they provide a contrast to traditional environments, can help facilitate . . . reexaminations [of demographic and cultural groupings]" (T. W. Taylor 124), the contrast between the networked classroom and the traditional classroom may very well be a function of the observer's own subjectivity rather than of the environment itself. Often, those we choose to meet online are only those who are already just like us:

> Is the Net, which brings together people from such different geographical locations, social settings, and intellectual disciplines, creating a global community of common interest and awareness? Or is the Net, which presents people to each other in the form of textual abstractions and offers a separate discussion group or conference room for every subsubsubcommunity of interest, fragmenting an already fragmented world yet further? ("The Net and Perdition")

Even in classrooms where teachers allow or even encourage students to work in nontraditional formats (using MOOs or other synchronous communication forums, WWW research, HTML authoring, and/or newsgroup and listserv discussions), we teachers may sometimes actually be resisting student resistance by disallowing them even the opportunity to attempt to resist. That is, while we may see ourselves as empowering students or as promoting liberatory learning by using technology in the writing classroom, the idea of cyberspace as democratizing is all too often only an ideal and not a reality. Online spaces are often designed to mirror traditional academic structures, as institutions build "offices" and "classrooms" online where programmers and wizards (and, usually to a lesser extent, teachers) possess the knowledge and power. Students are then more or less left to reside on the receiving end of knowledge. Thus online spaces become communities that exclude students (and others) from full participation rather than spaces to empower them.

Netiquette guidelines also sometimes work against our reasons for going online in the first place by ensuring that what is said is only that which is allowed to be said (or that which has already been said). Judy Anderson argues that newcomers to an online discussion list should attempt to fit in by adopting their ways of speaking and acting. "You don't go barging into an expensive restaurant and make a huge noisy scene," she says, "and you rarely wear your evening dress to Joe's Bar and Grill" (Tuesday Café). In the same vein, then, Anderson contends that, when joining a listserv discussion, we should, in effect, dress like the natives. In "Cocktails and Thumbtacks in the Old West: What Would Emily Post Say?" Laurel A. Sutton cautions newcomers that

"Each newsgroup has its own culture and its own social conventions, and unless it is a brandnew group, you must be prepared to behave like the native population" (174). Netiquette guidelines thus can also be a way of resisting resistance, working to further marginalize those who do not already fit in by promoting what almost amounts to a "separate but equal" vision of cyberspace.

MARKETING AND METAPHORS

The tendency to view the online world as "virtual reality" is itself essentializing, reductive, and perhaps, just plain dangerous. Metaphors such as this do not merely describe reality (virtual or otherwise); they also help to shape that reality. Furthermore, using the metaphors of the traditional classroom to describe online writing spaces may actually encourage teachers and students to unwittingly reproduce the very structures they seek to resist, even when these same structures are consciously resisted in the traditional classroom. Unless we carefully consider how our construction of cyberspace may unwittingly serve to reproduce structures of authority and dominance, with resistance allowed only within severely circumscribed boundaries, we may find ourselves creating spaces that work against our pedagogical goals. Student resistance in the classroom, of course, is already a consequence of "the complex range of ways that students understand their own institutional location and how it shapes, and ascribes value to, their work" (Mahala and Swilky 629). For instance, our assessment practices are often geared primarily to preserving the *status quo* (White, Lutz, and Kamuskiri; Shale; Faigley; Ohmann). Further, assessment practices may even determine what counts as knowledge in the first place (Murphy and Grant 286–87), since what we choose to assess reflects what we consider to be important. More and more, however, corporations rather than educators are determining how educational and assessment practices are implemented (Berlin; Johnson-Eilola). Thus, instead of a "well-rounded education," we may find that we are being asked to provide instruction in "marketable skills" (Berlin 185). Although it is possible to provide both, of course, it is also possible that our own attempts to resist the commercialization of the academy may lead us to resist even seeing how literacy practices themselves are, and always have been, in a state of constant change. That is, as we continue to try to find ways to force new forms into old molds, we may be hastening our own demise and delivering up the academy to those same commercial interests.

The intersection of computer technology and the writing classroom can help to foster an awareness of the classroom as an ideological construct rather than a physical space, of course, and of writing as more than a means of rendering thought into a commodity, marketable or otherwise. Johnson-Eilola, for instance, argues that, by focusing on the collaboration that electronic spaces can allow, and encouraging cognitive mapping of the spaces in the classroom and in texts (and hypertexts), we can foster a greater awareness of how we (and our students) write and are written by the ideologies informing the classroom. For example, technology is often regarded as all powerful, able in and of itself to effect change: in pedagogical practices, communicative and literacy practices, individuals, and even in societies themselves. In other words, simply by virtue of using technological "tools" for writing and reading, many people believe that the writing classroom will magically be transformed into a democratic space. Literacy itself, then, would also be transformed merely by virtue of the medium used to produce or access it. This, however, ignores the gatekeeping practices that work against such change. By examining how these gatekeeping practices work, we can come to have a better understanding of the ideologies that inform them and, perhaps by so doing, we can also help foster the necessary skills to approach them critically.

Hypertext, hypermedia, hyper-authoring (whatever we call it) is still in the process of becoming, but what it will become will remain a mystery unless we experiment with the possibilities. Some theorists see chaos study as helpful in trying to discern new forms that may be emerging from the primordial matter of electronic writing: "Chaos theory suggests that we should be asking different kinds of questions about these texts— that our traditional notions of authorship, coherence, and style are changing along with scientific theories and the technology of communication" (Paul Taylor 132). The interest in chaos theory perhaps at some level reflects our dis-ease not only with technology but with a perceived "shift from a world view based on Newtonian physics to a world view based on quantum mechanics" (Tornow 177). Our students are growing up in a world where television, computer games, and hypertexts are altering their ways of perceiving reality. This shift in turn "is bound to bring a shift in sensibilities such that a linear deterministic world will eventually become antiquated" (181). Michael Spooner and Kathleen Yancey argue that, as a result of the intersection of modern computer technologies on communicative practices, written, visual, and aural genres are collapsing "back into the collage of raw experience" (273) in what they call a "wonderful stage-managed chaos of virtual communication" (275). However, they contend, it is a "prepared rhetoric of chaos, a genre of chaos, perhaps designed to exploit more of our native ability to process many channels of information simultaneously" (273). Of course, in part this multi-tasking is what worries those like Sven Birkerts who fear that more extensive reading will be at the expense of intensive reading, bringing with it a "sacrifice of depth" (138). One problem with ascertaining new forms in new media, however, is that we begin by using terms—metaphors—that belong to existing ones (DeWitt; Ong).

SLOUCHING TOWARD THE MILLENIUM

In choosing to take my classes online, I recognized that I would lose a certain amount of authority. Of course, no teacher can entirely relinquish control as long as we continue to hold the grade book. But it is up to us to make "choices about that power—whether to use it to extend our authority or to empower our students" (Johnson-Eilola 108). The commercial development of cyberspace readily encourages the commodification of information, in the same way that the technology of print made "words into objects" (106). Future methods of research and delivery using online spaces are also "threatened by governmental directives designed to aid business rather than educational institutions" (126). Obviously, the ideologies behind these decisions also need to be seriously interrogated in light of the economic realities of the twenty-first century.

Some control is necessary, of course, if we are to function effectively and help our students to succeed in and beyond the academic arena. But we now have the option to create alternatives to existing pedagogical structures. At any rate, it is imperative that teachers carefully evaluate the online spaces they choose in order to ensure that any limitations or strictures fit their own pedagogical needs and goals. Otherwise, we may find that some online educational spaces are actually just as limiting for teachers as they are for students, forcing us, at least in part, to adapt to the rule of the administrators and programmers. Conversely, other teachers may find the chaos that can ensue without such rules equally daunting or limiting. At any rate, it is possible that the boundaries between virtual reality and real life are not so distinct as we may be inclined to believe. We can not simply avoid technology in the writing classroom: even the pencil is, of course, a technological tool and as such carries its own ideological implications. Nonetheless, we must continue to examine our own motives and methodologies in light of evolving pedagogical goals and theories of composing, and in light of the new opportunities for change, as well as the new opportunities for domination and control, that technology can allow or encourage. We must, therefore, actively engage the cyberworld and seek out ways that we can use it to help our students to think critically about the classroom, about technology, and about society. Only by exploring for ourselves the ideologies that inhere in the spaces we inhabit—online and off—can we empower our students to decide for themselves whether to accept or reject them, and allow them to resist any attempt—including our own—to impose on them a way of thinking or of being without their conscious reflection and choice.

NOTES

1. Domain names outside of the United States are usually keyed to the country of origin as well as to the type of organization. For example, <http://www.unimelb.edu.au> is the World Wide Web server (www) for the University of Melbourne (unimelb), an educational institution (.edu) in Australia (.au). Internet addresses for sites in the United States generally omit the ".us" country designator.

2. MOOs use a form of object-oriented programming and a hierarchical inheritance structure to designate objects. The $classroom represents a parent object with certain features that can be copied by creating a "child" of the object. Thus, users can build their own classrooms while retaining the features of the generic object. For more information on MOO inheritance, see "help inheritance" at <telnet://moo.du.org:8888> or the *Lambda MOO Programmer's Manual* at <ftp://ftp.lambda.moo.mud.org/pub/MOO/ProgrammersManual.html>.

WORKS CITED

Anderson, Judy. "Discussion with Judy Anderson." *Tuesday Café*. <http://bsuvc.bsu.edu/~00gjsiering/netoric/catalog.96atc052896.log> (29 May 1996).

Berlin, James. *Rhetorics, Poetics, and Culture: Refiguring College English Studies*. Urbana, IL: NCTE, 1996.

Birkerts, Sven. *The Gutenberg Elegies: The Fate of Reading in an Electronic Age*. Boston: Faber and Faber, 1994.

DeWitt, Scott Lloyd. "The Current Nature of Hypertext Research in Computers and Composition Studies: An Historical Perspective." *Computers and Composition Journal* 13 (1996): 69–84.

Epstein, Samuel Latt. "WOODS Web Object Oriented Distributed Server." *MOOniverse*. <http://sensemedia.net:8080/sprawl/MOOniverse.html> (31 Dec. 1995).

Faigley, Lester. *Fragments of Rationality: Postmodernity and the Subject of Composition*. Pittsburgh: U of Pittsburgh P, 1992.

Flores, Mary J. "Computer Conferencing: Composing a Feminist Community of Writers." *Computers and Community: Teaching Composition in the Twenty-First Century*. Ed. Carolyn Handa. Portsmouth, NH: Boynton/Cook, 1990. 106-17.

Grigar, Dene, and John F. Barber. "Defending Your Life in MOOspace: A Report from the Electronic Edge." *High Wired: On the Design, Use, and*

Theory of Educational MOOs. Ed. Cynthia Haynes and Jan Rune Holmevik. Ann Arbor: U of Michigan P, 1998.

Johnson-Eilola, Johndan. *Nostalgic Angels: Rearticulating Hypertext Writing.* Norwood, NJ: Ablex, 1997.

Lanham, Richard A. Foreword. *Computers and Community: Teaching Composition in the Twenty-First Century.* Ed. Carolyn Handa. Portsmouth, NH: Boynton/Cook, 1990. xiii–xv.

Mahala, Daniel, and Jody Swilky. "Remapping the Geography of Service in English." *College English* 59 (1997): 625–646.

Moulthrop, Stuart. "George P. Landow, Hypertext: The Convergence of Contemporary Theory and Technology." *Computers and the Humanities* 28 (1994): 53–62.

Murphy, Sandra, and Barbara Grant. "Portfolio Approaches to Assessment: Breakthrough or More of the Same?" *Assessment of Writing: Politics, Policies, Practices.* Ed. Edward M. White, William D. Lutz, and Sandra Kamusikiri. New York: MLA, 1996. 284–300.

"The Net and Perdition." *Netfuture: Technology and Human Responsibility for the Future* 36 (December 1996). <http://www.ora.com/people/staff/stevet/netfuture/1996/Dec1996_36.html#1c> (22 May 1997).

Ohmann, Richard. *English in America: A Radical View of the Profession.* New York: Oxford UP, 1976.

Ong, Walter. *Orality and Literacy: The Technologizing of the Word.* New York: Metheun, 1982.

Schweller, Ken. "MOO Educational Tools." *High Wired: On the Design, Use, and Theory of Educational MOOs.* Ann Arbor: U of Michigan P, 1998. 88–106.

Selfe, Cynthia L., and Richard J. Selfe, Jr. "The Politics of the Interface: Power and Its Exercise in Electronic Contact Zones." *College Composition and Communication* 45 (1994): 480–504.

Shale, Doug. "Essay Reliability: Form and Meaning." *Assessment of Writing: Politics, Policies, Practices.* Ed. Edward M. White, William D. Lutz, and Sandra Kamusikiri. New York: MLA, 1996. 76–96.

Spooner, Michael, and Kathleen Yancey. "Postings on a Genre of Email." *College Composition and Communication* 47 (1996). 252–78.

Sutton, Laurel A. "Cocktails and Thumbtacks in the Old West: What Would Emily Post Say?" *Wired Women: Gender and New Realities in Cyberspace.* Ed. Lynn Cherny and Elizabeth Reba Weise. Seattle: Seal, 1996. 169–187.

Taylor, Paul. "Social Epistemic Rhetoric and Chaotic Discourse." *Re-Imagining Computers and Composition: Teaching and Research in the Virtual Age.* Ed. Gail E. Hawisher and Paul LeBlanc. Portsmouth, NH: Boynton/Cook, 1992. 131–48.

Taylor, T. W. "Five Questions for Writing Programs in the Information Age. Diss. U of South Florida, 1997.

Tornow, Joan. *Link/Age: Composing in the Online Classroom.* Logan: Utah State UP, 1997.

White, Edward M., William D. Lutz, and Sandra Kamusikiri. *Assessment of Writing: Politics, Policies, Practices.* New York: MLA, 1996.

GLOSSARY

CD-ROM   Compact Disc—Read-Only Memory. A computer storage device designed to hold large amounts of information on a small round disc. Most CDROMs are read-only, which means that files cannot be written to them by users.

Chat room   A virtual "room" or address where multiple users may communicate with each other in real time, usually by inputting text on a keyboard.

Cyberspace   First used by William Gibson in his cyber-punk novel *Neuromancer*, cyberspace refers to the virtual spaces online where files, programs, and people reside and interact through electronic means.

Domain names   The domain name, usually the first part of an Internet address, designates the specific computer that hosts a Web site or e-mail server. For example, the Internet address *<http://www.cas.usf.edu/english/index.html>* represents a file named *index.html* in the *english* directory residing at the domain *www.cas.usf.edu*, the World Wide Web (www) server for the College of Arts and Sciences (cas) at the University of South Florida (usf), an educational institution (edu).

Emote   In addition to the ability to talk in MOOs, characters can represent nonverbal activities by use of the emote command. Characters can smile, frown, or otherwise express body language, thoughts, and so on (for example, "Kiwi smiles" or "Kiwi shuffles uncomfortably in her seat"). These commands help to lend a more lifelike atmosphere to communication in MOOs, but they can also be distracting. Imagine, for example, how it would feel during a dissertation defense to read the thoughts, emotions, facial expressions, and body language of your audience.

Graphical icons   Graphical-user interfaces (GUI) such as Windows and Macintosh use pictures, or icons, to refer to specific commands, allowing for the input of commands using a mouse or other pointing device, rather than a keyboard.

Hotmail   Web-based electronic mail that does not require the user to have an e-mail client or account on another server, and is accessible from any computer connected to the World Wide Web.

Hypertext   "Hot" spots, or designated text, graphics, or icons that, when pointed to and clicked on using a mouse or other pointing device, automatically access or open linked information elsewhere within the same document or file or open other documents or files, as designated by the hypertext author. For nongraphical interfaces, such as *Lynx* browsers, the "tab" key is often used to move between links in a document or file, and the "enter" key may be used in place of clicking a mouse button to follow the link.

Interface   Usually used to refer to the operating system that allows for communication between the computer and various software applications. Literally, an interface is anything that connects two separate entities (i.e., a user and a computer, for example).

MOOs/MUDs   Multi-User Dungeon, Object-Oriented. Originally a form of the Dungeons and Dragons game developed for multi-users on the Internet, various forms of MOOs and MUDs are used for role-playing games, synchronous conferencing, and distance education application.

Operating system   Any one of a number of operating systems used to allow communications between input, storage, and output devices. Common disk operating systems used by personal computers include MS-DOS, IBM-DOS, and OS/2. Other operating systems include Mac OS (for MacIntosh computers), *Windows*, Unix, and VMS.

Synchronous communication   Used to designate communication or commands that follow each other in succession. Internet chat rooms and MUDs are forms of synchronous communication sites; e-mail communications are asynchronous.

Technorhetoricians   A term coined by Eric Crump on the Alliance for Computers Listserv to designate rhetoricians who work with new and emerging technologies in and out of the classroom.

PART 4

Toward a Pedagogy of Resistance

CHAPTER 8

The Literalization of Metaphor
and the Boundaries of Resistance

Susan Wells

The work of teaching writing, solitary and virtually anonymous, is remarkably porous to desire, fantasy, ideology, and projection. This essay looks at an attempt to reconfigure the classroom's space of desire as a public sphere: I want to think particularly about my own desire as a writing teacher, manifested in the project of forming a relation between the class and the public sphere, and to trace in that project my resistance to reflection. I argue that our field's tendency to literalize metaphors makes it difficult to reflect critically on our experience, and that our wish that our students achieve public agency is, among other things, a displacement of our own anxiety about our professional efficacy. In both cases, the teacher opts for something less disturbing than a prolonged survey of professional and political anxieties: the satisfying click of metaphor seamlessly fitting into the real, the altruistic delegation of agency to a new generation. Both impulses console us: whatever the frustrations of this discipline, it allows us to hold in our hands the beating heart of language. We would not be English teachers, we would not be teachers at all, if these forms of resistance did not attract us. I want to think of them, not as delusions to be cast aside, but as formations where political and analytic work can be staged: how can these practices express desire and agency?

For me, metaphors become literal most easily at the difficult bound-

Thanks to Lauren Dobkin, and to the other students who gave me permission to quote from their written work. I am deeply indebted to discussions of the public sphere and composition with Rose Eberley, William Lalicker, Don Kraemer, and the floating public sphere study group organized by Susan Jarratt.

ary between teaching and writing. While sometimes research appears as my political work of the moment, and dusty newspaper accounts of women's club meetings are as compelling as anything that's happening in the world—or, I might as well acknowledge my biases—as anything that happened in the sixties, there are also weeks when writing is a pointless chore, but the classroom offers me the future—available, malleable, open to intervention. The boundary between my writing and my teaching, then, is a membrane across which the charged particles of political efficacy are always in passage. I have seldom folded that boundary in on itself to write directly about the work of the classroom: the unpredictable intensity of readers' responses to my infrequent pedagogical essays suggests that the borders were there for a reason. When I argued, in "Rogue Cops and Health Care: What do We Want from Public Writing?" that the public sphere was, for teachers, a domain of desire, an old friend wondered how I could possibly reconcile this position with my daily commitment to academic writing. (Who could blame him?—I wondered the same thing.) An overworked director of writing programs impatiently read "Rogue Cops" as the work of a mandarin theorist at an elite university who never had to sort out her own ideas in the classroom. (I could have used his help with the five sections of freshman comp I'd taught in the last twelve months.) And Patricia Bizzell took particular issue with my suggestion that rhetoricians, haunted by the image of the *agora*, might do well to imagine the classroom-as-public instead as a prison visiting room—a place where power relations are visible, but where something, still, can be exchanged, where something significant happens in the lives of both parties. Bizzell characterized this metaphor as "constricted and difficult" and argued that I was underestimating the discursive resources available to students and to other speakers in this culture. She found my Habermasian argument that a public sphere is not available to us, but is something we must reconstruct, far too pessimistic.

I myself considered the essay to be a piece of cockeyed optimism, but I was quite willing to abandon the metaphor of the prison visiting room. It obviously distracted readers, even readers as formidable as Bizzell, from my argument. Instead, I decided to take up the challenge posed by other restive readers: how could I work in the classroom to reconcile the project of reconstructing a public sphere with that of inducting students into the work of constructing academic knowledge? And the question was especially pressing since the norms of academic discourse informed the curriculum of the program in which I teach. Concretely, I wanted to use Bizzell and Herzberg's *Negotiating Difference*, a text that celebrates the historical efficacy of public speech and writing in the United States, to help students do two things: to understand the academic discourses they were encountering for the first time, and to imagine themselves as writers in a public space that they would help build. If I had underestimated the available rhetorical resources, *Negotiating Difference* certainly arrayed them in formidable detail. My first assignment asked students who had just read Frederick Douglass' *What to the Slave is the Fourth of July?* to describe what the Fourth of July meant (or did not mean) to a community or group they were a part of. And my class obligingly provided me with a full range of audiences: they argued to church groups, to youth groups, to sports teams, to ethnic associations, to a group of cigarette promoters, and to their extended families. They found a full range of arguments, writing that the Fourth of July was meaningless, or that their observance had a special meaning absent from official celebrations, or that their audience inherited the true meaning of Independence Day. One writer addressed the essay to a group of youth offenders: a corrections officer in the juvenile justice system, he was "running a group" for high school-aged boys. "I decided to kill two birds with one stone," this student wrote, "and hold group while I got some help on the assignment." The prison visiting room, in this case an antechamber of the corrections system, was not going to leave me alone: our classroom discourse was being reproduced there. And periodically through the semester, our class—and Bizzell and Herzberg's textbook—entered the discourse of the corrections system; the classroom project of common reflection and emancipation somehow became part of a regulatory discourse of surveillance that was also, ironically, one of the most sustained experiences of attention and care that many of the young men in the group had experienced. It was not a one-way street: my students' work of surveillance was replicated in my own insistence that his writing did not yet meet even the loosest of academic standards, that one could not speak of Douglass as attending the Continental Congress, that norms of narrative history had to be respected. Douglass spoke in the anteroom of the prison; academic surveillance spoke through me.

Nor was this the first time that prisons had disturbed the borders between public and private spaces in Temple's composition program. Several years ago, a teacher's decision to assign Mumia Abu Jamal's *Live from Death Row* (New York: Addison-Wesley, 1995) had provoked protests from the Fraternal Order of Police. Composition syllabi were, for a few days, front page news in Philadelphia, as they had been in Texas. And it is appropriate that this blurring of the boundary between the privacy of the classroom and public political debate concerned *Live from Death Row*, a text which invests the smallest detail of everyday prison life—the taste of water, the feeling of sunshine—with a public and political significance. In prison, diet is a political and legal question: a MOVE lawsuit sought a vegetarian diet for prisoners who argued that "our diet is unquestionably innocent" (73). The visiting room of such an institution is not the worst possible metaphor for the public sphere, especially since our culture so often writes political questions on the body.

I don't think that I'm alone in being pursued by these literalizations of metaphor: ours is a field in which the transposition from theory to institutionalized practice is exceptionally rapid, perhaps too rapid. Our metaphors are likely to appear before us in very palpable form: because we are constantly reinventing our work, a metaphor that can be literalized is a valuable tool, a map for the work we do. Thus, syntactic fluency becomes speed of inscription; ownership becomes copyright; the contact zone becomes the physical space of the classroom. This process is the normal activity of a discipline that must broker competing knowledge claims, that has yet to establish a secure domain of academic expertise, and that is heavily mortgaged to institutional commitments toward which we are all more or less ambivalent. But I am also interested in my own strong impulse to literalize this particular event: I felt that my student's summary of Douglass's speech to his youth offenders' group had verified Negt and Kluge's metaphor and vindicated my offhand argument. The realization of Negt and Kluge's image in my own professional space assured me somehow that I was on the right track. The youth offenders group, even—or perhaps especially—at one remove from my own classroom, had an aggressive urban chic that legitimated the argument for a problematic and constrained, rather than civil and legitimated, public classroom. How can we account for this tendency to literalize, to read the space of the classroom in a particular way? What does it tell us about our own resistance?

One of the most useful accounts we have of the rhetorical resources that were once available to American speakers and writers is Michael Warner's *The Letters of the Republic: Publication and the Public Sphere in Eighteenth-Century America*. Warner argues that "print discourse made it possible to imagine a people that could act as a people and in distinction from a state" and that, reciprocally, "when an individual reads in a manner that implicitly relates him or herself to the indefinite others of a print public, certain consequences follow for the nature of the individual who reads or speaks" (xiii). This argument poses several questions about how students in a writing class might enter something like a public sphere. Do these students inherit any historical tradition of discursive agency? Does the teacher mediate such an inheritance? Is it also transmitted to students outside of the academy? Is the classroom a reasonable translation of the "the indefinite others of a print public?" Will our public, if we ever manage to construct it, be anything like a print public? Why do we as teachers imagine agency as conversation, territorial encounter, or inheritance? As Warner's book demonstrates, our understanding of print literacy as inevitably associated with democratic citizenship does not correspond to any necessary implication of the technology of printing, but was a contingent and politically interested construction of, alternatively, absolutist imperial projects in aid of uniformity, and republican ventures that valued a subject formed in reading. Warner's essays reflect on a long literalization of the metaphor of print, as historians and literary scholars have seen in its legibility, openness, and reproducibility as a map of modernity. That literalization can shape a strategy for responding to students' resistance; it is, perhaps, a mark of our own resistance to both the pressures of the real and the possibilities of the metaphorical.

Like Warner's, my understanding of the public sphere is based on Habermas' *Structural Transformation of the Public Sphere* as modified in his recent *Between Act and Norm,* and developed further by Negt and Kluge's *The Public Sphere and Experience.* I see the public sphere as a political and historical formation which invites writers to make a dangerous and costly trade: they achieve political agency at the price of their own discursive particularity. The writer agrees to put forward reasons which would convince any reader whosoever, and renounces modes of argument that mark a discourse as relatively particular and situated. The writer can hope to redirect that abstracted political entity called "public opinion" at the price of a more or less costly surrender of any comfortable speech situation. Alternatively, a writer can address one of the multiple "counterpublics" battling for some piece of the discursive terrain. But even that fraught and limited bargain is not necessarily open to contemporary speakers and writers: the heavy price of media participation, the concentration of the means of communication, and the displacement of the culture of citizenship by a culture of clientage all have, in Habermas' terms, "refeudalized" the public sphere. I argue that if the public sphere has been refeudalized, then it is the work of institutions of culture, including universities, to reconstruct it, to engage in public discourse with some consciousness of its contradictory status and to make it accessible. The metaphor of the prison visiting room marks those contradictions, reminding us that in our own culture, Dewey's pragmatist idealization of education has been replaced by newer, retributive passions for correction from which neither universities nor writing programs are immune.

My work on this project has been modest: a trio of first-year writing classes in successive years that focused on the construction of a form of public space in the classroom. I have not tried to make the classroom a safe space for revelations about students' families or their personal beliefs, although some students have written about both of these topics. Instead, I wanted to investigate the possibility that students' writing about their experience could be an available resource for their construction of academic knowledge, specifically for an interrogation of experiences that illustrated social difference. And I wanted to think about the relation between academic knowledge and public discourse as classroom forms.

The materials I needed for this project were ready at hand, available in the practices of our field. Students read selections on the Declaration of Independence and slavery and on social and economic class from Bizzell and Herzberg's *Negotiating Difference*, including an address by Russell Conwell, the founder of Temple University, about our religious duty to grow rich. We walked over to the university archives to inspect Conwell's ceremonial sword. (The university, understandably, hushes up a nineteenth century account of the foundation of Temple: Conwell found the inspiration for his life's work in his young orderly, Billy Ring's, rescue of that sword from Confederate attack at the price of his own life. Conwell swore to do the work of two men—his own and Billy Ring's. The historical record is, as usual, even more interesting: Ring may have rescued Conwell's sword, but he could not protect him from court martial after the attack. And Ring—not a boy solider, but a recruit Conwell's age—died of "phthsis" or consumption, about six weeks after the attack.) Faced with these rich, determinate, and contradictorily persuasive materials, students wrote narratives of their own first understandings of social class, distributed them to the class, and then wrote analytic and reflective essays based on their essays, the text's materials, and library research. The range of experiences available to any one class was immense: running a small business, traveling as a migrant farm worker, schooling in Latin America, the Caribbean, or Africa. None of these essays changed anyone's mind about the relation between hard work and success, or the possibilities of upward mobility. But students did move through their initial understandings to arrive at more complicated questions: Was class the same as income? If money can't buy happiness, why does everyone want more of it? Are children outside class, or just naive about class? Does education raise your class status, or just make you not care about it so much? We mulled over details—for almost everyone in the room, shoes were an immediate class marker. As middle school kids, students had lobbied for an expensive prestige shoe, and everyone still noticed shoes—down to my own resentful observation of the Provost's brand new Joan and David's. We discovered that "what we knew about class" was deeply contradictory. Everyone believed that upward mobility either depends on hard work, or that it depends on who you know—and commitments to these theories were deep. But the class was also full of students who, in the words of one essay, "would pull you aside, and offer in a whisper the secret knowledge that 'it's really the *other* one.'" We worried about class as an injury, and therefore an intractable rhetorical problem: many students wanted to distribute their essays anonymously—the student who managed product promotions, and whose essay discussed the difficulties of hiring reliable workers, felt that she could not be frank unless she withheld her name. Given the frequency with which students reported that their first experience of class was one of humiliation, such caution seemed warranted. But what about the opposite problem, I asked—How would you feel reading something that you thought was offensive, if that essay were anonymous? Embarrassed silence, discomfort, and a rueful recognition that there was no easy way to talk about class: for these writers, there would be no simple assumption of the mantle of public rationality.

This embarrassment—my embarrassment, my students' embarrassment—was not accidental. Class, after all, is deeply associated with issues of ownership, and in these classes (the temptation to literalize degenerates into a temptation to pun) all that students unequivocally owned was their names; their writing having been taken up into the academic system, marked, workshopped, conferenced, and graded. Still, students found oblique and inventive strategies for dealing with the airless binary between anonymity and full ownership. One signed her work with a pseudonym that preserved her gender and her ethnicity, without identifying her personally to her readers. Another blocked out her name, but kept mine on the heading of the paper that was distributed to the class, so that students' footnotes in the next round of papers credit me with remarkable insights about suburban life in Chester county.

These experiments were rooted in students' responses to the controversy about slavery and the Declaration of Independence, the initial project of both semesters. The contradictions of class and the issue of slavery and the Declaration were logically homologous. How could Jefferson, the opponent of the slave trade, have inhabited the same body as Jefferson the slaveholder and racist ideologue of *Notes on Virginia*? Similarly, how could we believe both parents' stories of endless and scantily rewarded labor and children's insistence that their own hard work would surely lead to success. In both cases, the discontinuity between belief and experience was enshrined above reflection in our most cherished national myths and stories of origin. Nor is this conjunction between political agency and social class without its historical roots: one of Warner's most closely argued points, after all, is the causal connection between the development of the public and the development of the market:

> The mutual recognition promised in print discourse was not an inter-action between particularized persons, but among persons constituted by the negating abstraction of themselves. The impersonality ascribed to print as the public discourse developed the market and the public came to be capable of mutual clarification. . . . Market agents, though real, are in principle not identifiable in advance. . . . Given the context of the emergent perceptions of print, the print readership also represented an audience that was real but in principle not identifiable. The value of print and the value of currency equally required the potential for inexhaustible transmission while the character of publication and the character of economic exchange equally required norms of impersonal relations. (62)

The homologies and logical congruencies between the central political issues of American independence and individual upward mobility in a market economy were rooted in the deepest formation of an American public. There had never been an uncompromised public sphere; the political discourse of rational subjects and the self-seeking competition of the market have always been metaphors for each other, struggling toward literalization.

And so there were ways in which the contingent problems of these classes were, in their intractability, workable representations of the central issues in the historical construction of the public sphere. But, as Warner points out, the public sphere also implies a norm of impersonal relations between writers and readers—a norm that is intractable, even scandalous, for a contemporary writing teacher. Of course a pedagogy that imposed impersonal relations in the classroom would renounce one of its most powerful resources. And I am not sure that our public sphere, if we are able to construct one, will allow us to be as gleefully impersonal as Warner's self-righteous pamphlet-writers, sincerely publishing their views for the good of their country, without partiality, prejudice, or personal affection. The public is always a domain where unknown audiences react unpredictably: contemporary audiences use personal narrative for all kinds of political work. But, surprisingly, a strange form of impersonality did appear in my students' writing. Students suspended judgement, at least in general discussions, on the class position of their contemporaries. Their essays spoke repeatedly about experiences with peers when class was irrelevant, and all speakers were understood as equally privileged. The generalized citizenship that Habermas imputed to the eighteenth-century public sphere is transposed into a generalized cultural membership, a state in which class differences are both irrelevant and imperceptible.

> When I was about 16 years old, I fell in love with electronic music and the "rave scene" as it is called. As I began to attend more raves and

became engulfed in the rave culture, I met people from all walks of life. Sometimes I would meet someone and sit down and talk to them for hours. There was no way to judge other kids economic standing at these parties because no one really flaunted clothes and accessories. Like myself, most of the people there wore jeans, a T-shirt, and sneakers. There was no physical way to tell what kind of social or economic class each belonged to.

I attended Archbishop Ryan that was a catholic high school in northeast Philadelphia. The people who attend my school came from all over the city, but it still consisted of white middle class students. There were hardly four minorities in the whole school. Since we wore uniforms I did not know what kind of income or what class people came from. (Dobkin)

At this point, most readers of the essay suspect that the oblivion about social class these writers assert is nuanced and functional, rather than a natural side effect of the uniform or the rave scene. A class designation that can be disguised equally well by rave garb or a Catholic high school uniform is one that is bracketed because it is also easily available. High school, and the cultural sites connected with it, worked for these students as a counterfactual public space, in which a group of possible interlocutors took each other as abstract speakers, people whose class was *for the purposes of the present site*, unknown. For these students, as for Warner's pamphlet writers and Habermas' coffee house habitués, class, ownership, and impersonality were connected, but the vectors of the connection were unstable. A student could enact ownership of a name, a paper, and an experience by eliding part of his or her identity: a name, a knowledge, a class location. The elision of class did not mean, for these students, that the question of the other's class was held open: more normally, everyone was assigned a middle-class status by default. For many students, the first consciousness of social class emerged when a friend they had assumed to be middle class turned out to be much richer or poorer than them. For poor and working-class students, these complex elisions of what everyone knew carried high costs:

I attended a private Catholic school. The majority of my classmates were better off, financially and economically. Even though everyone wore uniforms, there was a sense of those who were not as financially equal. My clothes were not always in style, a factor which is hardly noticeable in a uniform, yet can be indicated. The shoes and sneakers which I wore may not have been name brand, nor was my jacket, but I didn't feel ashamed. I've discovered ways to blend with the "in crowd," without having to look like them. I developed a personality which wouldn't let my family's shortcomings keep me down or display a feeling of being ashamed.

Even though I developed this personality, I avoided confrontations that would reveal my status. I didn't go to parties, associate with friends outside of school, or invite people over, because my clothes weren't good enough and I was ashamed of my living conditions.

From the time I started school, I never really compared the way I lived or the way I dressed to other kids, partly because I went to Catholic school and partly because I was just naive. However, I did encounter a few different experiences. When I was in the first grade I joined the Girl Scouts. . . . The first event they were having was a costume party for Halloween. Because it was so last minute my mom threw together a princess costume. We used an old "flower girl" dress I had worn a year and a half before. Then we made a princess hat and wand out of tin foil and cardboard. Well, I thought I looked great till one of the other girls came in an expensive "store bought" dress. She took one look at me in my homemade hat and wand and my dress that was about two sizes too small and started making fun of me. . . . One of the adults heard her and told her that it was time for her to go but first she would have to apologize. Her exact words were, "I'm sorry your dress is ugly." She turned around laughing and left with her mother, who was also laughing.

For working class and poor students, class was often an injury, particularly an injury to the body. Middle-class students know what everyone's class is, but need not be aware of that knowledge; working-class students were always aware of class, even when they are not sure of someone's class position. The working-class student's ability to blend in with the "in" crowd without spending money enabled the middle-class student's assumption that everyone has the same resources. The body—specifically the clothed and publicly presented body—functioned analogously to the printed text in eighteenth-century America: it offered at once a depersonalized anonymity and a personalized abstract identity. For Warner's eighteenth-century writers, anonymity was based on the assumption that all readers and writers were white males—that the advocate of the disinterested public good could not, by definition, be a Native American or a woman, and neither could his reader. For these students, the various uniforms of the high school public offered every speaker the possibility of being taken as middle-class: all speakers are therefore equally credible, but only insofar as they support this assumption, and renounce any aspiration to speak from the material difficulties of their lives. A student could not, for example, express disbelief when one of his classmates quoted the family maid as support for a position on immigration.

In a political culture which sees a "national conversation on race" as a distraction from the serious business of discussing the president's sex life, advocating that class differences be explored in the classroom as a way of constructing a public seems like thin soup. And I cannot attest, with any confidence, that these discussions made much difference to my students. I can report that students took this opportunity to frame their thoughts about class, to see them as thoughts rather than as inescapable and immutable truths, and to notice that class, the stuff of common knowledge, was actually pretty hard to talk about. Sometimes, the classroom had something of the giddy energy that comes over a group when they find themselves able to say, for the first time, something that's on everyone's mind. For students, the chance to reflect on one another's experience transformed, in modest ways, their own sense of what they had undergone, of what they desired: reflecting on the rarity of conversations about class and class difference in families, one student remarked that if class was not discussed in the family, young people learned about it from their friends, and that such instruction is never gentle. Another student, a participant in a corporate mentoring program, repeated with full confidence his mentor's assurance that class is entirely a matter of personal choice—you can be who you want to be—but framed that maxim with an account of his youth and education that made gestures of choice derisory. A third student offered the story of his casual exploitation at a nearby elite institution: he did the sound work for a drama production, volunteering his time and spending his money, and was summarily dropped when the play was over. Reflecting on other papers, he was struck with the power of students' beliefs that friendship transcended class: "Even people who were royally screwed by somebody in another class from themselves seemed to agree" that people from different classes could be friends. In all of these examples, students continued to hold contradictory ideas about class; those ideas begin to whisper to each other, or to be incarnated in different bodies, or to be inflected in different moods and tenses. Such progress is indeed modest: undramatic for students, it is also entirely congruent with work in composition that suggests that students can learn how academic knowledge is created by undertaking forms of research that bridge disciplinary knowledge and their own experience.

But what about my other goals for this class: did this classroom, in any sense, form a public? Again, the answers and the gains are modest: in opening to reflection issues that are normally tacit, this classroom fulfilled some of the functions normally ascribed to the public sphere. But, as in all attempts to create a classroom public, an issue of exigence emerges: what were the consequences of the talk and writing we did over those semesters? Criticism in the public sphere, according to Habermas, created a discursive space outside the official bodies of the state, the church, and the authorized academy. We do not expect classroom work, particularly work in composition, to intervene in political life, however

broadly or locally political life is understood. To be sure, our understanding of efficacy may be too narrow; it is possible that moving a few
students a few inches beyond the polite and ignorant pluralism that
structures the life of a metropolitan university, into some acknowledgment of difficulty, limit, and difference, is a significant intervention into
cultural politics. It is a small but real gain for students to acknowledge,
for example, that not all white people were rich, that class divisions
extended far beyond the United States, and that aspiration, envy, and
resentment are inextricably connected. Not all of these realizations were
good news (it would even be legitimate to call them pessimistic) but they
were generally accompanied with outrageous joking, flagrant parodies,
and a marked increase in students' investment in their writing, and in
their curiosity and openness to academic discourse.

It is also possible that my demand for efficacy in the classroom says
as much about my own political anxiety as it does about the needs of
students. One of the main historical arenas for student political activity
has been the content of their own education. That activity has taken
many forms: in the 1960s students agitated for the foundation of
women's studies and African American studies; in 1837, students at the
Pennsylvania Institute for Colored Youth, a Quaker-run school for
African Americans, demanded to be taught Greek and Latin instead of
farming and skilled trades. Now, the strongest pressures on universities'
curricula and practices come, not from insurgent students, but from the
intransigent forces of globalization and corporatization (LaCapra). It is
not at all easy to see how, as teachers, we can shape an efficacious
response to those forces; it is reasonable for us, in a discursive space that
offers us few allies, to set about making some for ourselves. To use our
classrooms as a way of training students to enter a public sphere is to
make use of one of the most powerful, if indirect, tools of persuasion at
our disposal.

Even my limited experiment evoked elements of Habermas'—and
for that matter, Warner's—account. Students wanted to speak to all the
readers in the classroom and accepted, however tentatively and partially, the constraints of reciprocity that the rhetoric of the public
implies. "You are children," said the product promotion manager reading the fifth student essay repeating that money can't buy happiness,
"but I can't say that to you and ask you to listen." Because the members
of the class had all written accounts of their experiences, because they
had read each others' accounts, they accepted the risky bargain of public discourse. Rather than foregrounding an argument based on direct
experience, they would foreground arguments based on some provi-
sional construction of plural (if not universal) norms of rationality. But,
of course, this exercise did not create the freely circulating, unpre-

dictable discourse of Habermas' analysis: students knew that what they wrote would not be read by their parents or their future employers. They knew, by name and face, almost all of the potential readers of their work, even when they could not attach a particular text to a particular student.

In many ways the prison visiting room was only literally present in these classes; unlike the paired dialogue of the visiting room, talk in the class was continuously shifting, contentious, and multidirectional. Even the student's session with youth offenders, my initial literalization of the prison visiting room, modified Negt and Kluge's image: this was not an encounter between one prisoner and a relative or attorney, but between liminal "youth offenders," and the kindly, middle-aged returning student who led a group meeting for them. But we might also remember the voyeurism of *Dead Men Walking*, and wonder whether students' pleasures, my pleasures, in their accounts of class were not simply home-grown experiences of the exotic. I am not at all comfortable, for example, with my response to students essays that agreed with Conwell's gospel of wealth: many students felt that their social position would be entirely determined by their own efforts, and that anyone at all could grow rich through hard work. I had to recognize how functional this idea was for students whose education and upward mobility were precarious achievements. Insisting that they take seriously statistical information about their comparative chances of success would not be doing them a favor. But I also wondered about the price students would pay for their assurance, particularly the price they were paying in relation to their families, most of whom had quite palpably failed in the duty to grow rich. If the prison visiting room is a place for unconstrained discourse which is entirely defined by its location within a system of constraint, the public of this classroom was a domain of reflection entirely surrounded by ideas that no one could afford to think through. And this may be the final function of the literalized metaphor in the practices of the classroom: such literalization marks a place where reflection has temporarily stopped; it delineates the boundary between artistic and inartistic proof.

The decorum of that boundary, of course, was scrupulously observed in the professional criticisms of "Rogue Cops and Health Care" that I described at the opening of this essay: a theory about student writing is supported "artistically," in Aristotle's sense, by its explanatory power, its persuasive force, its productivity in suggesting new approaches. And my critics staged their arguments on that academic high ground. But at the edges of all such arguments, there is a potential demand for inartistic proof: the demonstration on the ground that the theory didn't just suggest something new, but that it could be realized—literalized, in fact—as curriculum, as a series of assignments, as a different kind of student writing or a new experience of student writing. Composition has a rich array of tropes for such inartistic proof: student performance outcomes, measures of writing skill, rubrics for assessment. Such proofs are professional equivalents of the Catholic school uniforms in my students' essays: they present student writing, and the experience of teaching, as everywhere the same. All colleges and universities become mid-ranked institutions, serving students from an upwardly mobile middle class, students described at every institution, from Harvard to the humblest state school, as "mostly first generation college students." But, like the savvy student who learned to imitate the "in" crowd without spending money, we know that our conditions of work are not the same, and that those conditions set the possibilities of our work and our reflection on it, draw the boundaries between what is gallows humor and what is a tasteless joke, between our politics as objects of reflection and research and as concrete goals for a particular class.

And of course, the demand to translate theory into practice, the notoriously impolite question about what an idea means, about what we do Monday morning, is the governing instance of literalization in our discipline. It is, in important ways, a destructive demand, a resistance that blocks thought, that withholds what Freud called the little piece of mental freedom that marks the difference between ordinary misery and real illness. There are many things about our work and our programs that we do not control, that are in the hands of deans and departments and layers of staff and students and their work schedules. But we have much more control over how we think about our work: no external force can effectively forbid us to think broadly, imaginatively and rigorously. The demand that we do that thinking only a half-step away from classroom implementation interdicts reflection; we become our own inflexible conditions of work.

The insistence on implementation, however, is not only a Freudian, but also a Marxist, resistance: it is a way of demanding that theory take into account the concrete conditions of our work, especially as they emerge in that most intransigent of sites, the classroom. It is, customarily, the critique lodged by the practitioner, by the overworked administrator, by the compositionist whose identity is formed in teaching rather than in disciplinary knowledge. It is a reminder of the class division of our profession, a division absolutely replicated in our field. The demand for implementation is a tactic whereby we call into question the credentials of those who speak to us from more elite institutions, or more advantageous disciplinary positions. And it is an effective strategy, although its effectiveness carries a heavy price, like the price of the working-class student who knows how to be in with the in crowd, but can't socialize outside of school.

Early in this essay, I said that our movement toward literalization was a strategy for containing our anxiety about the limits of our own political efficacy. And the figure of implementation-as-literalization can serve as a final example of anxiety and containment. Our own political efficacy is based on the importance of writing in the reproduction of basic productive relations in our society. By intervening in students' relation to the written language, we change their relation to work, to ideology, to their own subject formation. Whatever the limits of that project, it is situated on a new discursive terrain: a culture in which written discourse has become marginal to the formation of political opinion, and for which writing has simultaneously become critical to the organization of working life. While print culture was central to Warner's public, it seems minor, even ornamental, in contemporary spaces that resemble the public—and simultaneously critical in the corporate and technical settings to which the public sphere was a regulating counterweight. We find ourselves, then, simultaneously essential and powerless; constantly in demand but deeply perplexed about what we are in demand for. At the same time, issues of language and writing appear more and more often in the explicit domain of politics and cultural debate: was the Oakland school board right in the Ebonics program? Why was the Starr report so explicit? Can a Washington D.C. municipal official use the word "niggardly" without being offensive? And we find ourselves less and less able to intervene in these debates, to address them productively and influentially. In this setting, it is not unreasonable for us to hope that the tremor in our hand is indeed the beating heart of language and not our future slipping through our fingers. It is reasonable for us to read our own metaphors off the bodies of our students; it is totally understandable that we would hold each other accountable for the differences in our conditions of work. The alternatives, after all, are difficult, and almost surely embarrassing: talking about class as it affects us, talking about our own relations to the institutions of production and political power. But perhaps it would be a good idea for us to work these matters out within the family, as it were: we can be sure that instruction in them outside the family will never be gentle.

WORKS CITED

Abu Jamal, Mumia. *Live From Death Row*. Boston: Addison-Wesley, 1995.

Bizzell, Patricia. "Rhetoric and Social Change," CCCC 1997, <www.htu.mtu. edu/cccc/97/bizzell.html>.

Bizzell, Patricia, and Bruce Herzberg. *Negotiating Difference: Cultural Case Studies for Composition*. Boston: Bedford, 1996.

Habermas, Jürgen. *The Structural Transformation of the Public Sphere: An Inquiry into a Category of Bourgeois Society.* Cambridge, Mass: MIT, 1989.

La Capra, Dominick. "The University in Ruins?" *Critical Inquiry* 25.1 (Autumn 1998): 32–55.

Negt, Oskar, and Alexander Kluge. *The Public Sphere and Experience: Toward an Analysis of the Bourgeois and the Proletarian Public Sphere.* Minneapolis: U of Minnesota P, 1993.

Wells, Susan. "Rogue Cops and Health Care: What Do We Want from Public Writing?" *College Composition and Communication* 47 (1996): 40–55.

Warner, Michael. *The Letters of the Republic: Publication and the Public Sphere in Eighteenth Century America.* Cambridge: Harvard UP, 1990.

CHAPTER 9

"Bitch" Pedagogy: Agonistic Discourse and the Politics of Resistance

Andrea Greenbaum

CONNIE CHUNG: What has Newt told you about President Clinton?

KIT GINGRICH: Nothing, and I can't tell you what he said about Hillary.

CONNIE CHUNG: You can't?

KIT GINGRICH: I can't.

CONNIE CHUNG: Why don't you just whisper it to me, just between you and me?

KIT GINGRICH: She's a bitch. About the only thing he ever said about her. I think they had some meeting, you know, and she takes over.

CONNIE CHUNG: She does?

KIT GINGRICH: Oh, yeah, but with Newty there, she can't.

(*Eye to Eye with Connie Chung.*
Transcript. Online. Lexis. CBS, 5 Jan. 1995.)

Before Hillary Clinton stood-by-her-man through the Lewinsky spectacle, before she dreamed of being a New York senator, she held the distinctive and rather envious title of national überbitch. Not only, as Kit Gingrich lamented, did Hillary Clinton "take over" meetings, she also refused to be the kind of woman who stayed home and "baked chocolate chip cookies."[1] As I watched the now infamous Connie Chung interview with Kit Gingrich, I wondered why Ms. Chung had missed her journalistic opportunity to ask Kit a follow-up question to Newt's assessment of Mrs. (Ms? Senator?) Clinton: what *exactly* makes Hillary a "bitch?" Was it simply because, as Kit suggests, she "takes over" meet-

151

ings? And if so, by extension, are all women who speak their minds, assert positions, take control, and dare to assume authority, "bitches?" Is the assertion of female authority so offensive because it is—indeed— a cultural form of social resistance?

As a woman and a teacher, I find the epithet disturbing, not because it offends my sense of propriety—let's face it, most women are not strangers to the word—but because it is an invective designed, invented, not simply to denigrate (as all invectives are) but to corral, restrict, tame—silence. Typically, a woman who is labeled a bitch is a woman who is perceived to have overstepped her authority, and in composition studies, the question of women's authority—as teachers, scholars, administrators, and public intellectuals within the field of English—has permeated the conversation in four prominent journals: *College English, JAC, College Composition and Communication*, and *Rhetoric Review*. And while considerable space has been devoted to exploring notions of authority and resistance in the composition classroom (for example, Penrose and Geisler; Tompkins; Mortensen and Kirsh; Ewald and Wallace), I do not believe that we have adequately addressed what I consider to be key issues in the discussion, and I would like to reframe the conversation around three questions: (1) What is the perception of female authority in the writing classroom? (2) What implications does authority, or lack of it, have within the confines of the academy in general and in English departments in particular?; and (3) How can female instructors use their authority and argumentative strategies to create a socially conscientious pedagogy, a pedagogy of resistance, one that will help students not simply learn how to argue more persuasively, but that will assist in empowering women students outside the walls of the classroom?

Given that the word *bitch*, as it is socially constructed, is often used to refer to a woman who uses power and authority with ruthless indiscretion, I will, for the purpose of this paper, appropriate the epithet, as African Americans have appropriated *nigger* (Marriott 1), and gays have used *queer* (Watney 23)—as a form of social resistance, an attempt to strip the word, demystify it, displace its hegemonic power by co-opting the term and claiming it as women's own.[2] I would like to speculate on approaches to composition pedagogy that address issues of authority and power—especially as it relates to argumentation—and develop what I am calling, rather tongue in cheek, "bitch pedagogy"—which I envision as an enhancement to the conglomeration of rhetorical pedagogical strategies articulated by Dale Bauer and Susan Jarratt ("Feminist Sophistics"), bell hooks ("Engaged Pedagogy"), and Dennis Lynch, Diana George, and Marilyn Cooper ("Agonistic Inquiry and Confrontational Cooperation").

Bauer and Jarratt coined the term "feminist sophistics" to refer to a rhetorical pedagogy that examines the role of rhetoric within a self-conscious historical context. They suggest that, "While students are quick to notice bodies, they are less likely to attend to history. Central to our project, then, is the historical placement of the feminist rhetor and her students" (154). Feminist sophistics argues for a rhetoric that examines the conscious placement of "gendered" (as well as race/classed/abled) bodies in the classroom. Such an approach calls for reflection on "what it means for a teacher to exercise rhetorical authority toward ends of social transformation" (149). Likewise, hooks suggests that teachers should practice an "engaged pedagogy," one that recognizes that we should not merely be concerned with imparting information to our students, but understand that we have an ethical imperative to enable their spiritual growth as well. She is not suggesting that we become our students' gurus but, rather, that we take our roles as authority figures seriously, that we understand that when we educate, we educate the entire person—a mind, a body, and a spirit—and that we comprehend the scope and responsibility of engaging in such a task and rise to meet that challenge. Her "engaged pedagogy" is a pedagogy that is confrontational, honest, direct, and loving—always, always, loving. Above all, hooks claims, we need to view education for what it really is—"the practice of freedom"—and we need to demonstrate to students, through our actions, the power to resist the oppressive forces of racism, classism, and sexism (237).

Similarly, Lynch, George, and Cooper argue that we need to conceive of a pedagogy that enables students to "participate in serious deliberations on issues that face all of us everyday" (63). Part of the difficulty in conceiving of such a pedagogical strategy is that we have, through good intentions, tended to foster a pedagogy of cooperation and collaboration. Compositionists such as Patricia Bizzell, Susan Jarratt, Dale Bauer, James Berlin, Karen Fitts, and Alan France have argued that this gentler approach to argumentation disempowers students. Our job is to prepare students for action within the confines of a democracy, and the art of confrontation and debate is a critical and necessary skill for them to acquire. The authors argue for a reconceptualization of argument, one that,

> Includes both confrontational and cooperative perspectives, a multifaceted process that includes moments of conflict and agonistic positioning as well as moments of understanding and communication. We want to see argument as agnostic inquiry or as confrontational cooperation, a process in which people struggle over interpretations together, deliberate on the nature of the issues that face them, and articulate and rearticulate their positions in history, culture, and circumstance. (63)

While the authors recognize the oxymoronic coupling of "confrontational" with "cooperation," they contend that both are simultaneously possible, if one considers John Gage's reconceptualization of rhetoric and advocacy. He argues that the primary function of argument is not to express some part of our inner selves, but to accomplish some task, to get something done. And the means by which we get things done in a democracy is through the ability to engage in effective argumentation. Therefore, we need to teach students not to fall into the trap of debating from a stable, unitary position, but instead help them seek to continually negotiate and rearticulate a position as they develop more knowledge about the subject—thus, creating a dynamic approach to argumentation.

All three of these rhetorical pedagogical practices—feminist sophistics, engaged pedagogy, and agonistic inquiry and confrontational cooperation—are concerned with creating a holistic approach to education, teaching students not only to become effective thinkers, writers, and speakers, but to use their knowledge to transform social inequities. Bitch pedagogy embraces these three approaches to rhetorical instruction but enhances the discussion to address the responsibility feminist instructors have in teaching and modeling agonistic discourse. I will suggest that we need to utilize the muscularity of argumentative discourse to empower all students, but particularly women students who (as we know, and as I will further demonstrate) often lack the ability and confidence to assert positions; they are the primary beneficiaries of acquiring strategies of rhetorical combat, and I will suggest that such an understanding of rhetoric-as-advocacy will help them recognize that the instructor's exertion of rhetorical authority, as well as their own, has ramifications beyond the narrow boundaries of the classroom.

As studies from our sister field of rhetoric—speech communication—indicate, women who learn to resist the gendered prohibition against exhibiting argumentative behavior and who learn the *techne* of argumentation (what Protagoras referred to as *logon agonas*, contests in argumentation) are more likely to be perceived favorably, by both men and women. Women who engage in argumentative discourse are regarded as more persuasive, more respected as organizational leaders, and are less likely to be physically abused by a partner (Infante and Rancer).

This essay will examine the pedagogical implications of enhancing female authority through the engagement of agonistic discourse as a form of resistance to proscribed modes of female communication. First, I will examine the historical roots of the word *bitch*, and address how it stands as a contemporary metonymic representation of female authority; second, I will illustrate the political and economic ramifications of feminist authority in composition classrooms; third, I will explore the usefulness of argumentation theory and its application to composition; and fourth, I will suggest that there are several ways in which feminist instructors can reconstitute authority in the classroom.

ALL SHE WANTS TO DO IS DANCE:
AUTHORITY, POWER, AND THE
CASE FOR BITCH PEDAGOGY

While *bitch* has been fashioned into a verb, synonymous with grousing, and can be directed in this context to both men and women (as in, "stop bitching"), it carries with it an obvious feminine undercurrent. The original Anglo-Saxon meaning of the word referred to the female of the genus Canis, but developed figuratively to express a male's response to seeing the female dog in estrus (Kelly 2). It appears in print for the first time in a treatise on hunting, *The Maistre of Game* (c. 1410), which describes the dogs as, "As houndes 'folowyn after a bicche or a brach. . . . As houndes do after a byches, when she is Joly" (qtd. in Kelly 2). Edward Kelly traces the word through the Renaissance period, noting Shakespeare's use of the word in *King Lear*. Kent curses Oswald as "the son and heir of a mongrel bitch" (2.2, 1076). In *A Classical Dictionary of the Vulgar Tongue* (1785), Francis Grose labeled it the most "offensive appellation that can be given to an English woman, even more provoking than whore" (qtd. in Gross 147). The etiology of the word is relevant, since we need to remember that it was male perception of the power of canine sexuality from which the term emerged, and it was not too far of a metaphorical stretch for men to equate the voraciousness of canine sexuality with a woman's. But over the years the word has gone through a metamorphosis. In *The Thesaurus of American Slang*, *bitch* is defined as, "A woman one dislikes or disapproves of," and for further elaboration, the reader should "see ball-buster."

> n.   Someone who saps or destroys masculinity.
> ball-wacker
> bitch
> nut-cruncher (Chapman 10).

The contemporary usage of the word no longer constrains it to the sexual realm (female promiscuity), but has been transformed connotatively as being oppositional to masculinity: "Female sensuality, even carnality, even infidelity, have been supplanted as what men primarily fear and despise in women. Judging by the contemporary colorations of the word bitch, what men primarily fear and despise in women is power" (Gross 151). Unlike the equivalent contemptuous term to describe a man, *bastard*, bitch is relational, seen in opposition to an Other—namely, a male adversary. In a phallocratic worldview, power is inherently hierarchical, and therefore female empowerment can only be gained through emasculation—by being a nut-crunching, ball-wacking, *bitch*.

As teachers and scholars we need to understand how that generalized conception of female authority, as illegitimate and oppositional, is viewed in the writing class. Moreover, we should consider how women internalize cultural dictums that prohibit assertion and foster passivity which, according to Sandra Bartkey, result in "category confusion":

> Feminist consciousness is often afflicted with category confusion, an inability to know how to classify things. For instance, is the timidity I display at departmental meetings merely my own idiosyncrasy and personal shortcoming, an effect of factors which went into the development of my personality uniquely, or is it a typically female trait, a shared inability to display aggression, even verbal aggression? (18)

The answer to Bartkey's question may be found in the extensive studies in argumentation theory, which consistently maintain that there are marked gender differences in the display of assertion and argumentation. I would like, in the course of this chapter, to examine ways in which feminists can work toward closing that particular gender gap, and I will begin by tracing the evolution of feminist pedagogy in rhetoric and composition.

I WANNA HOLD YOUR HAND: FEMINIST PEDAGOGY AND THE ETHICS OF CARE

While it is difficult to pinpoint exactly when this trend toward feminizing the composition class arose, Elizabeth Flynn argues in her much quoted article, "Composing as a Woman," that compositionists have,

> replace[d] the figure of the authoritative father with an image of a nurturing mother. Powerfully present in the work of the composition researchers and theorists is the ideal of a committed teacher concerned about the growth and maturity of her students, who provides feedback on ungraded drafts, reads journals, and attempts to tease out meaning from seeming incoherence in student language. (424)

It is not surprising then that the field of composition would become more "feminized," given that it is a field, Flynn notes, that has been shaped, primarily, by women—Janet Emig, Mina Shaughnessay, Ann Berthoff, Maxine Hairston, Shirley Heath, Nancy Sommers, Linda Flower, Andrea Lundsford, Sondra Perl, and Lisa Ede.

Sharon Crowley?
Susan Miller?

As we know, three critical works by women researchers have been credited with influencing this trend toward feminization of the classroom—Mary Belenky's et al., *Women's Ways of Knowing*, Nancy Chodorow's *The Reproduction of Mothering*, and Carol Gilligan's *In a Different Voice*. All three have been used by scholars to suggest that women's ways of relating to the world are different from men's, and that this representation needs to be acknowledged and acted upon; scholars called for a restructuring of the phallocratic, oppressive classroom into a more nurturing one. Flynn stressed that teachers should encourage women students to be conscious of their experiences in the world and take note of how their experience relates to the politics of gender. The initial pedagogical implication of feminist pedagogy was the practice of collaborative learning.

Early advocates of feminist pedagogy considered collaborative writing a useful means to disrupt power relations in the classroom. As a pedagogical foundation, collaborative writing was, for the early advocates of feminist pedagogy, a kind of respite from the strictures of the traditional, phallogcentric, authoritarian approaches to teaching. However, while there is an appearance of equity, the truth is collaborative methods can in fact be construed as authoritarian and do not reflect conditions outside the parameters of the controlled environment of the classroom (Smit).

Gender disparity in argumentation strategies immediately calls into question the ability of female students to actively assert a position in a mixed-sex environment. Further, the female writing teacher who shares her authority in a collaborative environment does so at great risk:

> If she [the female writing teacher] chooses the non-directive approach and works to share authority, it might reinforce the men's devaluation of her as an authority figure (and invite them to turn that power differential in their favor . . .) and it might send the women a signal that power and authority are inappropriate for women (even though the women might feel comfortable with a coequal teaching situation). (Payne 108–9)

It was this recognition—that women are already positioned at a political disadvantage within the dynamic structure of the writing classroom—that made feminist instructors reconsider the value of perpetuating a pedagogy based on essentialism, one that does not further enhance a female instructor's authority nor enable women to become more competent at representing themselves in an agonistic environment.

Theresa Enos, in a recent study of gender inequity in the academy, suggests that gender stratification is strongly apparent within rhetoric and composition, with men more likely to hold the rank of full professor and to have tenure. She found:

> Women are more likely to be assistant professors, lecturers, or instructors, even when these women are faculty members with doctorates. For example, at research and doctoral institutions, 47 percent of the men were full professors, but only 14 percent of the women. The associate professor rank split evenly, with 28 percent of each gender holding the rank of associate professor. Women are more likely to be assistant professors: only 20 percent of the men, but 42 percent of the women are assistant professors. Tenure is held by 68 percent of the men, but only 38 percent of the women. (7)

Enos discovered that women outnumber men in only one rank—lecturer—and she makes note that nearly 64 percent of the full-time lecturers are women (7). While the scope of this paper is not to address the issue of gender inequity in academia *per se*, I bring up this topic to foreground the discussion of authority and power in the classroom, since it is relevant to understand that if women occupy more tenuous positions within academic structures, their pedagogy is likely to reflect their economic uncertainty; without the security of tenure or the support of their department, women are far more dependent upon positive teaching evaluations, and are probably less willing to challenge the curriculum or students' values. How I am perceived when I assert a position, willingly engage in conflict, and take control, is filtered through socially constructed lenses of gender perception. And my students' perception of me has a direct link to my effectiveness as a teacher. In fact, Koblitz's 1993 study, "Bias and Other Factors in Student Rating," supports this contention. He found,

> If female instructors want to obtain high student ratings, they must be not only highly competent with regard to factors indirectly related to teaching but also careful to act in accordance with traditional sex-role expectations. In particular . . . male and female instructors will earn equal student ratings for equal professional work only if the women also displayed stereotypically feminine behavior. (qtd. in Schell 79)

Dale Bauer's study of student evaluations of feminist teachers confirms Koblitz's findings. Moreover, Bauer takes the observation a step further, arguing that women must not only display the stereotypical feminine behavior of nurturer, but their bodies must also conform to students' expectations of femininity. "Many of the evaluations," she describes, ". . . address the literal embodiment of feminism: the site/sight of the teacher's body. Whether addressing her clothes, her hair, or her body part, students often dissect the feminist professor, trying to find something somatic with which to contain her intellectual difference"(66). Since teaching evaluations play a critical role in retention and tenure, feminist compositionists are placed in a precarious economic situation, since poor evaluations will naturally affect the advancement of their careers. Women who refuse to adopt the prescribed role of caregiver will face dire professional consequences that go "well beyond the classroom into the private spaces of women's lives" (Lewis 174). By reinforcing the character traits of nurturance and empathy, academia constructs a hierarchy that does two things: it systematically positions women writing instructors at an economic and political disadvantage; and, by doing so, it fosters an atmosphere of compliance—women cannot truly teach resistance and agonistic discourse because we cannot, we dare not, display it, because modeling argumentative behavior, something students might perceive as "bitchy," is, as Koblitz and Bauer suggest, fraught with job instability.

I'd like to argue, however, that we have an ethical obligation to model and teach young women agonistic discourse, to teach them not to do what they are socially constructed to do—to yield, concede, make nice, smooth egos, avoid friction, take on the emotional work—but to push, assert, insist, remove emotionality and position themselves as authoritatively as possible in order to become critical thinkers, speakers, and writers, fully capable of meeting the demands of a democratic society.

In an effort to counter the aims of cultural and institutional compliance, Nedra Reynolds offers a feminist approach to resisting such domination through the use of "interruption." She suggests,

> Interruption is most effective in the spaces where physical presence heightens the effect—at conferences, in classrooms, around tables. Those of us who teach writing or women's studies classes have the opportunity to discuss interruption directly—to share with students the research of linguistics, to analyze the possibilities for shifting power, and to encourage women and other students to interrupt the domination for students, both as a tactic of resistance and as overlapping support for a speaker. (71)

While I most assuredly agree with the theoretical value of Reynold's tactics, writing teachers need to be cognizant of the abundant research in argumentation theory that suggests that most young women are virtually incapable of enacting such strategies of interruption; they are incapable not because of some inherent intellectual or emotional flaw, but because they have not been trained in the art of argumentation and debate and have been acculturated into disbelieving their own ability to assert and maintain a position. Instead, they engage in what Bartkey calls "rituals of self-shaming"—speech that is marked by hesitation, false starts, questioning intonations, and excessive qualifiers (89). Interruption requires confidence, and, unfortunately, many women (faculty members included) seem not to have the same level of confidence and self-esteem as their male counterparts.[3]

The project of this essay is to suggest that speech communication research in argumentation theory is applicable and useful to compositionists. Further, our own research in feminist theory and pedagogy can be used to augment the discussion and help us to reconfigure issues of authority and power in and outside the writing class.

THE BITCH IS BACK:
ARGUMENTATION AND THE FEAR OF ASSERTION

Susan Jarratt, one of composition and rhetoric's more ardent advocates for the return of agonistic discourse, believes that feminist instructors, in an attempt to create a conflict-free environment, inadvertently do students a disservice, leaving them "insufficiently prepared to negotiate the oppressive discourses of racism, sexism, and classism surfacing in the composition classroom" ("Feminism and Composition" 106). Further, she calls the nurturing atmosphere of the collaborative classroom an "illusory fiction" that ignores real social divisions (110). Jarratt suggests that we can better prepare students to address these oppressive discourses by teaching the sophistic notion of eristic argumentation, *dissoi logi*, and the ability to take on conflicting positions in an argument. Such practice in argumentation, Jarratt believes, enables students, particularly women, to resist dominating voices in the classroom.

Study after study in argumentation theory supports Jarratt's position. Skill at argumentation has been associated with several positive attributes, including greater communication competence, a capacity for increased learning, a stronger sense of social perspective-taking and higher self-esteem (Rancer, Goff, Kosberg and Avtgis 1). Argumentation and verbal aggression are often collapsed into a unitary category, but, in fact, they are distinctly different communication traits: "Argumentativeness involves attacking the positions that others take on given issues; verbal aggressiveness involves attacking the self-concepts of those others, rather than their positions" (Infante and Rancer 342–43). The locus of the attack is what distinguishes the two characteristics: verbal aggression is hostile and directed at an individual, argumentativeness is directed at a particular issue.

There is strong evidence to suggest that men and women reveal significant differences in their abilities to engage in argumentation. Anne Maydan Nicotera and Andrew Rancer point out,

> While no biological differences were observed in argumentativeness, significant differences were found in argumentativeness when individ-

uals were classified according to psychological gender orientation. Individuals (regardless of biological sex) classified as instrumental (i.e. masculine) were significantly higher in argumentativeness than those classified as expressive (i.e. feminine), androgynous, or undifferentiated. Persons with a "traditional masculine" psychological sex-role orientation exceeded all others in argumentativeness. (n. pag.)

Several prevailing explanations account for these gender differences in argumentation. For instance, Andrew Rancer and Robert Baukus's study on sex and trait argumentativeness concluded that males and females do differ in their belief structures about arguing, with females believing that argumentation is a hostile and aggressive communication strategy designed to dominate and control others. Another explanation for these differences has to do with social conditioning. In general, men are encouraged to be more competitive, dominant, and aggressive than women, and such social factors get played out in communication interactions. Infante notes, "According to the cultural sex-role expectations models, arguing . . . is compatible with expectations for male behavior but incompatible with expectations for female behavior" ("Aggressiveness" 175). Women may simply be hesitant to be perceived as violating cultural norms of femininity.

We already know that women are prone to maintaining silence in the classroom, and that those who have higher status, by virtue of their gender, race, occupation, or organizational rank, "make significantly more verbal contributions and consequently take up significantly more time talking" (James and Drakick 290). Teaching women to hone and cultivate argumentation strategies does not only increase their ability to participate in the classroom, but elevates their perceived stature, since women who engage in argumentation strategies are viewed as more competent (by both men and women) than their less assertive sisters (Lewittes and Lipsitz 594). Similarly, Judith Anderson and her colleagues concluded, "both male and female observers perceive argumentative females as more highly credible than females who are low in argumentativeness" (59). Anderson et al. discovered that by using female trainers as positive role models for displaying argumentative behavior, the women themselves were more likely to engage in what I had referred to earlier as rhetorical combat. Having a female instructor display behavior that is characteristically considered "unfeminine," assertive, and risk-taking, and by the instructor showing a willingness to enter into conflict, the women in the group were more likely to mirror that assertive behavior. Further, and perhaps most interesting of all, Anderson's research demonstrates that despite the cultural bias to the contrary, "argumentative women in leadership positions may be viewed as highly effective" (59).

Consistently, studies in argumentation theory reveal that highly argumentative individuals are perceived more favorably when compared to individuals low in argumentativeness.[4] Nicotera and Rancer's study of 174 undergraduates (ninety-one females, eighty-three males) at a Midwestern university supports previous findings that, "Favorable perceptions of high argumentatives have been found to extend beyond any single argumentative episode, and tend to form a more lasting and global credibility perception" (13). They also noted that in an organizational context, superiors are viewed more favorably by subordinates when the superiors demonstrate high argumentative traits, and as a consequence, "females may not enjoy as favorable credibility perceptions due to their (general) lower motivation to argue." Nicotera and Rancer conclude, "Since argumentativeness is associated with expectations for effective task behavior . . . women in organizations may be at a disadvantage" (14). However, there is a far more dangerous consequence for women than being at a professional disadvantage; women who do not know how to engage in effective argumentation often resort to verbal aggression to resolve conflict. The result is that verbal aggression is a catalyst to spousal violence (Infante, Chandler, and Rudd), and I suspect other kinds of interpersonal violence as well. If we are to be engaged educators, as bell hook's urges us to be, then we have an ethical obligation to teach women and men how to resolve conflict without resorting to violence—an especially valuable lesson for men, since argumentation studies indicate that men score higher in verbal aggressiveness than women, and verbal aggression is often the precursor to physical abuse (Nicotera and Rancer 13).

YOU OUGHTA KNOW:
THE RESPONSIBILITY OF ASSERTION

What these studies suggest to me is that we need to reconfigure feminist pedagogical approaches by being aware that, (1) the character trait defined as "argumentativeness" as modeled by female instructors is viewed favorably by both men and women; (2) this modeling enables women students to assert more dominant positions inside the classroom, and (3) this ability to engage in effective argumentation empowers women and has significance beyond the boundaries of the classroom. The accumulation of research on argumentativeness conclusively indicates that skill in argumentative communication enhances persuasive outcomes. Those who are able to engage in effective argumentation strategies are:

- Perceived as more credible persuaders
- Use a greater diversity of influence strategies
- Are less willing to use compliance-gaining strategies that create negative feelings in perceivers
- Are more reluctant to use their power to force compliance
- Encourage other people to express their views on controversial issues
- Are more effective in upward influence situations
- Are judged by their superiors as having more constructive persuasion styles
- Are not easily provoked by obstinate opponents into using verbal aggression
- Are judged as more competent persuaders
- Are seen as leaders in group influence situations (Infante and Rancer 342–43)

I have used the bitch figure as an obvious metaphor for the phallogcentric perception that female empowerment and authority is seen as inherently corrupt, but the fact is that unless we can help women resist the social stigma against employing argumentation strategies, they truly will never be able to have the same institutional footholds as men do. Bitch pedagogy takes into account an historical analysis of *kairos*, positionality, and I concur with James Ladikta that our ability to be effective teachers lies in our willingness to "devise a college composition program, that will have ethical, epistemological, rhetorical, aesthetic and political dimensions" (368). As rhetoricians, we have the obligation to model advocacy—especially when we know that the risks are so great when we don't. Karen Fitts and Alan France point out, "Advocacy itself is necessary to any dialogue—to any authentic, therefore rhetorical exchange" (14). But advocacy always entails a sense of authority, and the feminist writing teacher does not relinquish authority, but rather manages "the meanings it has for our students (and ourselves) in its classroom enactments" (LaDuc 163). One of the ways to "manage" authority in the classroom is to reconstitute it, and bitch pedagogy is the recognition that the authority the female writing instructor brings to her class—what she models, and what pedagogical practices she employs—aids in transforming student passivity.

Ten years ago, Ellen Strenski recognized the enormous value in teaching students how to employ what she refers to as the "army" method of scholarly discourse: "Problems must be attacked, data mastered, evidenced marshaled, theses presented and defended against disproof. The purpose is to persuade a skeptical, potentially hostile audience and thereby win" (138). I like Strenski's military metaphor to express the rigorous, adversarial, muscular nature of scholarly investigation. For my own purposes, I would like to expand on her position by arguing that the appropriation of the robust character of what has traditionally been considered masculine discourse will not only fortify a woman's ability to succeed in the academy by further enhancing her capability to argue from a position of strength and confidence, but will translate into other areas of interpersonal interaction.

The acquisition of argumentative modes of discourse does not just assist female students in learning the craft of advocacy, it also empowers women faculty. Bartkey is not the only faculty member who wonders why she does not speak out at meetings; others—many other women—experience the same sense of self-doubt in the academy and within other organizational structures. A telling commentary comes from a respondent to Enos's study on gender roles in the academy. The woman writes: "Perhaps women don't have the networks and interviewing savvy that men do, and we have to work on that. But it seems to me that women still are not taken very seriously at higher levels in the academic world" (67). In order to be "taken very seriously" by other scholars, Jane Tompkins confesses that when she was writing her book, *West of Everything*, she felt obligated to "become a man," to adopt male modes of argumentation in order to succeed in the academy (qtd. in Olson, "Jane Tompkins" 14). If women academics—women who have been trained in articulating perspectives, in developing arguments, in defending positions—lack the confidence to assert their own authority, to speak with their own voices, how can we then expect to train other women, our students, to do so?

It is the obligation of feminist instructors to oversee the project of helping other women (as well as ourselves) learn how to speak out, how to have the ability, the rhetorical savvy and the confidence to assert positions—at our department meetings, with our partners, or to mechanics who want to overcharge us. We should resist the fear of assertion, and we should speak and teach others to do the same, despite the discomfort of hearing the ultimate epithet leveled against us, at any woman who dares to argue persuasively from a position of authority.

NOTES

1. Later, Hillary recanted her scandalous remark—perhaps a half-hearted attempt to de-bitch herself—and as proof of her domestic savvy, published her own recipe for chocolate chip cookies.

2. In the last several years, "bitch" has been reclaimed by American singer Meredith Brooks, who in her rant anthem, "Bitch," gleefully asserts that she's

"a bitch" and proud of it, and by Elizabeth Wurtzel in her pop-feminist treatise, *Bitch: In Praise of Difficult Women.*

3. This gender-gap in self-esteem as it relates to academic achievement is well chronicled, becoming apparent to educators as early as pre-adolescence. For a more thorough discussion of this topic, see the American Association of University Women's publication *Shortchanging Girls, Shortchanging America*, and Peggy Orenstein's book (also commissioned by the AAUW) *Schoolgirls: Young Women, Self-Esteem and the Confidence Gap.*

4. An extensive review of argumentation literature can be found in Dominic Infante and Andrew Rancer's article, "Argumentativeness and Verbal Aggressiveness: A Review of Recent Theory and Research."

WORKS CITED

American Association for University Women. *Shortchanging Girls, Shortchanging America.* Washington, DC: AAUW Educational Foundation, 1991.

Anderson, Judith, Beatrice Schultz, and Constance Courtney Staley. "Training in Argumentativeness: New Hope for Non-Assertive Women." *Women's Studies in Communication* 10 (1987): 58–66.

Bartkey, Sandra Lee. *Femininity and Domination: Studies in the Phenomenology of Oppression.* London: Routledge, 1990.

Bauer, Dale M. "The Meanings and Metaphors of Student Resistance." *Styles of Cultural Activism: From Theory and Pedagogy to Women, Indians, and Communism.* Ed. Philip Goldstein. Newark: U of Delaware P, 1994.

Bauer, Dale, and Susan C. Jarratt. "Feminist Sophistics: Teaching with an Attitude." *Changing Classroom Practices: Resources for Literary and Cultural Studies.* Ed. David B. Downing. Urbana, IL: NCTE, 1994. 149–66.

Belenky, Mary Field, Blythe McVicker Clinchy, Nancy Rule Goldberg, Jill Mattuck Tarule. *Women's Ways of Knowing.* New York: Basic, 1986.

Bizzell, Patricia. *Academic Discourse and Critical Consciousness.* Pittsburgh: U of Pittsburgh P, 1992.

———. "The Teacher's Authority: Negotiating Difference in the Classroom." *Changing Classroom Practices: Resources for Literary and Cultural Studies.* Urbana, IL: NCTE, 1994. 194–201.

Berlin, James. *Rhetorics, Poetics, and Cultures.* Urbana, IL: NCTE, 1996.

Chapman, Robert L., ed. *Thesaurus of American Slang.* 1st ed. New York: Harper & Row, 1989.

Chodorow, Nancy. *The Reproduction of Mothering.* Berkeley: U of California P, 1978.

Enos, Theresa. *Gender Roles and Faculty Lives in Rhetoric and Composition.* Carbondale: Southern Illinois UP, 1996.

Ewald, Helen Rothchild, and David L. Wallace. "Exploring Agency in Classroom Discourse, or Should David Have Told His Story?" *College Composition and Communication* 45 (1994): 342–68.

Fitts, Karen, and Alan W. France. "Advocacy and Resistance in the Writing Class: Working Towards Stasis." *Pedagogy in the Age of Politics: Writing and Reading (in) the Academy.* Ed. Patricia A. Sullivan and Donna J. Qualley. Urbana: NCTE, 1994: 13–24.

——, eds. *Left Margins: Cultural Studies and Composition Pedagogy.* New York: State U of New York P, 1995.

Flynn, Elizabeth. "Composing as a Woman." *College Composition and Communication* 39 (1988): 423–35.

Gage, John. "An Adequate Epistemology for Composition: Classical and Modern Perspectives." *Essays on Classical Rhetoric and Modern Discourse.* Ed. Robert J. Connors, Lisa S. Ede, and Andera A. Lunsford. Carbondale: Southern Illinois UP, 1984. 152–70.

Gilligan, Carol. *In a Different Voice.* Cambridge: Harvard UP, 1982.

Golub, Sharon, and Eileen Maxwell Canty. "Sex-Role Expectations and the Assumption of Leadership by College Women." *Journal of Social Psychology.* 116 Pt. 1 (1982): 83–90.

Gross, Beverly. "Bitch." *Salmagundi* 103 (1994): 146–56.

Harkin, Patricia, and John Schlib, eds. *Contending with Words: Composition and Rhetoric in a Postmodern Age.* New York: MLA, 1991.

Hooks, Bell. "Engaged Pedagogy." *Women/Writing/Teaching.* Albany: State U of New York P, 1998. 231–38.

Infante, Dominic. "Inducing Women to be More Argumentative: Source Credibility Effects." *Journal of Application Commuication Research* 13 (1985): 33–44.

——. "Aggressiveness." *Personality and Interpersonal Communication.* Ed. James C. McCroskey and John A. Daly. Newbury Park: Sage, 1987. 157–92.

Infante, Dominic A., Teresa A. Chandler, and Jill E. Rudd. "Test of an Argumentative Skill Deficiency Model of Interspousal Violence. *Communication Monographs* 56 (1989): 163–77.

Infante, Dominic A., and Andrew S. Rancer. "Argumentativeness and Verbal Aggressiveness: A Review of Recent Theory and Research. *Communication Yearbook* 19. Ed. Brant R. Burleson. Thousand Oaks: Sage Publications, 1996.

James, Deborah, and Janice Drakich. "Understanding Gender Differences in Amount of Talk: A Critical Review." *Gender and Conversational Interaction.* Ed. Deborah Tannen. New York: Oxford UP (1993): 281–312.

Jarratt, Susan. "Feminism and Composition: The Case for Conflict." *Contending With Words: Composition and Rhetoric in a Postmodern Age.* Ed. Patrica Harkin and John Schilb. New York: MLA 1991. 105–24.

Kelly, Edward Hanford. "A 'Bitch' by Any Other Name is Less Poetic." *Word Study* 45 (1969): 1–4.

Kobitz, Nat. "Bias and Other Factors in Student Ratings." *Chronicle of Higher Education.* Sept. 1 B3, 1993.

Laditka, James N. "Semiology, Ideology, Praxis: Responsible Authoring in the Composition Classroom." *Journal of Advanced Composition* 10 (1990): 357–73.

LaDuc, Linda. "Feminism and Power: The Pedagogical Implications of (Acknowledging) Plural Feminist Perspectives." *Pedagogy in the Age of Politics: Writing and Reading (in) the Academy.* Ed. Patricia A. Sullivan and Donna J. Qualley. Urbana, IL: NCTE, 1994. 153–65.

Lewis, Magda. "Interrupting Patriarchy: Politics, Resistance, and Transformation in the Feminist Classroom." *Feminisms and Critical Pedagogy*. Ed. C. Luke and J. Core. New York: Routledge, 1992: 167–91.

Lewittes, Hedva J., and Sandra Lipsitz Bem. "Training Women To Be More Assertive in Mixed-Sex Task-Oriented Discussions." *Sex Roles* 9 (1983): 581–96.

Lynch, Dennis A., Diana George, and Marilyn M. Cooper. "Moments of Argument: Agonistic Inquiry and Confrontational Cooperation." *College Composition and Communication* 48 (1997): 61–85.

Marriott, Michel. "Rap's Embrace of 'Nigger' Fires Bitter Debate." *New York Times* 24 Jan. 1993, natl. ed.: p1.

Mortensen, Peter, and Gesa F. Kirsh. "On Authority in the Study of Writing." ⟵ *College Composition and Communication* 44 (1993): 556–72.

Nicotera, Anne Maydan, and Andrew S. Rancer. "The Influence of Sex on Self Perceptions and Social Stereotyping of Aggressive Communication Predispositions." *Western Journal of Communication* 58.4 (1994): 283–307. Online. ArticleFirst. 1 May 1999.

Olson, Gary A. "Jane Tompkins and the Politics of Writing, Scholarship, and Pedagogy." *JAC* 15 (1995): 1–18.

Orenstein, Peggy. *Schoolgirls: Young Women, Self-Esteem, and the Confidence Gap*. Washington, DC: AAUW Educational Research Foundation, 1994.

Payne, Michelle. "Rend(er)ing Women's Authority in the Writing Classroom." *Taking Stock: The Writng Process Movement in the '90s*. Ed. L. Tobin. Portsmouth, NH: Boynton/Cook, 1994. 97–111.

Penrose, Ann M., and Cheryl Geisler. "Reading and Writing Without Authority." ⟵ *College Composition and Communication* 45 (1994): 505–20.

Rancer, Andrew S., Valerie Goff Whitecap, Roberta L. Kosberg, and Theodore A. Avtgis. "Testing the Efficacy of a Communication Training Program to Increase Argumentativeness and Argumentative Behavior in Adolescents." *Communication Education* 46.4 (1997): 273–86. Online. ArticleFirst. 1 May 1999.

Rancer, Andrew, and Robert A. Baukus. "Discriminating Males and Females on Belief Structures about Arguing." *Advances in Gender and Communication Research*. Ed. Lawrence. B. Nadler and William. R. Todd-Mancillas. Lanham, MD: UP of America, 1987. 155–73.

Reynolds, Nedra. "Interrupting Our Way to Agency: Feminist Cultural Studies and Composition." *Feminism and Composition Studies: In Other Words.* Ed. Susan C. Jarratt and Lynn Worsham. New York: MLA, 1998. 58–73.

Schell, Eileen E. *Gypsy Academics and Mother-Teachers: Gender, Contingent Labor, and Writing Instruction*. Portsmouth, NH: Boynton/Cook, 1998.

Schmidt, Jan Zlotnik. *Women/Writing/Teaching*. Albany: State U of New York P, 1998.

Shakespeare, William. *King Lear. William Shakespeare: The Complete Works*. Ed. Alfred Harbage. New York: Viking P, 1969.

Smit, David W. "Some Difficulties with Collaborative Learning." *Journal of Advanced Composition* 9 (1989): 45–58.

Strenski, Ellen. "Disciplines and Communities, 'Armies' and 'Monasteries,' and the Teaching of Composition." *Rhetoric Review* 8 (1989): 137–49.

Watney, Simon. "Queer Epistemology: Activism, Outing, and the Politcs of Sexual Identities." *Critical Quarterly* 36 (1994): 13–27.

Wurtzel, Elizabeth. *Bitch: In Praise of Difficult Women*. New York: Doubleday, 1998.

CHAPTER 10

Resisting Academics

Bruce Horner

Compositionists have long been ambivalent towards things "academic." That they should be so speaks most obviously to their tenuous place in academic institutions, their work simultaneously necessary to its life and denigrated as second-class, unbefitting the academy's sense of its true identity and purpose. In recent years, this ambivalence toward the "academic" has in composition taken the form of what I take to be a nostalgic desire for nonacademic work, writing, and institutional forms. Academic discourse, for example, is rejected as too constraining, as ill-equipped to represent the range of thoughts and experiences students and their teachers bring to the composition course, the concerns traditionally expressed in academic discourse pale in comparison to concerns of real political, economic, and/or personal significance for teachers, students, and the public at large (Bridwell-Bowles; Elbow). This ambivalence is at least part of what drives renewed interest among compositionists in "personal" or "experimental" discursive forms, and efforts to incorporate service-learning components into composition courses and otherwise to shape composition courses to engage in politically activist work of one sort or another, either through consciousness-raising or assigning students to engage in acts of public, as opposed to "academic," discourse on issues raised in that discourse (see, for example, Cooper and Julier; Heilker). Against academic work, these efforts pose work that is seen as social, real, experience-based, committed.

I would argue, however, that many such efforts mistake the official purposes assigned to academic knowledge and academic discursive and institutional forms for the full range of uses to which these can and have been put. As a consequence, they can end up reinforcing, rather than challenging, dominant, limited and limiting approaches to such categories as the academic and the real, the personal, and the institutional or

[handwritten margin notes: expressive driven by ambiv. toward "academic"]

social (see Carr 96). More importantly, they can lead to neglect of the potential of work to be accomplished at locations disparaged by the rubrics "Composition" and "the academic." To explain the basis for this danger, I use Marx's analysis of the relation between the exchange-value and use-value of a commodity in his critique of commodity fetishism, Anthony Giddens' critique of functionalism, and Pierre Bourdieu's typology of capital. In efforts to resist the academic, work performed in composition continues to be identified with, and evaluated in terms of the effects of, commodified forms of the individual semester, course section, student, or textual object. Insofar as such efforts remove academic forms from the social and material, they reinforce the hegemonic identifications of these with the dominant, and blind us to the counterhegemonic potential of writing, teaching, and learning taking strictly "academic" forms. To suggest alternative approaches implied by this analysis, I examine recent arguments concerning the use of service-learning in composition and academic discourse.

COMMODITY FETISHISM AND THE
CRITIQUE OF FUNCTIONALISM

Marx argues that both use and exchange value reside within the commodity: "nothing can be a value without being an object of utility. If the thing is useless, so is the labour contained in it; the labour does not count as labour, and therefore creates no value" (Marx, *Capital* I, 131). Thus, one cannot deny the continuing potential use-value of work even in its commodified form, for use-value is "only realized in use or in consumption" (Marx, *Capital* I, 126). Commodification itself occurs when the value of the work is identified not with the social relations of its production (including its consumption) but with the form of the product. As Marx explains, it is only when "the labor expended in the production of a useful article [is presented] as an 'objective' property of that article, i.e. as its value . . . that the product of labour becomes transformed into a commodity" (153–54). Thus, in what Marx terms commodity fetishism, "the products of the human brain appear as autonomous figures endowed with a life of their own, which enter into relations both with each other and with the human race" (164–65).

Giddens' critique of functionalism is aligned with the Marxian view of commodity fetishism. Functionalism "explains away" the unintended consequences of actions by renaming those consequences as fulfilling the needs of social systems. It thus imputes a teleology to those systems, which are imagined as operating behind the backs of social actors (Giddens 7, 112). For example, functionalist arguments explain the existence of a "reserve army" of unemployed in capitalist society by saying that because capitalism leads to the formation of such a reserve army, this must be because the reserve army serves a "function" within capitalism: capitalism is said to "need" such an army (Giddens 112–13).

Against such arguments, Giddens makes three charges pertinent here: first, they tend to perpetuate a noxious view of social actors as dupes of social systems; second, they assume that the posited system and its "functions" can be analyzed outside of history; and third, they assume a cohesive relation between part and whole (Giddens 110–12). Functionalist arguments assume a condition of systemic homeostasis and an (often) organic or homological relation between the system as a whole and elements within it. Contradictory and contingent effects are thereby rendered invisible or subsumed within a posited systemic "functionality." Historical specificity and change are thus effaced, for structures are imagined to operate outside and independent of such factors.

The debate in composition studies over discursive forms illustrates these limitations. A particular discursive form—say, the "personal essay"—is understood as having, in itself, a particular value: that is, it is treated as a commodity. The labor expended in producing that value—not just the labor of the writer, but of readers, as well as the labor involved in (re)producing the social relations and material conditions in which a particular "personal essay" is written and read in particular ways, labor which accounts for the particular effects that an essay may have historically—is seen as an objective property of the essay form itself, which is thus abstracted from social historical circumstance. The personal essay form is then said to "function" in a particular way. In other words, the historical effects of a given form in certain instances are seen as evidence that the form, by itself, has this function. Such claims are rampant in arguments both for and against particular discursive forms, i.e., whether the personal essay, for example, is praised or condemned for the particular effects and functions attributed to it, and so whether or not "it" should be taught.

Arguments over the abolition of freshman composition and basic writing sometimes lapse into similar functionalist errors. In these arguments, whether pro or con, the historically contingent effects of specific types of writing programs are "explained away," as it were, by naming these effects to be their inherent "function." So, for instance, in functionalist arguments, particular instances of basic writing programs having had the effect of increasing attrition among oppressed groups is said to show that basic writing programs have this "function" (see, for example, Shor "Our Apartheid").

There is a slippage in such arguments between the historical effects of specific programs and claims about a type of program in general, which is abstracted from history and disparaged for its purported functions. And in this way, the institutional form of the program is treated as a commodity. Its value is associated not with the labor expended in the production of that value (e.g., the specific teachers, administrators, students, publics working in, with, on, and through it) nor the conditions of that labor, but with the idea of the program itself. Rather than understanding the specific use-value of such institutional structures as being realized only in the specific instance of their use, these structures, "the products of the human brain," are seen as "autonomous figures endowed with a life of their own, which enter into relations both with each other and with the human race." The labor expended in the production and reproduction of social structures is thereby not recognized but viewed "as an 'objective' property" of the structure itself. Thus, "the product of labour becomes transformed into a commodity." Debate then turns on the specific exchange-value of that commodified institutional program or form. Ignored or effaced in such debate are the particular social historical circumstances and labor performed that would account for the actual production of specific values, in those specific circumstances, for specific people.

What makes such functionalist arguments difficult to resist are the historical effects of specific institutionalized forms. While we need to acknowledge this history—for example, the history of freshman composition *being used* as, or having had the effect of, a gatekeeping device in numerous instances—we also need to refuse the temptation to label those effects as evidence that those forms possess in themselves an autonomous "function. So, while we can and should recognize the historical effects of certain academic institutional forms, such as the universal requirement for freshman composition, we must beware of attributing to those forms an autonomous power to achieve such effects. To make such an attribution is to reify the forms and treat them as commodities: to remove them from the contingencies of material history, and to then let their supposed "functions" dictate how we attempt to bring about, or prevent, actual effects. In combating such arguments, we need to insist on analyzing the significance of discursive and institutional forms in terms of the specific historical circumstances of their use and effects.[1]

As this brief discussion should suggest, Marxian critiques of commodity fetishism and functionalism are relevant to composition's resistance to the academic in several ways. First, they pose a challenge to dominant views, both within and outside composition, regarding the value of the work performed by composition teachers, students, and courses. Second, they provide a perspective from which to better understand the mixed history of the effects of academic institutional forms in which composition programs are and have been located and associated, and a perspective from which to intervene in that history. And third, they can provide a better perspective from which to attempt to enable us to intervene in the mixed history of the effects of specific academic, and nonacademic, discursive forms associated with work in composition.

VALUING WORK IN COMPOSITION

The debate on the value of the work performed by composition teachers, students, courses, and programs is vexed by a confusion concerning the relation between the exchange-values of commodifications of that work, contingent on a host of factors, and their potential use-value. Most broadly, however the exchange-value of the commodifications of composition's work may be defined, that exchange-value is often thought to entirely displace or exhaust the potential use-value of that work. For example, in debate on the "skills" composition courses are imagined to produce in students, those opposed to work in composition aimed at producing those skills sometimes confuse the commodification of that work with its full value. Understandably disturbed by the social relations associated with the commodification of workers obtaining when they are treated as so many bundles of abstracted skills, some argue against teaching the skills themselves.

But this confuses the denigration of those skills and those using them with the skills themselves—as if, for example, one were to conclude (as some have) that there is something inherently degrading about the "skill" of typing because those who are hired to use their skill at typing have often been subjected to degrading, exploitative social relations in their places of work. And it ignores the potential use-value to be realized in the specific uses to which that skill may be put—typing manifestos, say, or a legible letter (or, more likely, e-mail nowadays) to one's friends or relatives. In short, it accepts the commodification of the skill: treating the skill as an abstract entity and attributing to it values that in fact derive from specific work and conditions of work reduced to and named as a "skill." So, for example, attention to teaching the "skills" associated with the "mechanics" of writing—i.e., using conventional notations in writing—is sometimes condemned as demeaning to students and complicit with the dehumanizing treatment of workers judged on their mastery of such mechanics. While this dehumanizing treatment should indeed be condemned, it is wrong to then condemn any attention to conventional notations as itself demeaning. That is to say, we can challenge the exchange-value attributed to mastery of such matters without denying the particular use-values to be realized, in specific instances, by such notational practices.

Pierre Bourdieu's distinctions between economic, social, cultural, and symbolic capital, and the relations among these, help make sense of the variations of such arguments. As Allan Luke has observed, Bourdieu's typology of capital makes possible the "analysis of *relations* of power and knowledge" otherwise often understood monolithically (326; my emphasis). In Bourdieu's formulation, the value of a given form of capital is not fixed but contingent. As Bourdieu puts it, "The kinds of capital, like trumps in a game of cards, are powers which define the chances of profit in a given field. . . . The conversion or transformation of capital is mediated by one's position within the relations of power and knowledge in a social field" (*In Other Words* 230, 231). For example, as Luke explains, economic capital may be readily transformed into cultural capital (training, cultural artifacts) and social capital (e.g., social circles, institutional facilities). In capitalist societies, one can "literally buy his or her way into particular social networks and goods" (Luke 327). However, one's ability to convert such social networks and goods into economic capital "depends in part on her or his embodied competence, a key form of *cultural* capital" (Luke 327; my emphasis). The historic inability of African Americans to convert their literacy training into either economic or symbolic capital can in this way be explained by their "position within the relations of power and knowledge in a social field": specifically, as a caste-like minority in the United States, they lack, by definition, any social capital (see Ogbu). Capital is only capital, Luke warns, "if it is recognized as such . . . realization of one's economic, cultural and social capital is contingent on institutional pre-conditions which delimit and authorize what one is 'entitled' to do, and whether one has 'recognized authority'" (329).

Bourdieu's typology of capital enables us to see the debate over teaching writing skills as one between types of capitalization and commodification advocated (or denounced). For those opposed to the teaching of writing skills, it is the economic capitalization of writing "skills," and the exploitative social relations common to the process of that capitalization, that is rejected. Further, these opponents observe that such teaching ignores the roles which racism, sexism, classism, etc., play in students' ability to capitalize on their writing skills. That is, such teaching may mask the degree to which the value of these skills, and the ability of students to realize that value, are contingent on the students' social and cultural capital.

But then, confusing the use-value of those skills with their economic exchange-value, those making these arguments often offer as an alternative writing that is seemingly use-less—i.e., seeming to lack any economic exchange value in the economy of employer and "real world" demands. Peter Elbow articulates this position in arguing that we reserve first-year writing courses for giving students a chance to "take some time for themselves" away from the demands of readers ("Being" 76–77). But, first, teaching writing as what Susan Miller has termed an essentially "intransitive" activity whose value is ostensibly "inherent" to that activity (97) can be seen as itself producing cultural capital, in the form of an aesthetic disposition appropriate to, and recommending those displaying it as, members of a leisure class capable of maintaining "an active distance from necessity" (Bourdieu, *Distinction* 5). More- [*leisure*] over, the possibility of achieving this form of cultural capital, and exchanging it for economic capital, is no less contingent on the social, cultural, and other forms of capital of those pursuing it than is the value of writing skills. Not all are positioned socially to be able to capitalize economically on this intransitive writing (i.e., to convert the cultural capital into economic capital): the ability to do so is contingent on the other forms of capital—cultural, social, and economic—one already possesses. Hence the counterarguments that efforts to teach writing as use-less are "elitist" and irrelevant to the needs of many students not so positioned. We have here, then, not so much a clash between whether to capitalize or not to capitalize, to commodify or not to commodify, but a clash between two different forms of capitalization and commodifica- tion of the work of writing and of composition: work commodified into the production of abstract "skills" with economic exchange-value (which may potentially be converted into other forms of capital), or work commodified into the production of abstract "art" with cultural exchange value (which likewise may potentially be converted into other forms of capital).

While it should be clear that I am particularly interested in chal- lenging condemnations of the production of writing "skills," the point to be made here is that both sides in this debate overlook the potential use-value of the work conducted. Recognizing work only in the com- modity form—an abstract skill or art—both arguments seem to take the exchange-value of that work for its full value. The use to be realized from the work by particular individuals in specific circumstances gets ignored because the work is understood only in commodified form. If this is granted, the question we face is how to recover that use-value in order to value the work of composition differently. And the difficulty here is that the use-value of work cannot be specified in advance: use- value, recall, is "only realized in use or in consumption." What the spe- cific use-value of work in a composition course may be cannot be known in advance, as the praise former students sometimes, seemingly belat- edly, offer their former teachers attests. *Exactly*

If we attempt to judge work in composition by its use-value, then, and if we recognize the contingencies of the value of the various forms of inevitable capitalization of that work, we will have to put aside issues of attrition or retention, students' subsequent academic performance and employment history, as, if not irrelevant, not a direct indication of that work. This means, of course, refusing the commodification of the institutional forms of the teacher, the course section, the student as FTE, academic credits, forms we regularly use in defining our work and in terms of which we as workers are seen and evaluated. Our work and that of our students does not conform and is not restricted to these, nor do the uses to which that work is or can be put.

However, that does not mean that we reject out of hand all the material conditions of academic life associated with these institutional forms. To do so would be to make the functionalist error and recognize only the official, and not the unofficial, purposes and uses to which these forms may be put, and to read the significance of these forms outside of material history. Instead, we have to look at the specific uses to which we and our students might put such forms. This means, too, that in teaching within these institutional forms, we should investigate, with our students, both the restrictions the conditions associated with these forms seem to impose on our work, and the uses to which those conditions might be put. And this means that we must resist institutional evaluations of the work we perform—in annual performance and tenure and promotion reviews—that recognize only the immediate exchange-value of what is produced, neglecting the potential use-value of the work for the students, faculty, the institution, and the community at large.

To suggest what this might mean in concrete terms, let me address the issue of teaching the "mechanics" of writing. First, and perhaps most obviously, we cannot let the fact of attempts to commodify the work of producing, and learning to produce, conventionally notated writing, or the attempt to capitalize economically on the "skill" so commodified, deter us from teaching students ways to produce writing conventionally notated. But our awareness of the gap between commodifications of this sort of editing as a "skill" and the actual work involved in such editing, and of the lack of transferability of one's ability to edit one sort of writing, in one situation, and one's ability to edit other sorts of writing in another, will have to inform how we teach this "skill," how we represent the learning of it to our students, and how (or, rather, whether) we are evaluated on our ability to "transfer" this "skill" to our students. As I have argued elsewhere, we do our students a disservice in pretending that we are "giving" them a "skill" in teaching them proofreading, or the conventions of "correct" English ("Rethinking"). What "works" in one instance, and indeed what is deemed "correct," may not work or be deemed correct in other circumstances (see Russell 65–67). And as many have argued, we cannot, in good faith, subscribe to or encourage in our students belief in the myths that associate the ability to produce writing deemed by some authority to be "correct" in its notation with a writer's intelligence, cognitive style or maturity, or place along the putative oral/literate divide (Rose).

What we can do is teach the techniques of proofreading, and the conventions of notations, as themselves socially and historically contingent—not to discourage attention to them, but to encourage the appropriate sorts of attention to them, to demystify what are all too often viewed as Platonic Absolutes, as unfathomable in their logic as they are thought to be immutable. Similarly, courses assigned the task of teaching such "skills" would be judged not in terms of the notational forms the writers might produce on a given test but in terms of students' growing awareness of the need for flexibility in manipulating and challenging the legitimacy of notational forms, with the understanding that this awareness, and the students' actions growing out of that awareness, will continue to be subject to change long after the course is over.

VALUING ACADEMIC INSTITUTIONAL FORMS

The neglect of the use-value of work traditionally assigned to the composition class, such as the teaching of proofreading, or the rejection of such work on the basis of the history of its commodification and economic capitalization, has its counterpart in arguments to abolish the institution of freshman composition, at least as traditionally understood, in favor of work outside that institutional frame: work associated with writing in other academic disciplines or in the workplace, or work conducted in service-learning activities. These abolitionist arguments make the functionalist mistake of taking the historical effects of, or official purposes assigned to, first-year composition programs for their inevitable and complete functions. Arguments to adapt composition courses to conform more completely to the demands of writing activities in the workplace ascribe both a dysfunctionality to traditional composition courses and a normative functionality to writing and work outside such courses. In so doing, these arguments treat such programs as themselves commodities, viewing as objective properties of these programs specific effects that can in fact be attributed to the labor of specific individuals, and thus abstracting the programs from material social history. And often, in place of these programs, commodifications of the work of writing in the workplace are heralded, commodifications which again treat as effects of the commodity as autonomous agent the labor involved in the production of that writing and the material social circumstances of its use.

This dynamic is illustrated in some of the essays collected in *Reconceiving Writing, Rethinking Writing Instruction* advocating the abolition of freshman composition. The essays rightly condemn what they term "General Writing Skills Instruction" (GWSI) for the lack of validity to claims of "general writing skills" (i.e., what I would term a commodification of the work of writing), or at least the lack of transferability of such skills, and the consequent failure of such instruction to prepare students for writing in specific circumstances of other disciplines and the workplace. However, as Charles Bazerman argues in a response included in the collection, while institutions may well have charged composition programs with GWSI, an admittedly "unpromising curricular space," "the pages of the composition journals have been filled with ways in which writing teachers have developed to turn their first-year writing classes into situated and meaningful occasions that engage students in motivated writing" (252). In other words, the work of such programs has not been restricted by the official purposes ascribed to them. Conversely, a normative functionality is in some of these arguments attributed to nonacademic writing. That is, nonacademic writing, as nonacademic, is assumed by definition to be inherently situated and meaningful to writers. In such arguments the "academic" is inevitably opposed to the "real," imagined as discrete from actual work in and on the social (see, for example, Petraglia 91–92).

Arguments for incorporating service-learning into composition curricula often make a similar case. For example, Paul Heilker, while acknowledging that "simply changing the where of teaching writing . . . will probably be of little consequence," argues nonetheless, "Writing teachers need to relocate the where of composition instruction outside the academic classroom because the classroom does not and cannot offer students real rhetorical situations in which to understand writing as social action" ("Rhetoric" 71). In this argument, students "desperately need real rhetorical situations, real audiences and purposes to work with, real people to become in writing," a need which the academic setting of the traditional composition classroom apparently cannot, by definition, meet.

Part of what concerns Heilker is the unpromising, if perhaps common, practice of asking students to write in ways addressing hypothetical situations: to "*imagine* an entire rhetorical world, to conjure up an appropriate audience, subject matter, an ethos out of thin air" (71; see Petraglia 92). But he also seems to reject out of hand the reality of academic audiences, concerns, subject matter, and work. However, as Bazerman reminds us in his response to similar arguments, "If we start analyzing the first-year writing course we find it is a very real place" (254). And many of the concerns of first-year writing students—for instance, defining who they are, exploring how they might participate in university life, and how that participation might change who they are—are indeed quite real to them. While it would be futile to claim that all first-year writing courses address these and similar concerns, it would be equally wrong to deny that many can and do.

This is not to argue against service-learning in composition but to reject its use as a means of making composition more "real," more socially connected, than it is. Raymond Williams has warned that "what the dominant has effectively seized is indeed the ruling definition of the social" (125). This ruling definition inevitably falls short of including or exhausting all human practice: it simply fails to recognize it, or identifies it falsely as not social but private, natural, metaphysical, personal (Williams 125). A belief in the divorce of composition, and the academy generally, from the real and the social is not only dominant but indeed serves the dominant by acquiescing in the neglect of the social potential of the "academic" realm generally and composition in particular. We should not, therefore, reinforce this belief through specious claims about the greater reality of writing in service-learning outside the academy.

What service-learning can do is make more visible to students the specific and various uses to which they might put the resources available to them *as students* working in an *academic* setting: time available for studying social problems and indeed for engaging in "service-learning"; the luxury of reflecting on one's position about such problems; access to paper, computers, and libraries; the focus provided by a particular course. And service-learning projects can make visible the specific relationships of the realm of the academy, and work and workers deemed "academic," to these other realms of the social. Bruce Herzberg's description of the experience his composition students had tutoring in a homeless shelter gives a sense of how service-learning led to increasing the visibility of such relationships. The experience, Herzberg reports, gave them a greater understanding of "the social and cultural reasons for the existence of illiteracy—the reasons, in other words, that the students needed to perform the valuable service they were engaged in" (66). What seems to have occurred here is not that the composition class was made more "real" in some abstract sense through sending students out of the academy, but that the students developed a greater sense of the real, if ordinarily denied, social relation between themselves as students in a private college and the homeless they visited in a nearby "community" shelter. Herzberg himself describes this program not as relocating the composition class from the academy to some other realm but as an effort "to reach *into* the composition class with a curriculum aimed at democracy and social justice" (66). Students remain students, but with a changed sense of what it means, in present historical social circumstances, to be students, as well as what it means to be homeless.

One obvious objection to this way of valuing service-learning in composition is that changing the social consciousness of these students, however laudable, is hardly an adequate response to the social problems of homelessness, racial oppression, environmental destruction, etc., we now face, and that the real value of service-learning resides in the immediate, concrete results to the community from the work students may perform. This is a tempting argument. It highlights the disparity between the urgency of addressing these problems and the luxury of consciousness-raising, and implicitly calls into question the elitism of a focus on the consciousness of those socially already well positioned. Far better to work at helping the homeless, and at removing the underlying causes of homelessness, than to worry about the feelings of late-adolescent members of the middle and upper class towards the homeless.

Without denying that disparity, I would argue that this objection is misguided, and in several ways. First, it falsely assumes one must choose between the goals of addressing these social problems and raising social consciousness, forgetting that the two are inevitably intertwined. It is difficult, after all, to imagine how the experience of working with problems of homelessness would not affect one's consciousness. What this argument instances is a reinforcement of the dominant's exclusion of practical consciousness from its definition of the social which Williams warns against. Second, and relatedly, it denies the materiality of the academy and traditional academic work in a way that, again, reinforces rather than challenges the dominant's ascription of such work to social insignificance.

That denial occurs in two senses: first, it denies the material conditions of academic work, proposing instead a march on social problems that is utopian in its failure to recognize both the material conditions limiting the work students and teachers can do as well as the existence of other actors on the social scene materially better positioned and already at work on these problems. Second, it denies the materiality of the consequences of such traditional academic work as the writing of student papers that circulate primarily within the composition classroom. This second denial accepts dominant definitions of the social as limited to commodities with seemingly guaranteed and visible effects—programs that lead immediately to physically demonstrable changes in people's lives; writing that is public because it is published. Recognizing the official purposes and impacts claimed for such "social" work and the disparity between these and the official purposes and uses claimed for traditional academic work in composition as, say, the production of commodified writing skills, it neglects the unofficial purposes and uses made of work with seemingly immediate social impact, as well as the actual potential social use-value of work officially designated as merely "academic." It ignores, for example, the economic exchange-value of nonprofit agency work—a growing part of the U.S. economy—pursued by students' interest in service-learning as a means of beefing up their résumés. And it accepts the official means of measuring the value of academic work, which is recognized only in its commodified form—say, in academic credits—rather than in the uncommodified form of active minds and changing consciousnesses.

Again, this is not to deny the potential use-value of service-learning or service work, nor the obvious economic and other forms of exchange-values of traditional academic work, realized by students, exchanged in the currency of academic credits, diplomas, and jobs. It is to reject taking the exchange-value of these commodified forms of both types of work for their full potential use-value. That service-learning is often used as a means of beefing up résumés does not vitiate the use-value of the work conducted in its name; nor does the economic and cultural capitalization of traditional academic work in composition vitiate the potential use-value of that work for students and others.

VALUING ACADEMIC DISCOURSE

The need to recognize the potential use-value of the work of traditional composition programs ordinarily understood only in terms of its commodification and exchange value has its parallel in the need to be alert to both the exchange—and potential use-value of nonacademic and academic discursive forms. I have argued elsewhere that recent calls for composition teachers and students to pursue experimental, non-"academic" discursive forms can confuse specific writing forms for practices and conditions involved in the production (and reception) of these (Horner, "Students" 519–20). But disparagement of the production of traditional academic discursive forms instances the same confusion. In other words, the specific discursive form—the seemingly impersonal academic essay or report, say—is understood only in terms of its current exchange value (at least for some) in the economy of academic credits and grades. This occludes the labor of specific writers, readers, practices, and material social conditions of practice contributing to the realization, in a particular instance, of a particular use-value for a given essay, and other potential use-values to be realized through other concrete labor. The form, instead, is treated as a commodity with properties identified as objectively residing in that commodity. In a recent critique of standards in higher education, Tom Fox makes this point, observing that the issue he and his students face in composition classes is not, in fact, which

discursive form to use but how to participate in continuing literate traditions of using a variety of discursive forms, traditions ordinarily hidden from view by the dominant (Fox, ch. 5). Introducing his African
American students to examples of writing for social action, Fox shows
how discursive forms ordinarily understood in dominant culture as irrelevant to social and personal concerns are malleable in their use, for they
can be and have been put to different uses: for example, the use to which
David Walker, African American slave author, put nineteenth-century
traditional American prose style in composing his 1848 insurrectionary
Appeal in Four Articles (Fox 102, 30–32). It is thus manifestly not academic discursive forms in themselves which have properties of impersonality and removal from social concerns. To believe so is to engage in
commodity fetishism. Rather, it is the dominant's reification of academic, and other, discursive forms that is to be combated: the treatment
of these as fixed in meaning, purpose, and use, unsusceptible to human
labor.

This is not to argue for or against teaching traditional academic discursive forms in lieu of other forms, it is to argue against teaching forms
as commodities, and to argue for teaching the practices and the conditions of practice—i.e., the labor of readers and writers and of those contributing to the conditions for specific reading and writing practices—
that account for and make possible the realization of specific use-values
through certain textual forms, as well as those leading to the commodification and realization of various types of exchange-value from them.
This shifts the focus of the composition course from discursive forms in
themselves to the responsibilities and practices of readers and writers,
and to the conditions making possible those practices and the work to
which readers and writers so situated may put them.

I have been arguing that compositionists' understandable ambivalence toward academic institutional and discursive forms threatens to
cut us off from the potential uses to which those forms might be put. To
tap their potential, we need to resist not academic work but commodifications of that work, and to reject concluding that the exchange-values commonly realized from such commodifications have supplanted,
rather than masked, the full potential uses to which composition teachers' and students' academic work may be put. As Jean Carr has warned,
we should not "leave the academic world behind as if it offered no evidence of alternative literacies, of resistance or differential uses for reading and writing, as if it were, in fact, a story already known and known
fully" (96). In this sense, insofar as one academic tradition is to resist
orthodoxy, exploring the potential uses of the academy and resisting
commodifications of its work is fully in conformity to, rather than a
break from, the academic. Thus, rather than attempting simply to resist

the "academic," we, and our students, can refuse the dominant's implicit denigration and commodification of the academy and academic work. Instead of resisting the "academic," we, and our students, can carry on as resisting academics.[2]

NOTES

1. For illustrations of such analyses, see the essays gathered in the February 1996 issue of *College Composition and Communication* on institutional "mainstreaming" of basic writing (Anokye, Duffey, Grego and Thompson, Rodby, Soliday).

2. The arguments presented here are developed in my *Terms of Work for Composition: A Materialist Critique* (Albany: State U of New York P, 2000).

WORKS CITED

Anokye, Akua Duku. "Housewives and Compositionists." *College Composition and Communication* 47 (1996): 101–03.

Bazerman, Charles. "Response: Curricular Responsibilities and Professional Definition." Petraglia, *Reconceiving Writing*, 249–59.

Bourdieu, Pierre. *Distinction: A Social Critique of the Judgement of Taste.* Trans. Richard Nice. Cambridge: Harvard UP, 1984.

———. *In Other Words: Essays Towards a Reflexive Sociology.* Trans. M. Adamson. Stanford UP, 1990.

Bridwell-Bowles, Lillian. "Discourse and Diversity: Experimental Writing within the Academy." *College Composition and Communication* 43 (1992): 349–68.

———. "Freedom, Form, Function: Varieties of Academic Discourse." *College Composition and Communication* 46 (1995): 46–61.

Carr, Jean Ferguson. "Rereading the Academy as Worldly Text." *College Composition and Communication* 45 (1994): 93–97.

Cooper, David D., and Laura Julier. "Democratic Conversations: Civic Literacy and Service-Learning in the American Grains." Kassner, Crooks, Waters, 79–94

Duffey, Suellynn. "Mapping the Terrain of Tracks and Streams." *College Composition and Communication* 47 (1996): 103–07.

Elbow, Peter. "Being a Writer vs. Being an Academic: A Conflict in Goals." *College Composition and Communication* 46 (1995): 72–83.

———. "Reflections on Academic Discourse: How it Relates to Freshmen and Colleagues." *College English* 53 (1991): 135–55.

Fox, Tom. *Defending Access: A Critique of Standards in Higher Education.* Portsmouth, NH: Boynton/Cook, 1999.

Giddens, Anthony. *Central Problems in Social Theory: Action, Structure and Contradiction in Social Analysis.* Berkeley: U of California P, 1979.

Grego, Rhonda, and Nancy Thompson. "Repositioning Remediation: Renegotiating Composition's Work in the Academy." *College Composition and Communication* 47 (1996): 62–84.

Heilker, Paul. "Rhetoric Made Real: Civic Discourse and Writing Beyond the Curriculum." Petraglia, *Reconceiving Writing*, 71–77.

Herzberg, Bruce. "Community Service and Critical Teaching." *College Composition and Communication* 45 (1994): 307–19. Rpt. Petraglia, 57–69.

Horner, Bruce. "Rethinking the 'Sociality' of Error: Teaching Editing as Negotiation." *Rhetoric Review* 11 (1992): 172–99.

———. "Students, Authorship, and the Work of Composition." *College English* 59 (1997): 505–29.

Kassner, Linda Adler, Robert Crooks, and Ann Waters. *Writing the Community: Concepts and Models for Service-Learning in Composition*. Urbana, IL: National Council of Teachers of English, 1997.

Luke, Allan. "Genres of Power? Literacy Education and the Production of Capital." *Literacy in Society*. Ed. Ruqaiya Hasan and Geoff Williams. New York: Longman, 1998. 308–38.

Marx, Karl. *Capital, I: A Critique of Political Economy*. Trans. Ben Fowkes. New York: Vintage, 1976.

Miller, Susan. *Textual Carnivals: The Politics of Composition*. Carbondale: Southern Illinois UP, 1991.

Ogbu, John U. "Literacy and Schooling in Subordinate Cultures: The Case of Black Americans." *Literacy in Historical Perspective*. Ed. Daniel Resnick. Washington, DC: Library of Congress, 1983. Rpt. *Perspectives on Literacy*. Ed. Eugene R. Kintgen, Barry M. Kroll, and Mike Rose. Carbondale: Southern Illinois UP, 1988. 227–42.

Petraglia, Joseph. *Reconceiving Writing, Rethinking Writing Instruction*. Ed. Joseph Petraglia. Mahwah, NJ: Erlbaum, 1995.

———. "Writing as an Unnatural Act." *Reconceiving Writing*, 79–100.

Rodby, Judith. "What's It Worth and What's It For? Revisions to Basic Writing Revisited." *College Composition and Communication* 47 (1996): 107–11.

Rose, Mike. "Narrowing the Mind and Page: Remedial Writers and Cognitive Reductionism." *College Composition and Communication* 39 (1988): 267–302.

Russell, David R. "Activity Theory and Its Implications for Writing Instruction." Petraglia, *Reconceiving Writing*, 51–77.

Shor, Ira. "Our Apartheid: Writing Instruction and Inequality." *Journal of Basic Writing* 16 (Spring 1997): 91–104.

Soliday, Mary. "From the Margins to the Mainstream: Reconceiving Remediation." *College Composition and Communication* 47 (1996): 85–100.

Williams, Raymond. *Marxism and Literature*. New York: Oxford UP, 1977.

A F T E R W O R D

Resisting the Politics of Insurrection

Dale Bauer

readings

In an era when we are increasingly defined by accountability, our renewed attention to "resistance" in general is a necessary and refreshing reality check at the millennium. To that end, the essays in this collection might be titled "What We Talk About When We Talk About Resistance." Every essay in this collection questions the meaning of the term "resistance," and it proves to be the most dialogic of terms. It's not something any author takes for granted, whether in terms of the agency involved or the political effects of opposition and refusal. The essays in *Insurrections* suggest how resistance is at once (1) romantic, (2) historic, (3) narrative, (4) radical, (5) antiracist, (6) mythic, (7) moral, (8) tragic, (9) heroic, (10) class-inflected, (11) gendered, (12) racialized, (13) agonistic. And that's not even as comprehensive a list as the authors have shown in this volume.

More important, academics can resist (1) their students (and, as we know, vice versa), (2) second-class institutional citizenship, (3) metaphors, (4) technological urgency or ignorance, (5) academic discourse or disciplines themselves, (6) the goals of the university, (7) capitalism, and (8) doing the academic housework of the university (the use-value of our work that gets discounted in the university's accounting of its exchange-values). The effects of resistance range from joy through ambivalence to despair; above all, resistance is a coping mechanism (Brown). Thus the dialogism of "resistance" is dizzying.

Perhaps it's useful to say what these essays don't do: they eschew theorizing abstractly about the "politics of" *whatever*. For example, look at any account of critical pedagogy and you'll find a laundry list of "politics" to which we need to attend: the "politics of identity and difference," "politics of cultural difference," "the politics of personal location," "politics of experience," "a politics of representation," "a politics of articulation," "politics of hope and possibility." The notion of the "politics of" anything begins to seem more like the left's mantra than a call to action. Arguably we've all been guilty, more or less, in presenting certain abstract notions of resistance rather than particular examples of social action.

"Resistance"—as a concept—has a romantic history, as Trimbur suggests, one that fosters a sense that classroom life is not outside history but firmly in it. The ubiquity of the term demonstrates, in Trimbur's words, the "divergent ways individuals and groups seize a degree of relative autonomy within the institutions of schooling, articulating identities and purposes that in one way or another withhold consent from the dominant enterprise and its hegemonic aims." Case studies of positive and negative resistance abound. Trimbur's essay worries the term effectively in order to analyze its "appeal" to educators as they try to imagine how to discuss their work.

In fact, the essays challenge exactly what can be done *within* the university that can be labeled as politically effective, true resistance in the form of "counterhegemonic" practice. Beth Flynn categorizes the possibilities: strategic, counter-strategic, and reactive resistances. Yet, as Tom Fox declares, such defining of resistance fails, since resistance is context-dependent. Some of the essays, like Fox's, even talk about resistance to resistance. As Susan Wells describes it, her "resistance" is to reflect on her job: "a displacement of our own anxiety about our professional efficacy." (On the next page of her essay, however, those anxieties are about "political efficacy," a clue to how easily we shift between the two, and then on the next page to "historical efficacy.") Throughout this collection, there is a healthy anxiety about what we should resist and, more important, why we should do it. Are the days of resistance—in the post-capitalist university—over?

One example of the current hegemony is technology: the newly technological classroom may "erect borders that, in effect, resist students' attempts to resist" (Walker). Ellen Strenski disagrees: we only resist information technologies at our peril; all systems need some resistance in order to avoid implosion. About resistance, Strenski takes the philosophical view: "For the sake of discussion, let them be perceived as 'resistors' in the electronic sense, as components in a complex circuit board analogy." (Is this one of the metaphors Susan Wells would resist?) The relevant Bakhtinian question is whether this built-in resistance is "allowed carnival," a safety-valve that drains counterhegemonic practice, or "true" or "authentic" revolutionary thinking? A utopianism at the crux of the bureaucracy?

Essays like Keith Gilyard and Elaine Richardson's on Students' Right to their Own Language, for example, address the problem through the study of (rather than the theorization of) the use of African American vernacular in academic language. "Black discursive style," as the authors conclude, "rather than a quality to be merely appreciated, is essential to the development of a Black, formal, public voice." As Tom Fox also argues, African American students on traditionally white campuses resist not only white racism, but also promote academic writing as a means of resistance. Both of these essays suggest the need for teaching resistance through historical cases of revolutionary rhetorics, testifying to the importance of teaching "historical and contemporary scholars of color" (Fox). In the same way, as Greenbaum argues, feminist teachers use "agonistic" resistance to avoid the appearance of weakness. This sort of resistance is not resistance *to* students, but to their categorizing female teachers as "bitches" or, what is sometimes worse, "mothers."

Only one contributor—Bruce Horner—disagrees with "Composition's resistance to the academic," arguing that we should not confuse "use-value" of writing skills with their economic exchange-value. For Horner, the same is true of the teaching of composition itself: the university uses up our "use-value," but finds no exchange-value in the teaching of writing (hence its feminization or second-class status). Horner's point, then, is that resistance is misplaced: it should not be against the use-value, but the way in which American culture only values writing's exchange-value. In Horner's terms, "we must resist institutional evaluations of the work we perform—in annual performance and tenure and promotion reviews—that recognize only the immediate exchange-value of what is produced, neglecting the potential use-value of the work for the students, faculty, the institution, and the community at large." We will thus become "resisting academics."

Yet as these essays in *Insurrections* already suggest, we are always "resisting academics," ever in the process of accommodating and refusing the systems we create. The question is not whether there is a good or bad resistance, an authentic or allowed counterhegemony, but whether the institutions in which we work allow differing values instead of a singular value, whether it allows resistance in the first place. In arguing our resistance, we should use the language of vocation—of our calling—or even the language of accounting that many of us despise most? Or is it time to launch an aggressive defense of the liberal arts as a critical force in the culture? Would the language of passion, commitment, ethics, or morals communicate what we need to say?

Let me offer my own example: What do the late Bill Readings and

Jane Tompkins have in common? One decried the end of the university; the latter, tried to resuscitate the Ophelia-like academy from its precipitous death. Also common to both is a rejection of the resistant or oppositional stance that has become so habitual for many of us in the 1990s. Readings and Tompkins offer two different approaches in lieu of oppositionalism—one focused on Thought, the other on Emotion, tropes once more for the mind-body split that many encounter in the academy, but which has been the target of feminist pedagogy for decades.

These two models—dwelling in the ruins of the university *and* rejecting teaching performance for a more affective approach—are two ends of a new spectrum of resistance to accountability. In one of his final chapters, Bill Readings recommends that we examine more closely "the scene of teaching" since truly *ethical* teaching involves "an accountability at odds with accounting" (154)—a phrase that he repeats with emphasis throughout his book. He asks, "To whom or what are teachers, students, and institutions accountable? And in what terms?" (150). He wants to define this accountability as a question of value, but not the value inscribed within the "logic of accounting" that fuels the bureaucratic post-1968 University.

Pedagogy, for Readings, has no "accountable" time. Teaching operates as a "specific chronotope"—a function beyond the time-space compression of late capitalism—that exceeds accounting (151); as such, teaching cannot be evaluated from the centered perspective of administrators, professors, or students. Teaching is more complex than any unilateral account and must be conceived, Readings argues, as a *decentered* activity. In short, he reminds us that the act of teaching is ungrounded (161) and, hence, cannot be counted or accounted for. It is an act of justice, a respect for the other, that is not measurable by relations of students to faculty FTE, evaluation numbers, or cost effectiveness of TAs and adjuncts versus full-time faculty.

Rethinking the pedagogical mission for which we are accountable is also Jane Tompkins' project. Tompkins embraces an emotional accountability to students, not in any consumerist way that many of us in public and private institutions now face routinely. To circumvent the omnipresent call to be accountable, she claims that she began to stop "performing" teaching. Without ironic effect, I want to quote her directly: "To know nothing, nothing solid, pre-existing, nothing that would deflect the course of events from its unpredictable past" (123). For Readings, teaching's transcendental signifier is Thought; for Tompkins, it is the Emotion (125).

Think of how Readings and Tompkins both resist the ideal of "excellence" as a raison d'etre for the University, and both search for a cornerstone that is "something besides an ideal of individual excellence"

(193) or, as Readings has it, of institutional excellence. Instead, they both suggest pedagogy as a united solution. To this end, we might ask what is a pedagogical model that bypasses accountability and instrumentality (Tompkins 205)? The next stage—perhaps for the millennium—is to find a way to integrate this split "scene of teaching." That is, to resist the bureaucratic rationality of "excellence" or "accountability" or even the "exchange-value" of what we do when we teach.

use value
Horner

CONTRIBUTORS

Dale Bauer is Professor of English at University of Kentucky. She is the author of *Feminist Dialogics* (1988) and *Edith Wharton's Brave New Politics* (1994), along with editions of "The Yellow Wallpaper" and a collection of essays on Bakhtin and feminism. She has written on feminist theory, pedagogy, and American literature.

Stephen Brown is Assistant Professor/Director of the First-Year Writing Program at the University of Tampa. His recent book, *Words in the Wilderness: Critical Literacy in the Borderlands*, is published by State University of New York Press. His articles have appeared in *JAC, College Literature, Review of Education*, and *Journal of Florida Literature*.

Elizabeth Flynn is completing a book manuscript entitled *Feminism beyond Modernism* and coediting a book entitled *Reading Sites: Gender, Race, Class, Ethnicity, and Sexual Orientation*. She is coeditor of *Gender and Reading* (Hopkins 1986), *Constellations* (HarperCollins 1992, 1995), and *Reader*. She has published numerous articles and book chapters and is a member of the Executive Committee of the Division on the Teaching of Writing of the Modern Language Association (MLA), a representative on the MLA Delegate Assembly, and former chair of the Committee on the Status of Women of the Conference on College Composition and Communication.

Tom Fox is Professor of English at California State University, Chico. He teaches undergraduate and graduate composition courses and administers various parts of the university composition program. He is the author of *Social Uses of Writing* (Ablex 1990) and *Defending Access* (1999) and numerous articles and book chapters on the politics of writing instruction.

Keith Gilyard is Professor of English at Pennsylvania State University and former Chair of the Conference on College Composition and Communication (CCCC). He has also taught at Syracuse University, where he directed the Writing Program, and at the City University of New York, and New York University. He has served as Vice President and

President of the NCTE/CCCC Black Caucus. Gilyard has written extensively and lectured widely on language and education. His books include *Voices of the Self: A Study of Language Competence*, for which he received an American Book Award, *Let's Flip the Script: An African American Discourse on Language, Literature, and Learning*, and the edited collection, *Race, Rhetoric, and Composition*.

Andrea Greenbaum is Assistant Professor at Barry University. Her essays and reviews have appeared in *Composition Studies, Writing on the Edge, JAC, Composition Forum, Humor: The International Journal of Humor Research, American Studies, Studies in American Jewish Fiction, Teaching English in the Two-Year College*, the *Journal of Men's Studies*, and *Film and History*. Her recent book project, *The Emancipatory Movements: Liberal Politics and Composition Studies* examines the infusion of cultural studies, sophistic rhetoric, and feminism within the discipline of composition studies.

Bruce Horner is Associate Professor of English and currently Associate Chair of the Department of English at Drake University, where he teaches courses in writing, literacy studies, and song criticism. His essays on composition have appeared in *College English, College Composition and Communication, English Education, JAC, Rhetoric Review*, and *Writing on the Edge*. He is author of *Terms of Work for Composition: A Materialist Critique* (State University of New York Press, 2000), and co-author, with Min-Zhan Lu, of *Representing the "Other": Basic Writers and the Teaching of Basic Writing* (NCTE, 1999). He has also published in the field of music criticism, in *MOSAIC* and the *Journal of Musicology*, and is coeditor, with Thomas Swiss, of *Key Terms in Popular Music and Culture* (Blackwell, forthcoming).

Gary A. Olson is Professor of English and coordinator of the graduate program in rhetoric and composition at the University of South Florida. His most recent book is *The Kinneavy Papers* (with Lynn Worsham and Sidney I. Dobrin).

Elaine Richardson is Assistant Professor of English at Pennsylvania State University. Her research interests include computer technology, discourse analysis, and African American language, culture, and literacy. She has published in the *Journal of English Linguistics*, the *Journal of Pidgins and Creoles*, and the *Journal of Commonwealth and Postcolonial Studies*. She is currently working on a book that focuses on the theory and practice of composition relative to African American rhetoric.

Ellen Strenski is Assistant Writing Director in the Department of English and Comparative Literature at the University of California, Irvine. She is coauthor and coeditor of *A Guide to Writing Sociology Papers* (St. Martin's, 1998, 4th ed.), and coauthor of *The Research Paper Workbook* (Longman, 1993, 3rd ed.).

John Trimbur is the Paris Fletcher Distinguished Professor of Humanities and Director of the Technical, Scientific, and Professional Communication program at WPI in Worcester, MA. He began teaching writing in the mid-1970s in basic writing programs at inner city community colleges in Philadelphia and Baltimore. Since then, he has directed writing programs and writing centers at Rutgers in Camden and Rhode Island College and has published extensively in writing theory and cultural studies of literacy. The collection of essays he coedited, *The Politics of Writing Instruction*, received the Outstanding Book Award from the Conference on College Composition and Communication in 1993. He has written the textbook *The Call to Write* and cowritten two others, *Reading Culture* (3rd ed.) with Diana George and *A Short Guide to Writing About Chemistry* with Herbert Beall. His work in progress focuses on visual design and the materiality of literacy.

Janice Walker is Assistant Professor in the Writing and Linguistics department at Georgia Southern University, where she teaches courses in professional writing, technical communication, and composition. She is the creator of the Columbia Online Style for citation of electronic sources and coauthor of *The Columbia Guide to Online Style* (Columbia UP, 1998). She is also coauthor (with John Ruszkiewicz) of two books on writing and research in the modern age, *Bookmarks: A Guide to Writing and Research* and *writing@online.edu* (Longman, 1999). Currently, she is working on a collection of essays on the effect of modern technologies on our conceptions of text and literacy.

Susan Wells teaches English at Temple University and has just finished *Out of the Dead House: Nineteenth-Century Women Physicians and the Writing of Medicine* (Wisconsin, 2000), and has recently published *Sweet Reason: Intersubjective Rhetorics and the Discourses of Modernity* (Chicago, 1996). Currently, she is working on Habermas' theory of the public sphere as it applies to issues of teaching writing.

INDEX